Manipulating Authoritarian Citizenship

Studies of the Walter H. Shorenstein Asia-Pacific Research Center

Andrew G. Walder, Series Editor

The Walter H. Shorenstein Asia-Pacific Research Center (APARC) in the Freeman Spogli Institute for International Studies at Stanford University sponsors interdisciplinary research on the politics, economies, and societies of contemporary Asia. This monograph series features academic and policy-oriented research by Stanford faculty and other scholars associated with the Center.

Manipulating Authoritarian Citizenship

SECURITY, DEVELOPMENT, AND LOCAL
MEMBERSHIP IN CHINA

Samantha A. Vortherms

Stanford University Press
Stanford, California

Stanford University Press
Stanford, California

© 2024 Samantha A. Vortherms. All rights reserved.

No part of this book may be reproduced or transmitted in any form or by any means, electronic or mechanical, including photocopying and recording, or in any information storage or retrieval system, without the prior written permission of Stanford University Press.

Printed in the United States of America on acid-free, archival-quality paper.

Library of Congress Cataloging-in-Publication Data
Names: Vortherms, Samantha A., author.
Title: Manipulating authoritarian citizenship : security, development, and local membership in China / Samantha A. Vortherms.
Other titles: Studies of the Walter H. Shorenstein Asia-Pacific Research Center.
Description: Stanford, California : Stanford University Press, 2024. | Series: Studies of the Walter H. Shorenstein Asia-Pacific Research Center | Includes bibliographical references and index.
Identifiers: LCCN 2024007545 (print) | LCCN 2024007546 (ebook) | ISBN 9781503640184 (cloth) | ISBN 9781503640832 (ebook)
Subjects: LCSH: Citizenship–China. | Domicile–China. | Local government–China. | Authoritarianism–China.
Classification: LCC JQ1517.A2 V678 2024 (print) | LCC JQ1517.A2 (ebook) | DDC 323.60951–dc23/eng/20240316
LC record available at https://lccn.loc.gov/2024007545
LC ebook record available at https://lccn.loc.gov/2024007546

Cover design and art: David Drummond
Typeset by Newgen in 11/14 Adobe Garamond Pro

To my family, for your unfailing faith in me

Contents

	Acknowledgments	ix
	Introduction	1
1	The Institutional Evolution of China's Local Citizenship	21
2	Manipulating Citizenship: Rights and Membership in Authoritarian Citizenship	54
3	Internal Citizenship Regimes: Pathways of Local Naturalization	85
4	Balancing Security and Development: Municipal Variation	113
5	Voluntarism and the Naturalization Decision	148
	Conclusion: Beyond *Hukou*	176
	Appendix A: Defining the *Hukou*: Key Terms	187
	Appendix B: Methods, Data, and Sources	193
	Appendix C: Policy List and Results Tables	213
	Notes	217
	Works Cited	239
	Index	273

Acknowledgments

In 2007 in Shenzhen, over dinner, a friend lamented that she wanted to marry her long-time boyfriend, but her parents would not support the match because he had neither household registration locally nor in her hometown. The wide-ranging conversation that followed touched on social inequality, public order, family and birth planning, economic reform, and labor markets. Little did I know then that I would spend the better part of my early career studying China's other little red book, the *hukou*.

First and foremost, I am grateful to my mentors at the University of Wisconsin–Madison who helped me turn my interests in inequality, development, and migration into this book. Melanie Manion pushed me to develop expertise in Chinese politics and in political science more broadly. Simply put, she taught me how to be a scholar and a mentor. Rikhil Bhavnani challenged me to think about my project in more comparative and rigorous ways. Scott Gehlbach graciously provided detailed feedback and general mentoring support throughout the project. Yoshiko Herrera encouraged me to better contextualize the comparative nature of the project. David Weimer provided essential guidance for the design and analysis of the experimental survey used in this book.

I thank Peking University's China Center for Health Economic Research for providing me invaluable institutional support during two of my three years of field research. I thank Gordon Liu, Guan Haijing, Yao Yao, Zhou Qin, He Yangyang, and Chen Yunwei for all the support they provided and the professional home they provided me in Beijing. A special thanks to Professor Guo Zhonghua for sending me down the path of citizenship

x *Acknowledgments*

research. I am grateful for the University of Chicago Center at Renmin University and the Universities Service Centre at the Chinese University of Hong Kong for welcoming me into the community there and providing me workspace.

This research would not have been possible without significant help from research assistants in China and the United States. I thank the numerous research assistants in Beijing, Changsha, Guangzhou, and Hangzhou who implemented the survey presented in this book. Three research assistants from Renmin University assisted in collecting the local *hukou* data drawn on heavily throughout the book. John Deacon, Boyun Kim, and Ben Raynor also provided valuable research assistance for the project. A later version of the manuscript benefited greatly from comments made by Mary Gallagher, Nita Rudra, and Jeremy Wallace during a book conference that they generously attended remotely during the summer of 2020.

Multiple institutions provided institutional and financial support for this project. The University of Wisconsin–Madison's political science department will always be my academic *laojia*. Visiting research positions at Peking University and Sun Yat-sen University supported nearly three years of research in China. I benefited greatly from the academic community at Stanford University while I was a Shorenstein Postdoctoral Fellow on Contemporary Asia at the Shorenstein Asia-Pacific Research Center. In particular, Jean Oi and Andrew Walder provided great insight into my project and welcomed me into the West Coast China community. At University of California, Irvine, I found a supportive community with numerous scholars who provided feedback on this book and continue to provide excellent mentorship, including Sara Wallace Goodman, Jeffrey Kopstein, Kamal Sadiq, and Dorothy Solinger. The Long US-China Institute at UCI keeps me grounded in China research across disciplines, and this book benefited from the guidance and community of fellow Long Institute faculty.

This project was funded by the Social Science Research Council, Fulbright-Hays Program, National Science Foundation (1323974), China Medical Board, Ford Foundation (New Generation China Scholars), the University of Wisconsin–Madison, and the Institute for Humane Studies (IHS017071). Portions of this book appear in "Dividing the People: The Authoritarian Bargain, Development, and Authoritarian Citizenship" (*Comparative Politics* 56, no. 1 [2023]).

I give special thanks to Dan LoPreto, Andrew Walder, and the production team at Stanford University Press for their support and guidance in

Acknowledgments xi

the review and publication process. The book benefited greatly from three anonymous reviewers. Beth Riley and Jonathan Cohen provided excellent editorial assistance. All remaining mistakes and typos are my own.

My peers provided essential support throughout this process. I am indebted to members of the Madison Mafia—Sarah Bouchat, Meina Cai, Dominic DeSapio, Brandon Lamson, Ning Leng, Ruoxi Li, Kerry Ratigan, and Zuo Cai, among others—for their comments and support throughout the years. A special thanks to the Women Who Write Awesome Things writing group, including Hannah Chapman, Rachel Jacobs, Anna Meier, Susanne Mueller-Redwood, Anna Oltman, and Rachel Schwartz, who read half-formed chapters throughout the project's lifespan. Fiona Cunningham and Ning Leng read and improved many portions of the book along the way. Wendy Leutert gave insightful comments on many chapters and provided immeasurable personal and professional moral support from the early stages of research and beyond.

The research and writing of this book spanned many different phases of my life, from the early days as a graduate student in UW's library cages to late nights in Peking University's empty classrooms, to writing in fast-food chains in a small town in rural Wisconsin, to tables around UCI's Aldrich Park. My work through this time would not have been possible without the unwavering support of my friends and family. I give special thanks to my fellow researchers from the Provincial Dinner Club, the Beijing Broads, the Monday Night Trivia crew, and my friends in Beijing and Shenzhen, who are too numerous to name. My Chinese family provided logistic support and dinner conversations that helped me stay grounded, both in life and in research.

Finally, none of this work would have been possible without the support of my family. I gained strength from my parents' unwavering belief in my abilities, even when they did not understand what I was doing or why I had chosen to go halfway around the world to do it. Shirley, Dan, and Tony endured countless phone calls of frustration and exhaustion, holidays celebrated remotely, and at times lack of communication while I was, and still am, far from home. Ellie's mere presence helps make this work feel worth it. And I thank Chris for patience, understanding, and months of feeding me and giving me the space I needed to complete this book. Chris, who you were, are, and will be inspires me every day.

Manipulating Authoritarian Citizenship

Introduction

Moving from one place to another is a common experience. Although moving across towns or states creates exciting prospects for new jobs and new lifestyles, bureaucratic headaches can result: establishing a new address and proof of residency, the dreaded visit to the Department of Motor Vehicles to change driver's license, registering children in new school districts, and more. But routine internal migration found in many parts of the world operates differently in China. A person moving from Shanghai to Beijing, for example, is building a new life but faces additional barriers more usually associated with international migration than with internal migration. Chinese internal migrants can rent an apartment, but in most places, they cannot automatically register their children in their neighborhood school. They can establish utilities for their home, but they cannot directly sign up for the same health insurance, unemployment benefits, or minimum livelihood guarantees offered to the locals they now live among. In short, China's 376 million internal migrants lack *local* citizenship—entitlements to local-government-provided rights—because they do not have official local urban household registration.[1]

Internal, domestic migrants in China are a distinct population legally separated from their local neighbors via the household registration, or *hukou*, system. The Chinese *hukou* is an internal citizenship institution: an exclusive, hereditary identity document that predicates rights entitlements in one subnational location. Local citizens, those with locally registered *hukou*, are entitled to services and redistribution provided by the local government, whereas internal migrants who live and work outside their place

2 *Introduction*

of registration are not. This internal citizenship distinguishes China from many contexts in which national citizenship creates equal membership in the state internally. The only way for internal migrants to gain permanent access to government services is to formally relinquish their previous *hukou* and its entitlements to register in a new location. But in contrast to the experience of moving between cities or provinces in other countries, obtaining a new *hukou* requires not just notifying but obtaining approval from the local government. Local governments, with control over who has access to local services, became particular about who and how many migrants they allowed to gain local citizenship in the early twenty-first century. As a result, how restrictive or permissive municipalities are when it comes to allowing migrants to gain *hukou* and thus access local-government services varies significantly. Some created open policies, allowing more migrants to naturalize locally—formally transferring their *hukou* to local urban status and canceling their old *hukou*—whereas others remained closed, making it nearly impossible for migrant workers to gain permanent access to local citizenship rights.

To illustrate, take the examples of Xi'an and Chengdu, two provincial capitals in China. In Xi'an, local officials targeted high-skilled workers from other provinces to whom to grant *hukou*. In 2010, the city's official *hukou* population grew by 5,900 net migrants, approximately 0.07 percent of the total population (Shaanxi Statistics Bureau 2011). Chengdu, just southwest of Xi'an, had looser regulations on who was eligible to change *hukou* and targeted local migrants, those who had long ago arrived in the city from the local countryside but had been living as outsiders, to give local citizenship through *hukou*. In 2010, Chengdu's *hukou* population grew by 96,196 net migrants, or 0.8 percent of the total population (Sichuan Statistics Bureau 2011). Across the country, municipalities varied in *which* migrants could become local citizens and in *how many* could gain *hukou* and thus entitlements to local citizenship rights (figure 0.1).

Why do some local governments open their doors and actively integrate migrants into the local citizenry while others remain closed? Why are some migrants welcomed in one city and not the next? What explains variation in access to local citizenship *within* China?

This book argues that access to citizenship rights, and therefore, access to government redistribution, results from both security and economic motivations. Specifically, officials at multiple levels of the Chinese bureaucracy

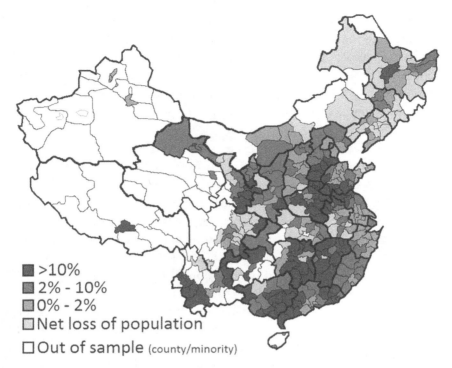

FIGURE O.1. Estimated net *hukou* acquisition rate of migrants in mainland China in 2010. Source: Estimated using MPS (2010) and NBS (2010). Naturalized population size is estimated as growth of local urban population not attributed to natural growth.

faced a trade-off between security-driven incentives to exclude migrants and economically-driven incentives to include migrants to support development. On the one hand, the need to provide public security and social stability created incentives to remain restrictive, protecting local resources from outsiders—that is, limiting autocratic redistribution. On the other hand, economic development imperatives created countervailing pressures to operate open citizenship regimes to manage local labor markets.

Internal citizenship regimes vary across the country because local economic development strategies differ in ways that change who the local state wants to incorporate into the permanent population. Outward-oriented development—driven by engagement with the international economy—increases incentives for high-skilled labor recruitment through migration. Bottom-up development—driven by local resources and agricultural

4 *Introduction*

upgrading—increases the need to integrate more local, rural populations to support transformation of the old urban-rural dual management economy. Top-down policies—in which development depends on central-government support—encourage expansion of citizenship to meet central policy targets. Internal citizenship regimes are, then, the downstream result of security concerns and variation in development policies at multiple levels of government.

This balancing act between security-based conservatism and development-supporting liberalization created a highly institutionalized form of authoritarian citizenship. Without democratic institutions creating broad accountability mechanisms, autocratic systems can—and do—limit redistribution. They do so substantively, by redistributing socioeconomic rights rather than political rights, and mechanically, by redistributing to those whose inclusion benefits the state. *Internal citizenship institutions*—rules governing *who* is entitled to redistributed rights within one national polity—allow autocratic systems to ensure both security and economic incentives behind redistribution. These internal citizenship regimes subdivide the population into different classifications of citizens with differentiated rights entitlements. Only full citizens are entitled to the most socioeconomic rights. The result is a form of autocratic citizenship defined by particularistic membership that predicates socioeconomic rights.

Who, in the end, gains access to citizenship also depends on migrants themselves. Policy reforms of the early twenty-first century create institutional space for voluntarism, in which migrants can choose to change their *hukou* or not, analogous to an international naturalization decision. No longer subjects of central and local policies dictating one's identity, individuals choose to naturalize and access local citizenship or remain outsiders. This individual-level decision-making about *hukou* identity increasingly determines overall variation in access to citizenship rights after *hukou* reform, because some migrants choose not to naturalize and become local even when given the opportunity to do so by liberalizing local governments.

Unequal Redistribution and Autocratic Citizenship

Autocratic states rely on redistribution to stay in power. Often framed as the authoritarian bargain, autocratic systems exchange socioeconomic rights and redistribution for at least tacit political support. A state that does not provide redistribution may face threats to its power because even autocratic systems rely on popular support (Przeworski 2022). But redistribution is inherently unequal because political power is unevenly distributed in society. Political supporters receive the most redistribution (Bueno de Mesquita et al. 2003; Haber 2006), and political challengers receive redistribution to buy their support or ingratiate the regime with them (Albertus, Fenner, and Slater 2018; Gandhi 2008; Haggard and Kaufman 2009; Knutsen and Rasmussen 2017; Pan 2020). But extant theories fail to explain who counts as a member of the selectorate—the privileged group of those who receive at least some redistribution—and how autocratic leaders use institutions to define and change hierarchies of inclusion. As a result, theories of authoritarian redistribution focus on the security imperative—redistribution as a coercion, co-optation, and repression mechanism—overlooking concurrent economic incentives and how redistribution incentives vary within one polity. The arguments laid out in this book use citizenship institutions to fill these gaps.

Citizenship institutions constitute not only rights but also an exclusive membership identity—formal belonging in the polity with rights entitlements from the state (Brubaker 1992; Tilly 1995). Traditionally, citizenship conjures up the image of national-level membership: we are citizens of China, the United States, or South Africa. But when institutions divide a population within one polity, allowing access to citizenship rights to some nationals but not others, citizenship must be relocated below the national level. These internal citizenship regimes—institutions that define membership in citizenship within a national polity—create hierarchies of belonging within one country and are a core feature of citizenship in authoritarian contexts.

One of this book's most important contributions is a framework for understanding citizenship in authoritarian contexts. Other studies of citizenship focus on direct political rights, often equating democracy and citizenship (Distelhorst and Fu 2019).[2] From the perspective that elections make citizens, in which the concept of citizenship applies only if there are direct political elections, nondemocratic nationals are relegated to subjecthood and individuals are merely subject to imperial power without rights entitlements.[3] This assumption of subjecthood mischaracterizes the nature of individual-state relations for more than half the world's population.[4] By limiting the study of citizenship to cases with direct political participation, the study of individual-state relations ignores other forms of what Tilly

6 Introduction

(1995) calls transactions between people and the state—the fundamental basis of citizenship.

Citizenship in authoritarian contexts has not gone unstudied, but existing research emphasizes the application of democratic definitions of citizenship in authoritarian contexts and individual-level rights claiming. Some scholars use existing, democracy-focused conceptions of citizenship to identify patterns of democratic practices in authoritarian contexts.[5] Other scholars focus on citizens themselves: citizenship is not only the institutions that bestow rights but also the individual identity and the practice of claiming rights from the state.[6] The arguments presented here contribute to the systemic understanding of citizenship in authoritarian settings, of membership in the polity that predicates rights and responsibilities—the fundamental institutions that define citizenship. Autocratic systems design citizenship institutions, particularly citizenship membership rules defining who is and is not entitled to state resources, to manage and manipulate populations and redistribution.[7]

VARIETIES OF CITIZENSHIP

Fundamentally, citizenship is a special membership category: an identity that bestows on its holders rights and responsibilities determined by belonging to a particular political community (Brubaker 1992; Turner 1990, 1993). It is an exclusionary status of entitlement that connects the individual and state through a series of transactions (Brubaker 1992; Soysal 1994; Tilly 1995). The most important and fundamental purpose of citizenship is to delineate membership that entitles some individuals—citizens—to allocation of resources provided by the state while excluding others—noncitizens (Brubaker 1992; Turner 1993). Membership institutions are the rules and structures that dictate who is entitled to citizenship rights. Citizenship membership creates boundaries defining citizenship as a special class.[8] Defining citizenship by entitlements—*what* members are entitled to from the state defining citizenship rights—and exclusion—*who* is and is not entitled to these benefits defined by membership institutions—is not inherently related to regime type and provides a rubric for comparing types of citizenship across different political regimes.

In its ideal democratic form, citizenship is a universal, inclusive membership that bestows democratically defined individual rights, epitomized by electoral rights that distribute political power across society. Universal membership in citizenship is a necessary condition for a functioning ideal-type democracy in which individuals have power over the state through political participation (Dahl 2005).

But the democratic citizenship of civil, political, and social rights envisioned by Marshall (1950) and others who followed is just one form of citizenship rarely fully realized. In practice, most democracies do not ensure full, ideal-type inclusive democratic citizenship because "democratic norms are not *perfectly* realized anywhere" (Schedler 2002, 38, emphasis in original). Citizenship rights and membership are truncated, interrupted, and selectively protected (Chung 2017; Lohr 2012; Starr 2021). The fundamental rights of political participation in democracies are regularly restricted. Throughout history and across country contexts, laws and policies reduce the ability of women and racial and religious groups to vote, stripping them of the most important democratic political right (Keyssar 2009). Strict voter registration laws in the United States during the twentieth century, for example, interrupt the practice of citizenship by imposing high administrative burdens (Highton 2004). When equitable democratic rights clash with traditionalist cultural values, women's rights are often restricted.[9] Informal institutions such as corruption and clientelism prevent the full realization of political rights. For example, clientelist regimes in Colombia combined with economic precarity characteristic of unprotected social citizenship leads to vote buying, undermining representative democracy (Escobar 2002).

Even when political rights are well established, access to social rights depends on a group's ability to lobby. Social rights and economic protections in one-person, one-vote systems mean some groups gain socioeconomic rights and redistribution from the government when they represent strong political groups. When interest groups lose the ability to influence elections, they lose the ability to ensure social citizenship outlays.[10] Formal democratic institutions also channel discriminatory practices that limit social citizenship. For example, in the United States, de jure discrimination in segregation policies in the nineteenth and twentieth centuries formally stripped political and social citizenship rights from people of color. Even after school integration, legal segregationist housing policies prevented people of color from enjoying the benefits of urban spaces with higher quality of social rights, such as education (Rothstein 2017), creating a de facto limitation on membership in social citizenship.

The highly varied experience of citizenship in democracies and general lacunae in theories of citizenship in nondemocracies highlight the need

8 *Introduction*

to expand the study of citizenship beyond its ideal and dominant forms. Developing a better understanding of how citizenship institutions operate beyond ideal-type democracies creates a more inclusive concept with global application.

THEORIZING AUTHORITARIAN CITIZENSHIP

Non-democratic Rights and Membership

Unlike its democratic counterpart, citizenship in authoritarian contexts is premised on unequal entitlements to rights. Both defining features of citizenship—rights and membership—exist in nondemocracies, but their content varies: socioeconomic group-based rights dominate and membership is particularistic rather than universal.

Unwilling to redistribute political rights, autocrats redistribute socioeconomic rights as citizenship rights (Mann 1987; Meijer and Butenschøn 2017b; Perry 2008). Many authoritarian systems, China included, premise state legitimacy on the provision of economic well-being, income growth, and the provision of some basic welfare such as education and pensions (Hu and Saich 2012; Keane 2002; Perry 2008; Shi and Lu 2010; Solinger 1999). Although political rights do exist, such as voting in local elections, socioeconomic redistribution defines the individual-state relationship.

Citizenship rights describe *what* individuals are entitled to from the state; membership defines *who* is entitled to those rights. Unlike universal membership in ideal-type democracies, membership in nondemocratic citizenship is inherently particularistic, creating boundaries of belonging within a national polity in which some have access to citizenship rights and others do not. Autocratic systems are not rooted in universalistic expectations of the state-individual relationship. Instead, autocratic systems can, and do, create internal citizenship regimes that subdivide the national political community into members and nonmembers.

Internal citizenship regimes are sets of membership policies used to divide populations within a country dictating people's eligibility for citizenship rights.[11] Some individuals are marked as members in the policy, having entitlements to rights provisions, and some are nonmembers, restricted from accessing rights. Internal citizenship regimes can divide the population along economic,[12] racial,[13] religious,[14] and geographic lines. These regimes create hierarchies of citizenship with differentiated membership statuses within one national context that consequently dictate who has access to citizenship rights and who does not. This disaggregation allows autocratic leaders to target different redistribution provision to specific groups, helpful for fulfilling the authoritarian bargain without providing more than necessary. The resulting institutional arrangements are fragmented, layered, and subject to manipulation by autocrats to strategically redistribute enough while limiting the provision of rights.

Hukou *as a Citizenship Membership Institution*

The *hukou* is the paramount internal citizenship institution in China on which access to rights provided by the local state depends. All individuals have a *hukou* that identifies each as a citizen of a particular location and with a particular type, either urban or rural. All are citizens of the specific county where they are registered, and the local government is responsible for providing access to citizenship rights. Most conventional elements of citizenship entitlements, such as public schools, state-run health insurance, and registration of children to establish their citizenship, are reserved for the local population, identified through *hukou* (Vortherms 2015, 2019; Zhang 2012). Only those holding a local *hukou* are permanently entitled to these rights (Chan 2009; Cheng and Selden 1994; Vortherms 2015). Non-*hukou* populations—those with *hukou* registered in some other city or county—do not have permanent access to locally provided social housing, social security, unemployment compensation, minimum livelihood guarantees, employment training, and small-enterprise subsidies where they live and work (Zhang 2012; Zhang and Wang 2010).[15]

Right to a particular *hukou* follows jus sanguinis lines: *hukou* is registered at birth and *hukou* identity is hereditary; children inherit their status from either one of their parents.[16] Unequal citizenships are not only defined at birth but also carry on generationally, and children receive the same privileged or nonprivileged status as their parents, regardless of where they are born or what their parents do. Because of this birthright citizenship, there are no automatic ways to change *hukou* status. Instead, to obtain local citizenship in another location, a person must naturalize locally by applying for formal permission from the local government to change *hukou* and permanently relinquishing a previous *hukou* identity.[17] Naturalization is the process of acquiring citizenship rights. I use the term *local naturalization* to refer to the processes whereby individuals gain citizenship status within internal citizenship regimes. Local naturalization processes are the rules that

10 *Introduction*

dictate the manner of selection of individuals to gain rights entitlements. Just like the *what* and *who* of authoritarian redistribution, naturalization policies are essential tools for manipulating *how* a person gains access to redistribution.

The Chinese *hukou* system operates similarly to other infamous internal passport systems, such as the Soviet *propiska* and its Central Asian descendants and the Vietnamese *ho khau*. In each of these settings, entitlements to government services, socioeconomic rights, and in extreme cases, livelihoods depend on holding local citizenship.

Varying Access to Local Citizenship

For decades, the central government strictly controlled local naturalizations, limiting who and how many people could change their *hukou* status, as a legacy of central economic planning. Even in the early reform years, the *hukou* remained integral to the dual urban-rural system of economic management.[18] Decentralizing reforms in the first years of the twenty-first century attempted to break down the persistent urban-rural divides in the economy. As local governments gained greater autonomy, naturalization policies proliferated and diversified. Especially at the municipal level,[19] governments manipulated local citizenship regimes, changing who was eligible for full citizenship and how many people could naturalize locally. Some municipalities targeted classically defined desirable migrants, including high-skilled workers and those with formal professional training. Others remained restrictive toward high-skilled workers and instead targeted more local migrants with family connections to the local urban center. Small cities, which often saw the strongest pressure from the central government to open naturalization pathways, varied greatly in *hukou* policies; some opened doors and others resisted reform and remained closed. The result was a highly varied landscape of access to citizenship rights across the country, and hundreds of millions of migrant workers faced dramatically different access to local citizenship rights. What explains variation in access to citizenship?

Some argue that the *hukou* is used to control the population, ensuring the regime's security and stability.[20] Traditionally, redistribution in authoritarian systems follows security threats, and socioeconomic goods are used to coerce, co-opt, or repress potential challengers to the regime.[21] Migrant workers isolated by the *hukou* system in China lead many of the labor protests seen across the country because they often face significant discrimination and exploitative working conditions. In a system with socialist goals, such labor-based protests could be destabilizing, especially if protestors emphasize workers' rights consciousness. This security pressure to avoid protests could filter down to local governments and encourage the use of *hukou* policies to protect security.

But since the first years of the twenty-first century, the *hukou* system has seen significant subnational variation and reform that cannot be explained by security alone. Of the two cities, Xi'an and Chengdu, mentioned earlier in the chapter, Chengdu faces higher security concerns than Xi'an yet naturalizes ten times, proportionally, as many migrants.[22] Labor protests may fail to challenge the regime if they are rules oriented rather than rights oriented.[23] And inequality, once presumed an existential threat to regime stability, finds mixed results in survey research (Whyte 2010, 2016). The security imperative of limiting and controlling the population no doubt encourages the continuation of the *hukou* system in some form but cannot explain variation alone.

Others have argued that access to citizenship rights resulted from marketization of *hukou* and the success of neoliberal economic models transforming the system. According to this perspective, as the country introduced market forces, *hukou* itself became a pseudo good, exposed to market supply and demand.[24] Although the introduction of market forces increased incentives to reform the *hukou* system, especially reducing migration controls, market forces cannot explain why some cities remain fairly closed to some of the most economically productive migrants or why some smaller cities, with relatively weak market economies, see an expansion of citizenship rights but others do not. A purely market-based understanding of *hukou* ignores the active role state policy makers take in manipulating policy to benefit local development and the continuity of *hukou* as a state-directed form of development.

The Argument: Explaining Internal Citizenship Regimes and Their Outcomes

I argue that both security and economic logics drive variation in local citizenship membership, defining who can become a local citizen and who cannot. The central government long used the *hukou* system to protect

12 *Introduction*

government resources, by restricting access to services, and to promote economic development, by managing and distributing labor in either urban or rural economies. These forces encouraged exclusive membership and restrictive access to redistributive citizenship rights, especially in economically productive urban spaces. But as economic policy changed with the dismantling of the command economy, development policies encouraged greater openness in internal citizenship membership: granting more people access to citizenship rights in the pursuit of economic development. The central government reformed *hukou* management, decentralizing authority to local governments alongside control over other factors of production to match the shift toward a decentralized and adaptive economic development model. Local governments, in turn, used local citizenship regimes to target migrants for integration through naturalization when they benefited local development policies.

Variation in internal citizenship regimes, and therefore access to particularistic, expanded access to citizenship rights, resulted from balancing exclusion, driven by security concerns, and openness, driven by economic incentives, at both central and local policy-making levels. Security, prioritized by the central government, supported the *hukou* system's continuation. But economic motivations for supporting development drove institutional change and greater openness. Central policies continued to emphasize maintaining the system while allowing bottom-up variation in *hukou* policy management. Local variation proliferated with new ways internal migrants could gain local citizenship and differing barriers for groups among municipalities, changing who could naturalize. A migrant with desirable characteristics, such as educational background or wealth, might be welcomed in one city but not in the next.

Granting of *hukou* and expanding access to citizenship redistribution continued as a primary tool for managing labor in China's market socialist system. When control over economic development policies decentralized, so too did *hukou* policies so that labor market management could match local development needs. Local governments, through their control over membership policies—the rules of who was and could become a local citizen—used these internal citizenship regimes to strategically manipulate their population to align with local development strategies: migrants whose skills supported local development could naturalize, and everyone else remained excluded.

Variation in access to citizenship resulted from divergent development strategies because strategies were not monolithic across the country. I present three broad categories of development strategies that target different types of migrants for inclusion: Outward-oriented development strategies, dependent on foreign firm production and foreign capital, create greater demand for high-skilled workers. Bottom-up development strategies depend on rural upgrading and land-centered urbanization, two processes that dislodge rural residents from their land and create incentives for the local government to target the most local migrants for inclusion, regardless of their skill level. Top-down development in impoverished areas, in which development goals are set and financed from outside the municipality, lacks the underlying economic mechanisms to drive naturalization, unless it is directly related to policy goals, such as poverty alleviation resettlement. As shown in other new regionalism studies (Rithmire 2013b), the overarching driver of variation is that similar policies implemented from the top down interact with existing institutional arrangements—namely, development policies—and result in subnational variation.

Finally, because local citizenship regimes expanded access to citizenship rights by creating more opportunities for naturalization, individual choices became increasingly important in understanding who, in the end, gets access to citizenship. Internal migrants, no longer dispatched to labor assignments by central planners, have agency to naturalize or not, depending on individual cost-benefit decisions. Even the most open and inclusive policies will not expand citizenship rights if migrants choose not to naturalize.

Key Contributions

MEMBERSHIP IN AUTHORITARIAN REDISTRIBUTION

A primary contribution of this work is its application of the citizenship framework to identify who enjoys authoritarian redistribution. By focusing on the manipulation of local citizenship membership within one policy, this book adds a dynamic perspective of who benefits from authoritarian redistribution. This book shifts the focus from the *what* and *why* of redistribution, which dominates the authoritarian welfare literature, to the connection between *why* and *how* redistribution occurs.

Most of our understanding of authoritarian redistribution through welfare stems from the basic logic of the selectorate theory. Although autocracies

14 *Introduction*

redistribute less than democracies (Acemoglu and Robinson 2006; Ansell 2008; Boix 2003; Haggard and Kaufman 2009), redistribution through welfare provision benefits autocratic longevity. Redistribution through welfare helps pay off supporters and buy off would-be challengers[25] or enmeshes populations in state institutions to repress, co-opt, or coerce support.[26]

This book contributes to this literature in two key ways. First, it concentrates on the who and how of authoritarian redistribution. Who receives welfare regularly boils down to regime insiders versus outsiders, to elites versus the masses.[27] It breaks down these general inclusion and exclusion criteria to provide a more nuanced explanation of variation within the masses. The focus on internal citizenship institutions and how membership defines entitlements to redistribution provides a broader yet still practical understanding of how authoritarian redistribution functions and, perhaps more importantly, how redistribution changes.

Second, this book contributes to the field of authoritarian welfare as a tool for economic development. Autocratic systems can provide welfare to advance development outcomes, including in the context of globalization.[28] This study expands on the security and economic imperatives for welfare distribution, showing how multilevel policy making complicates the motivations for redistribution by allowing multiple drivers to coexist and interact. Specifically, I argue that security concerns of the central government drive the continuity in China's internal citizenship regimes, but security alone cannot explain variation in policy outcomes. Economic development policies encouraged the center to decentralize redistribution. Local authorities benefit from the system's security-enhancing features but drive variation in policy implementation to support local economic development.

This book relocates exclusion in citizenship below the national level. Studies of citizenship across regime types take the national level as the most important location for inclusion and exclusion in citizenship. Although this is sometimes appropriate, membership operates below the national level in many contexts.[29] And local-level exclusion occurs both in rights and in membership, such that local limitations to citizenship membership undermine the value and protections of national-level citizenship. I argue that this local level of exclusion is inherent in nondemocratic citizenship, but lessons can be drawn for democratic contexts as well, where laws and regulations formally or informally segregate populations, limiting their access to government services and protections.

Introduction 15

HUKOU AND LOCAL CITIZENSHIP

The citizenship framework also adds to our understanding of the *hukou* specifically. While others have also described *hukou* as citizenship, this analysis contextualizes *hukou* as a comprehensive citizenship institution, concentrating on membership from a theoretical perspective.

The Chinese *hukou* is one of the most important institutions in modern Chinese society. It is often blamed for being the root of structural inequality in China, while also identified as one ingredient in China's economic rise (Chan 2009; Cheng 1991; Liu 2005; Solinger 1999; Wang 2005). Scholars in many disciplines have studied the *hukou* system because of its social, political, and economic impacts. The bulk of studies on *hukou* concern *hukou*-constrained migration, both explicitly through migration controls and implicitly because of migration's welfare consequences.[30] Scholars identified the institutional changes[31] and durability through periods of reform.[32] Research from the reform period after 1980 focuses on how the *hukou* institutionalizes inequality to affect social identity,[33] labor market outcomes,[34] and access to welfare and government services.[35]

Framing *hukou* as a citizenship institution also has its origin in existing research because it defines membership in the polity that provides the bulk of citizenship rights (Smart and Smart 2001; Vortherms 2015, 2021). As Solinger (1999) argues, the state commodified migrants when it introduced market forces but never fully considered, or treated, them as citizens. This expanded the urban-rural inequality seeded during the command economy era, keeping rural migrant workers eager to improve their situation as second-class citizens and limited by the exclusionary structure imposed by local states.

My focus on membership, and in particular the incentives to expand membership in this formerly closed system, adds complexity to existing understandings of *hukou* as primarily an institution of exclusion.[36] The *hukou* no doubt provides the state with powerful exclusionary tools that allowed continued social stability and economic growth through inequality, but the previous focus on exclusion and control creates an excessive dependence on the security incentives for local citizenship.

This study moves beyond security and the continuation of the national-level regime to explain the highly fractured subnational functioning of control, which necessitates an added economic lens. Economic development encourages exclusion to make resources stretch further, but it

16   *Introduction*

also stimulates expansion when development depends on greater inclusion. Thus, this work examines strategic inclusion—*who* gains the privileged included status *when*—and inherent, security-driven exclusion.

I argue that development creates incentives to liberalize the *hukou* system.[37] But unlike previous studies, my study disaggregates this economic mechanism. I contend that economically driven liberalization is not a question of a state retreating from economic management but rather one actively participating in labor allocation through the decentralized management of the *hukou* system. This added, more nuanced role played by economic development necessitates a multilevel analysis, of understanding the *hukou* system from both the central and the local levels. This book shows that the subnational level is where these security and economic logics collide to create a highly varied system of local citizenship.

CENTRAL, LOCAL, AND INDIVIDUAL EFFECTS ON ACCESS TO CITIZENSHIP

Multilevel factors drive access to citizenship rights. Variation in access to citizenship rights, this study's key outcome, depends on central-, local-, and individual-level interactions with *hukou* policies. Each level of analysis provides its own perspective. The central perspective tells a story of security maintenance and macrolevel economic development coordination. The local perspective highlights the rising importance of local economic development policies in generating variation in the day-to-day functioning of the *hukou* system. Because central policy encourages voluntarism, or eligible individuals' ability to choose to change their *hukou* or not, individual cost-benefit calculations provide the final piece of the puzzle explaining variation in who gets access to citizenship rights and who remains excluded. Understanding variation in access to citizenship depends on all three levels of analysis. Limiting analysis to only one level oversimplifies the complexity of China's internal citizenship regimes. This multilevel analysis incorporates not only the often-ignored individual level but also the interplay among levels to provide a more holistic picture of citizenship in China.

Consideration of the interactions among these three levels of analysis is essential for understanding how and why access to citizenship varies. Omitting any one level ignores the interplay of incentives for expanding or restricting local citizenship membership. A focus on the center would lead to an oversecuritized understanding of variation. A focus on the local level would lead observers to a principal-agent framework, in which variation occurs because of improperly controlled local governments. But as I argue here, local variation is not itself a bug but a feature of central-government management. By drawing on an original, representative survey from two cities, I show that the individual level sketches a generalizable picture of the vast variation in demand for *hukou* and provides context for the consequences of these policies. Without this level of analysis, the decline of the *hukou* system might seem more likely than warranted.

Research Design

I began research for this project in 2012, interviewing local bureaucrats and academics involved in policy experiments in southern China and reviewing government policy across bureaucratic levels. At the time, a 2011 national *hukou* reform had just trickled down through the bureaucracy, and those involved in *hukou* policy experimentation were certain that the change would be the watershed moment for *hukou* reform. It was not. Through these early interviews I saw the clear gap between national and even provincial policies and local implementation. Conversations with policy working group members made clear local officials' latitude in adapting policies. Throughout this book's chapters, I discuss five levels of analysis as they interact with each other: the center, provincial, municipal, county, and individual. This multilevel approach helps show the interaction of security and economic incentives in determining access to citizenship.

Over approximately thirty-seven months between 2012 and 2017, I completed more than a hundred semistructured interviews with government bureaucrats at the county, municipal, provincial, and central levels; *hukou* police officers and detectives, who are the grassroots bureaucrats and state agents responsible for day-to-day implementation of *hukou* policy; and firm managers, human resources workers, and factory headhunters. I had scores of conversations with migrant workers themselves across the socioeconomic spectrum. These conversations illuminated the thousands of government policy documents I collected at four levels of government, highlighting how *hukou* institutions were supposed to be versus how they normally operated.

In Guangdong, one eager bureaucrat turned academic exclaimed that I did not need to leave Guangdong for research, that as a province, it had it all: migrant sending and receiving areas, municipalities on the cutting edge of policy reform, and laggards (Interview 44120801). Indeed, this

18 *Introduction*

sentiment of being the future of *hukou* reform was a repeated phenomenon in other provinces as well. How key migrant hubs like Beijing, Shanghai, and Guangzhou manage their *hukou* policies is important, which is why they are the focus of existing research.[38] But every city in every region in China excludes migrants from citizenship. I designed my project to provide a broader picture of citizenship regimes across the country to understand how the system operates nationally. To this end, I conducted semistructured interviews in six provinces in four regions.[39]

I relied on the municipal—also called prefectural—level to measure internal citizenship regimes. This level of government is the highest level tasked with policy implementation that is also involved in policy formulation. Municipal governments directly manage municipalities' core urban districts and oversee rural counties and satellite cities below them. Provincial-level aggregation, despite its greater data availability, is less helpful in evaluating *hukou* policies because belonging and service provision usually occur at the municipal level and below.[40]

To understand the bottom-up perspective, my surveys in Beijing and Changsha used a multistage spatial probability sample of migrant and rural residents to understand attitudes toward and demand for local *hukou*. The survey used experimental questions to evaluate variation in demand for local urban *hukou*. As I argue in chapter 5, the function of local citizenship regimes cannot be understood without understanding how migrant and rural residents themselves see their citizenship and whether they desire to change it.

Book Outline

The book begins with a conceptual framework for understanding authoritarian citizenship and its manipulation. Chapter 1 traces the evolution of the *hukou* as a citizenship institution. I outline the key features of citizenship institutions—membership, rights, and responsibilities—as they operate in nondemocratic settings. I then apply these to the Chinese context. The *hukou* became a citizenship institution when the state used it to implement the Soviet-style command economy. Central-state planners used the *hukou* as a redistribution mechanism to support planned labor allocation to drive urban development at the cost of rural development, in furtherance of the dualist economy keeping urban and rural management separated.

Decentralized reform did not deconstruct *hukou* as citizenship but shifted the management of labor and redistribution to the local level, creating varied local citizenship regimes.

Chapter 2 examines the means and motivations for manipulating access to citizenship to explain variation in internal citizenship regimes. It presents my central argument, that the simultaneous task of balancing security and economic incentives at multiple governmental levels resulted in varied internal citizenship regimes. Generally, security incentives motivated a closed system, creating particularistic membership in China's citizenship, whereas economics motivated a selective, strategic expansion of access to citizenship rights for migrants who benefited economic development. When development was centrally managed through the command economy, and the central government managed *hukou* policies. When economic policies decentralized, especially control over the factors of production, so too did control over *hukou* policies. Local officials, juggling the trickle-down security incentives inherent in the *hukou* system and the pressure for development, used local citizenship regimes to achieve locally driven development strategy by expanding targeted redistribution.

Chapter 3 describes variation in *hukou* policies at the local level. I disaggregate the country's internal citizenship regimes into the pathways to local citizenship allowed by municipal governments. Using a near census of municipalities, I code local *hukou* transfer processes into a quantitative index of government policies in 2016. These data provide information on the implementation of local naturalization. These pathways purposely mirror international pathways to citizenship and target different types of migrants for local citizenship, allowing local governments to act strategically, disaggregating migrants into desirable and undesirable populations.

Chapter 4 defines and explains variation in local citizenship openness—how easy it is to naturalize locally—through security and economic lenses. I identify what makes a migrant desirable, based on the local security-economic trade-off. Security, social stability, and fiscal chauvinism create incentives to remain closed. Variation in local development policies creates incentives to open policies to some migrants but not others. I outline three development pathways—outward oriented, bottom up, and top down—and assess how they create incentives to target different migrant groups for local naturalization. To add to the breadth of inclusion defined by local citizenship policies, I also estimate the depth of inclusion, or net

20   *Introduction*

naturalizations: how many people changed their *hukou* across the country. This chapter draws on a wide range of quantitative and qualitative evidence, including the original index of *hukou* policies discussed in chapter 3, official statistics, and estimated population and *hukou* transfer projections.

Chapter 5 provides the last empirical piece of the puzzle: who wants local citizenship? Variation in access to citizenship is not only a question of who local governments allow to change their *hukou* when given the chance. When institutional reform includes voluntarism, or individuals being able to choose to interact with policy change or not, understanding policy outcomes depends on understanding demand for institutional change. Drawing on an experimental, probabilistically sampled survey implemented in Beijing and Changsha in 2015 and 2016, I highlight how individuals make cost-benefit decisions on becoming citizens or remaining outsiders. This potentially risky decision to naturalize locally and detach themselves from their hometowns is based on their rights endowments and financial support. The survey shows significant variation in desire to obtain *hukou* among the excluded populations. This variation is a missing link needed for understanding the potential for *hukou* reform.

The conclusion discusses the continued consequences of China's internal citizenship regimes. It explores the potential mismatch between reforms and bottom-up demand for reforms, from both individuals and local governments. Lessons from China's local citizenship regimes are extended to other comparative contexts, such as former Soviet republics whose welfare rights are still influenced by subnational citizenship contexts.

ONE

The Institutional Evolution of China's Local Citizenship

China's *hukou* system, like many Chinese social and political institutions, has a long history with many imperial ancestors. Over the course of the *hukou*'s implementation, the system shifted from an institution of responsibilities and extraction during the imperial era to a local citizenship institution that bestowed citizenship rights. This chapter traces the historical evolution of China's *hukou* institution from the perspective of citizenship. The *hukou*'s history is well trodden, and previous scholars used the concept of citizenship when understanding *hukou* in its modern form. This chapter adds to this discussion by tracing the evolution of local citizenship explicitly and contextualizing the process holistically from the perspective of authoritarian citizenship. I lay out four periods in this chapter—the imperial, Mao, early reform, and decentralized reform eras—each representing the shifting meanings and implications of a citizenship institution. I identify in each how *hukou* interacts with the three key elements of citizenship—membership, rights, and responsibilities—to analyze the institutional development of citizenship in China.

The imperial era saw the rise of local membership, used by imperial powers to enforce responsibilities of taxation and conscription, aligning with the concept of subjecthood under the imperial order. The Mao era defined by the spread of communist ideology saw a redefinition of individual responsibilities as socialist work, organized and enforced through the *hukou* system. The *hukou* system transformed into a local citizenship institution in conjunction with the command economy and industrial-centered development, as the *hukou* became an essential tool to implement the dual

22   Chapter 1

urban-rural development model of the command economy. Development policies necessitated government redistribution of socioeconomic rights to industrial workers, identified through the *hukou* system.

The early reform period triggered by market reform dismantled the command economy and removed internal migration restrictions related to the *hukou*. The rise of internal migration dramatically altered the implications of local citizenship created in the Mao era, but it did not fundamentally reform the *hukou* as a citizenship institution. Finally, as state-led development evolved to a more decentralized form, *hukou* naturalizations—processes that allowed internal migrants to change their *hukou*, thus granting access to local citizenship rights—decentralized, and internal citizenship regimes manipulated by local governments emerged.

Citizenship Institutions under Authoritarianism

Full, liberal democracy depends on inclusive citizenship in which all individuals in society, on the basis of membership in the national polity, have access to political rights. Democracy and inclusive citizenship are mutually constitutive: without inclusive citizenship, democratic institutions fail to function properly (Dahl 2005; Shaw 2017). Thus, inclusive membership and individualistic political rights define democratic citizenship. These rights ensure equal access to democratically defined political participation, such as voting, with political rights at the core of ideal-type democratic citizenship.[1]

But this internally consistent, elections-driven democratic citizenship is just one form of citizenship. Assuming that elections make citizens means citizenship is codetermined with regime type and ignores the varieties of citizenship not only across the democratic-nondemocratic dichotomy but also within each of those sets of regime types (Heisler 2005; Mann 1987; Murphy and Fong 2006). Scholars have long argued that citizenship operates in nondemocratic contexts with variation in the content of citizenship institutions—membership, rights, and responsibilities—dependent on regime type (Mann 1987).[2]

AUTHORITARIAN RIGHTS AND RESPONSIBILITIES

Socioeconomic redistribution dominates citizenship rights in nondemocracies because autocratic leaders are more willing to redistribute socioeconomic rights than political rights (Mann 1987; Meijer and Butenschøn

2017b; Perry 2008). Favorable government performance, such as the provision of economic development, increases popular support for authoritarian rule.[3] Protection of socioeconomic rights, especially as demographics change as a population ages, underlies popular conceptions of citizenship in Russia (Henry 2009). In the transition to dictatorship, citizenship rights in Spain and Portugal shifted away from direct political participation to socioeconomic rights, including access to housing, which fundamentally reshaped the meaning of citizenship (Pinto 2012).

Citizenship rights in China also center socioeconomic redistribution. Citizens expect the state to provide collective socioeconomic goods rather than the individual rights traditionally expected in western European countries (Perry 2008; Shi and Lu 2010; Solinger 1999). State provision of protective redistribution is deeply rooted in the political philosophy of welfare for the people (Janoski 2014; Perry 2008). The early Chinese Communist Party (CCP) embraced this notion, emphasizing economic rights above all others. It developed socioeconomic rights as the basis of citizenship rights provided by, and demanded of, the state, aligned with communist ideology. Throughout the 1990s and 2000s, the Chinese state itself purposely defined citizenship rights as socioeconomic benefits to tie state legitimacy with the provision of these rights (Hu and Saich 2012; Keane 2001). The dominance of socioeconomic rights internalized as well, as the general population demanded greater socioeconomic protections as a basis of state legitimacy (Gilley 2007; Shi and Lu 2010). To this day, socioeconomic rights that include social protections, such as the right to education, health care, pensions, and old-age care, make up the bulk of Chinese citizenship rights. Political rights, including direct elections, do exist at the local level in China, but they are dwarfed by both the provision and expectation of socioeconomic rights.[4]

Responsibilities of citizenship also vary by regime type because fundamental state institutions vary. Citizenship responsibilities, such as paying taxes and conscription, largely do not change by regime type, but duties to work or support a central party are more likely in nondemocracies. Communist regimes, for example, see work as an essential citizenship responsibility because economic planning is an essential portion of state function. Additionally, citizens of nondemocracies often have, either implicitly or explicitly, a responsibility to support the regime. This can be viewed as the seemingly unlikely overlap between the authoritarian bargain and Tilly's transaction model of citizenship. Autocrats provide socioeconomic

24 Chapter 1

redistribution, or rights, for at least tacit political support, or responsibilities. This mirrors Tilly's transaction model of citizenship, whereby a series of transactions between the state and the individual define citizenship (Tilly 1995).

CITIZENSHIP MEMBERSHIP IN AUTHORITARIAN CONTEXTS

Socioeconomic rights dominate authoritarian rights but these rights are not universally provided in nondemocratic settings. Because political power is not evenly distributed in society, membership is also not universalistic but instead is particularistic, with some individuals gaining access to rights and others facing significant exclusion. Compared with expected universalistic membership in democracies, particularistic membership allows the autocrat to manipulate citizenship selectively and strategically by defining who counts as a full citizen entitled to redistribution and who is not. Authoritarian citizenship creates internal division, locating membership within the polity rather than across polities. Within the authoritarian state, internal citizenship regimes create lines of division that form hierarchies of citizens within a country. Insiders and outsiders are defined not by nationality but by belonging to internally defined groups.

This picture is far from Brubaker's (1992) conceptualization of citizenship as an "internally inclusive and externally exclusive" category where national citizenship "define[s] a region of legal equality" (21). But using this inequality to relegate all Chinese nationals to subjecthood mischaracterizes the experience of citizenship in China. Instead of declaring citizenship inoperable in autocratic contexts like China, the understanding of citizenship must shift away from national state-dominated frameworks. In China, citizenship membership—the space of internal inclusivity identified by Brubaker—is at the local level. Local citizenship, defined by belonging to the local polity, entitles individuals to rights and responsibilities provided by the local state rather than the national state.

Localized citizenship defines the polity of belonging, not at the national level, but at the subnational unit, where "processes of belonging, entitlement and exclusion are accomplished locally rather than through national-level frameworks" (Smart and Lin 2007, 281). When national governments delegate to subnational governments through federal arrangements, devolution leads to localized citizenships.[5] A localized citizenship institution is a political institution that formally defines citizenship membership at the local level, where provision of and access to rights and responsibilities of citizenship occur at the local level (Vortherms 2015, 2021). Subnational citizenship is neither new nor isolated to China but rather is often the appropriate conceptualization of citizenship in federal states around the world in democratic and nondemocratic, historical and modern contexts (Aiyede 2009; Brubaker 1992; Helbling 2013, 149; Turner 1993; Wallner 2009; Wincott 2006).

The Chinese *hukou*'s closest institutional cousins are the geographically defined local citizenships of other (former) communist states. The Soviet Union used its internal citizenship regime, the *propiska*, to privilege urban industrial centers and strategic state-owned farms (Buckley 1995). Often called an internal passport system, the *propiska* limited migration, housing, and government redistribution to those who held local *propiska* paperwork and was an essential institution for implementing state planning. Most Central Asian states continue to operate *propiska* systems to this day, restricting access to the largest, most economically important cities but also limiting who can access the most generous government systems of redistribution. The Vietnamese *ho khau* system similarly divides people by their internal migration status, distinguishing between local, non-local long-term, and non-local short-term migrants with different entitlements to citizenship rights.

Local citizenship develops (1) when significant inequality exists among members of different subnational units in the content of rights and (2) as local authorities, such as subnational governments, gain more control over membership institutions used to exclude individuals.[6] In short, local citizenship is more than simply decentralized provision of goods; it is instead a political community where bounded membership defines entitlements to these goods.

China is an example of highly institutionalized local citizenship where formal institutions—the *hukou*—define membership and are controlled by local governments. The *hukou* system divides every city's population into groups defined by having a local urban *hukou* or not, creating a hierarchy of belonging with formal boundaries between the included and excluded. Internal citizenship regimes define who is allowed to become full local urban citizens and who lacks full or partial citizenship. Only belonging through the *hukou* system ensures permanent social and political rights. The focus on membership, the rules controlling it, and variation in outcomes

26   *Chapter 1*

distinguishes this study from much of the existing multilevel citizenship literature. The following sections explain the institutional development of *hukou* as a local citizenship institution as it developed in conjunction with state-managed economic development.

Imperial Origins from a Citizenship Perspective

Like many modern institutions in China, the *hukou* system traces its roots to multiple imperial structures. These imperial structures created institutions of local membership designed explicitly to control and manage the population for security and extraction. The imperial ancestors of the household registration system created historical legitimacy for the institution and laid the foundation for the modern institutional arrangements adopted by the People's Republic of China (PRC) government (see table 1.1 for a dynastic time line).[7] The imperial origins of the *hukou* system created institutional divisions linking individuals to one subnational polity and laying the groundwork for locally defined membership as a means of enforcing responsibilities.

The first ancestors of the household registration system developed as early as the Zhou dynasty (1046–256 BCE), when the Western Zhou dynasty instituted the *xiangsui* system. Households on rural land registered in a *xiang*, and urban households registered in a *sui*, and each was organized by geographic hierarchy, like nested subnational governments. These groups helped imperial leaders manage resources and used population registers to enforce exile. The use of the *xiangsui* registration system as a means of implementing exile was the first clear implementation of membership regimes in China. Imperial subjects sent into exile lost their membership rights in the imperial system. Relatively early in its development, household registration also became an institution to enforce responsibilities of individuals to the imperial state. Under the Qin dynasty (221–206 BCE), urban and rural records of the *xiangsui* system provided a means of implementing taxation and conscription. Imperial subjects were registered by household and assigned tax and conscription responsibilities, depending on the number of eligible men in the family. Paying taxes and participating in national defense through military conscription were and continue to be two of the most common forms of responsibilities demanded by the state of citizens.

The Institutional Evolution of China's Local Citizenship   27

TABLE I.I.

Time line of household registration as a citizenship institution

Dynasty	Years	*Hukou* development
Zhou	1046–256 BCE	Western Zhou began urban-rural distinction in the *xiangsui* system of hierarchical social control.
Qin	221–206 BCE	Unified system of taxation, conscription, and internal migration control. Family based (inherited).
Han	206 BCE–220 CE	Further development of nested levels of local control (central, prefecture, county, town, district, neighborhood) over system. Included the record of people's physical appearance. Family based (inherited).
Six Dynasties	220–589	Partial breakdown of the system. Southern and Northern dynasties reinstituted with de facto location (*tudan*) rather than place of birth after war-driven migration. Northern Wei dynasty began the equal-land (*juntian*) system.
Sui	581–618	Explicitly made registration about paternal family and narrowed the definition of extended family to exclude cousins. Rise of the importance of the nuclear family.
Tang	618–906	Nationalization and standardization of registration form. Equal-land system tied to *hukou*. Urban and rural residents demarcated as different classes. Local officials rated on quality of *hukou* control and records. Migration allowed, but only from low tax rate locations to high tax rate locations. Repatriation campaigns to return floating populations to place of registration.
Five Dynasties	907–960	No cohesive system.
Song	960–1279	Formation of the *baojia* system tying registration with taxation, conscription, and internal migration control with three-tier hierarchical system.
Yuan	1279–1368	Continued Song dynasty system, but created categories based on race and ethnicity, profession, and family to create exclusionary policies reducing the role of the Han majority. System complexities reduced its effectiveness.
Ming	1368–1644	Household card, direct ancestor of the *hukou* booklet, used for the first time. Households were divided by profession: military, peasants, merchants, and handicraft workers. Lower-class clans excluded from the system. Late Ming: tax reform severed the importance of *hukou* for tax collection. Required public pronouncements of *hukou* registration to control the population.
Qing	1644–1912	Late Qing institutional enforcement declined as market forces increased. Creation of special classification for criminals.
Republican Era	1912–1949	Used primarily to ensure political ideological support and to identify communist sympathizers. Internal migration allowed but required a 3- to 6-month wait before registration status could be transferred. Basis for modern Taiwan's household registration system.

SOURCE: Cheng (1991); Wang (2005); and government documents.

28 *Chapter 1*

The Han dynasty (206 BCE–220 CE) transformed the hierarchical *xiangsui* structure to what is now recognized as the subnational hierarchical governments of China, disaggregating central, provincial, county, town, and neighborhood responsibilities for registering and reporting the population. Officially called *hukou* for the first time, the new household registration system paired bureaucratic information gathering with subject duties, all organized and managed by subimperial governments. During these earlier imperial periods, extraction and control continued to be the most important functions of the system.

The first time *hukou* became associated with rights in the form of redistribution came in the Northern Wei dynasty (386–535 CE), during the Five Dynasties period. The Northern Wei empire, recovering from years of violent conflict, implemented a land distribution system known as the equal-land system (均田制). To prevent large, untaxable estates from accumulating land and threatening the Wei dynasty's centralized power, the state allocated land plots to peasants for life.[8] This land distribution system allowed better implementation of registering *hukou* at a time when the region had a highly mobile population fleeing war. The land distribution system grew in its geographic spread in the subsequent Sui and Tang dynasties, reaching its height during the Tang dynasty.[9] Before breaking down at the end of the Tang dynasty, this system represented the institutional origin of tying property use rights—a commonly defined political right—to household registration status (Zhang and Fan 2004).[10]

The imperial version of the household register began to decline in the Ming dynasty (1368–1644 CE), as market forces arose and a crumbling bureaucracy diminished the incentive to control the system throughout the Qing dynasty (1644–1912 CE). By the Republican Era (1912–1949), the system primarily provided ideological control over the population as the leaders of the Kuomintang (National People's Party)—the rulers of the republic from 1927 until 1949—rooted out members of the opposing CCP with the help of the system's information gathering function during the country's civil war (Wang 2005).[11]

The imperial origins of the *hukou* laid the basis for local citizenship, especially membership and responsibilities, before the development of local citizenship rights. Membership dictated citizenship responsibilities—primarily taxation and conscription—more than rights, aligning with what we would expect from an imperial system of government that treats its people as subjects rather than citizens. The rise of rights tied to registration status began with access to land in the Northern Wei dynasty, but these rights were limited and largely outweighed by responsibilities. The imperial *hukou* functioned primarily as a means of exile enforcement, population control, and resource extraction. It was not until the Mao era that entitlements to government services developed in tandem with population management. These institutions created the groundwork for the development of local citizenship.

Mao Era and the Rise of Local Citizenship

With the victory of the CCP and the founding of the modern PRC, the *hukou* underwent two important changes. First, communist ideology redefined individual responsibilities as labor contributions to society in support of the command economy. Second, Stalinist-style development increased redistribution to urban workers, defined by their urban *hukou* status, to fuel industrial-driven development at the cost of rural development. These changes cemented local membership policies while elevating *hukou* to an internal citizenship institution that distributed rights.

LABOR ALLOCATION AND THE CRYSTALLIZATION OF LOCAL MEMBERSHIP

After winning the Chinese Civil War in 1949, the CCP faced a fundamental survival challenge: cementing authority over a largely disjointed territory and repairing and industrializing a largely agrarian economy broken by international and civil wars while establishing the new socialist state.[12] For the first goal, the young PRC government continued the *hukou*'s imperial function to identify and persecute those who did not support the regime. During the early years of the Mao era, the CCP could root out enemies— those who supported the losing Kuomintang—from the population using information in the *hukou* (Wang 2005).

The second and third goals, establishing a stable industrialized state, required a more significant institutional shift in economic systems and the policies that supported them, including the *hukou* system. China's industrial development suffered long-term underinvestment and significant inequality, both of which stood antithetical to the new state's communist ideology, which championed state-directed development. Taking lessons from the Soviet Union's industrial policy, China implemented a command economy to spur development led by urban centers at the cost of the agricultural sector.[13] Under a command economy, the central planning committee directed the production and redistribution of goods to achieve a socialist form of development, replacing market forces. Central planning included labor allocation, whereby planners assigned workers to locations and jobs through the *hukou* system.[14] By 1958, every individual was assigned a *hukou* with a specific location and type, either agricultural or nonagricultural. This documentation allowed central planners, first, to know where people were for work assignments and distribution of economic goods and, second, to allocate more people to areas where more labor was needed to make production goals. Distributing labor by assigning specific *hukou* and controlling who could be where ensured sufficient labor needed for central planning while restricting access to urban, industrialized spaces. When labor was reallocated, more *hukou* changes occurred. Central authorities controlled the number of *hukou*s transferred and the methods of transferal to keep strict control over not only population movement but also population settlement.

Under the command economy, work, and explicitly work that supported the central planning office's economic development plan, became the core citizenship responsibility. The command economy required citizens to work wherever central planners allocated their labor. Labor discipline (劳动纪律)—the code of conduct that ensures production for the common good as a necessary element of social labor (社会劳动)—was the second citizenship responsibility listed in the 1954 constitution, preceded only by the duty to follow the constitution (Article 100). To fulfill this citizenship duty, to support the state-planned development, workers should abide by their work assignment, defined by their *hukou*, rather than following individual, household, or market-based decisions on employment and productivity.

To maintain the system of labor and goods allocation that prioritized urban industrial processes at the expense of rural development, strict migration controls enforced local membership. The Soviet-model planned economy required pouring resources from the rural agricultural sector into China's fledgling urban centers, including state provision of daily necessities. Central planners feared migrants from the countryside would flood into cities, demanding government redistribution and destabilizing industrialization efforts. Blind migration (盲流)—migration driven not by socialist planning but by individual cost-benefit analyses without consideration for the social and collective good—of peasants into the cities could

The Institutional Evolution of China's Local Citizenship 31

potentially undermine the entire system by subverting central planning and siphoning redistribution away from the industrial sector. To prevent this overdraft of government resources, officials made unauthorized migration untenable through the *hukou* system's membership and rights provisions. This process mirrored the development of the *propiska* in the Soviet Union: an internal passport system in which only urban, industrial workers were granted *propiska* to enter, work in, and settle in urban industrial settings so as to separate urban and rural economies.[15]

Under the planned economy, the state implemented a monopoly on buying and selling grain from the countryside and redistributed it to urban workers through food rations (粮食统购统销制度) (State Council 1953). Urban workers who were organized into work units, or *danwei* (单位)— identified as a nonagricultural *hukou* holder—received daily necessities from the *danwei*. Anyone in the city whose *hukou* was not registered in a *danwei* would not receive food. The state maintained control over the urban population's size to prevent excessive demand on government supplies.

The redistribution system propped up the industrial sector through rural extraction and buffered these areas from the rural masses. Without access to grain rations provided by the local government, rural and nonlocal *hukou* holders had no access to sustenance in the cities, thus deterring them from migrating (Ministry of the Interior and Ministry of Labor 1954). "Without registration, one [could not] establish eligibility for food, clothing, or shelter, obtain employment, go to school, marry, or enlist in the army" (Cheng and Selden 1997, 24).

At the same time as urban *danwei* development, rural communities began collectivizing. Rural collectivization became a major ideological goal during the Great Leap Forward (1958–1960) as a key element of China's "leap" into socialism. The state encouraged people to work, and eventually live, in larger and larger collective units, to the point that collectivization fervor signaled political correctness. These rural units failed to industrialize rural areas and allowed state forces to extract resources, such as grain, from the countryside and redistribute it to urban workers. Unlike in urban areas, where the state directly participated in distributing welfare rights, the rural collectives themselves were responsible for providing for rural populations.

Urban *danwei* and rural communes created the two collective administrative units on which the command economy was based, laying the foundation of China's dual urban-rural economic system. These organizations

32   *Chapter 1*

structured individuals' lives: the collective allocated housing, mess halls provided food, and higher-up leaders dictated work quotas and production targets, all defined by the central planning committee. The *hukou* system codified belonging and entitlements to urban *danwei*, defining membership in one of these economic units. The national implementation of the *hukou* law in 1958 identified all individuals by their assigned unit or commune's location and segregated the population by their registration type, agricultural (rural) or nonagricultural (urban). Changing status, especially by moving between urban *danwei* or from the countryside to an urban core, was strictly controlled through central planning. Implementing *hukou* policy that tied people to the countryside was contentious, given the "neofeudal hierarchy based upon the location of one's permanent job assignment" that the system created (Perry 2002, 213). But central planners believed the new *hukou* system was a necessary element of the command economy and implemented it nationwide.[16]

INCREASING (URBAN) CITIZENSHIP RIGHTS THROUGH REDISTRIBUTION

To support the socialist model of development, the state provided goods and services—from food to pensions—to urban *hukou* holders through their *danwei* of employment, meaning that those without formal employment—and thus without local urban *hukou*—could not access the benefits provided with it (Chan 2009).[17] Rural citizens, approximately 85 percent of the population in the early Mao era, lacked many of these basic protections so that the state could maintain redistribution in urban centers.[18]

The Great Leap Forward and its aftermath illustrates the push and pull of membership and urban rights interactions. During the Great Leap Forward, state investment flowed into industrial centers to encourage industrial development. Migration controls were briefly relaxed to allow greater rural labor recruitment for urban state firms (Wang 1997). But the Great Leap's industrial policy resulted in economic disaster, with food shortages leading to famine and more than thirty million deaths.[19] The state, without sufficient food rations to feed all rural *hukou* holders temporarily working in cities, let alone the countryside, restricted food rations for urban residents (Wang 2010). The three years after the Great Leap Forward saw twenty-six million workers from urban areas repatriated to the countryside to ensure sufficient food rations for the remaining urban workers (Wang 1997). The right to food redistribution, the most fundamental right in a command economy, became inextricably linked with local citizenship.

Thus, implementing the command economy by using *hukou* as a tool of labor allocation created extreme local membership and rights entitlements. Citizenship rights centered on the right to work, and worker status entitled individuals to socioeconomic rights. Workers, often defined as those formally employed in urban *danwei* and explicitly different from general citizens, had constitutionally protected rights of rest and leisure, health care, old-age care, social insurance, and social assistance (1954 constitution, Articles 92 and 93). The tying of these broader socioeconomic rights to the worker identity created inherent divisions between urban and rural citizenship rights, because urban *hukou* holders were workers and rural *hukou* holders were peasants.[20]

These services were purposely severely underdeveloped, underfunded, or completely absent in the rural areas in order to support industrial development in the urban economy (Chan and Wei 2019). Even though the central government divided resources for some benefits to rural populations, welfare systems, such as education entitled to all citizens, remained fundamentally different in the countryside from that in the urban centers (Croll 1999). This differentiated system created two classes of people within each locality: local nonagricultural *hukou* holders with government-provided services and agricultural *hukou* holders without.

Hukou-dependent rights allocation cemented the *hukou* as a citizenship institution because it not only made membership categories consequential for individual responsibilities to the state but also ensured that the rights and socioeconomic redistribution individuals were entitled to derived from the state. This change marks the *hukou* of the Mao era as fundamentally different from household registrations of the past, because it entitled holders to claims on the state.[21] Local membership and labor allocation became synonymous during the height of the command economy, and through this system, citizenship rights entitlements flowed.

Economic Reform and a New Meaning of Membership and Rights

The reform era (post 1979) ushered in three significant changes that altered how local citizenship membership and rights provision functioned. First, when the Reform and Opening Up policy, announced in 1979, introduced

34   Chapter 1

market forces to the Chinese economy, strict migration controls no longer served national economic interests.[22] Without strict migration controls, people began to move, and more people started living away from their place of *hukou* registration, dramatically increasing the implications of local membership. Second, as the central state dismantled the centrally planned economy, local governments became the primary providers of citizenship rights, making local citizenship even more consequential for access to rights and redistribution. Third, decentralized reform, launched nationally in 2001 and accelerated in 2014, allowed local governments to control membership policies, specifically local naturalization pathways, leading to varied local citizenship regimes.

EARLY REFORM AND CHANGING IMPLICATIONS OF LOCAL MEMBERSHIP

The early reform period (1979–2000) marked one of the most significant institutional reforms to the *hukou* system because the Mao era's near-complete migration restrictions gradually lifted. As out-of-plan migration grew in the late 1970s—and political will to restrict it declined along with the role of the centrally planned economy—the central government allowed reforms to gradually increase flexibility in the *hukou* system. Reforms allowed greater internal migration but did not fundamentally alter local membership. This relaxation of the *hukou* system, allowing migration but not extending citizenship rights, continued the use of the *hukou* system to support the urban-rural dual economy management, in which local economies benefited from cheap labor moving from the countryside.

In a series of reforms, the right to move developed without dismantling *hukou* as a local membership institution. In 1984, the State Council created a new *hukou* category, "self-supplied grain *hukou*" (自理口粮户口), that allowed rural migrants with their own food supply to live in urban areas (State Council 1984). This status allowed partial institutional change: migrants could live and work outside their registration location but were not entitled to local citizenship rights, including fundamental food rations.

Internal migration reforms of the early 1980s culminated in the 1985 temporary residence policy (Ministry of Public Security 1985).[23] Temporary residence permits allowed migrant workers to legally reside in cities but did not ensure access to government services, much like the self-supplied grain *hukou* (Chan 2004). All migrants had to secure a temporary residence permit from local authorities within three days of arrival, but they were not guaranteed formal rights beyond the right to stay in the city (Interview 44150701).[24] These reforms increased migration and the size of the floating population (流动人口)—those moving across township lines without naturalizing into the local *hukou* system (figure 1.1). Nationally promulgated temporary residence permits allowed people to move physically but did not alter fundamental citizenship membership. Migrants moved, but their *hukou*, and thus entitlements to citizenship rights, did not move with them. Without altering who was entitled to government redistribution, these reforms created a larger class of migrants excluded from citizenship rights.

During the Mao period, every municipality's population fell into either the local urban or local rural category, with very few exceptions. The rise of internal migration created four groups of populations within every municipality in China, defined by *hukou* location and type: local urban, local rural,

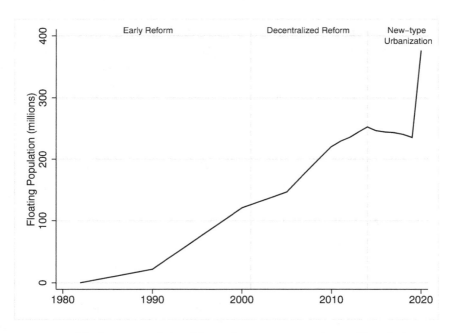

FIGURE 1.1. The floating population. Measured as cross-county migrants. The spike in 2020 is likely due to falling naturalizations and increased migration. See appendix A for definitions of types of *hukou* and populations. *Source:* 1982 and 1990 estimates from the census as reported in Liang and Ma (2004); 2000 through 2019 from NBS, *China Statistical Yearbook*; 2020 estimates from NBS (2021b).

36 *Chapter 1*

nonlocal urban, and nonlocal rural (figure 1.2). All nonlocal populations are, by definition, internal migrants as we traditionally think of individuals who move from one location to another. Local rural residents could also be migrants, because they move from the local countryside to urban centers, or nonmigrants, because cities grow around rural villages and expand into suburbs.[25]

Naturalization pathways increased in the early reform period. These pathways allowed migrants to change their *hukou* and gain entitlements to citizenship rights in a new location—that is, move from one of the non- or partial-citizenship categories to full citizenship categories shown in figure 1.2. During the Mao era, central planners strictly controlled *hukou* transfers, which were tied directly to central planning. This meant that most migrants could not change their *hukou* registration, especially when moving from rural to urban categories.[26] But the introduction of market reforms encouraged greater use of naturalization to manage local labor markets as employment needs shifted and grew in urban centers.

Some minor reforms allowing more naturalization occurred at the national level. For example, the central government, through the Ministry of Public Security, the Ministry of Food, and the National Bureau of Personnel, allowed family reunification naturalization, enabling cadres with

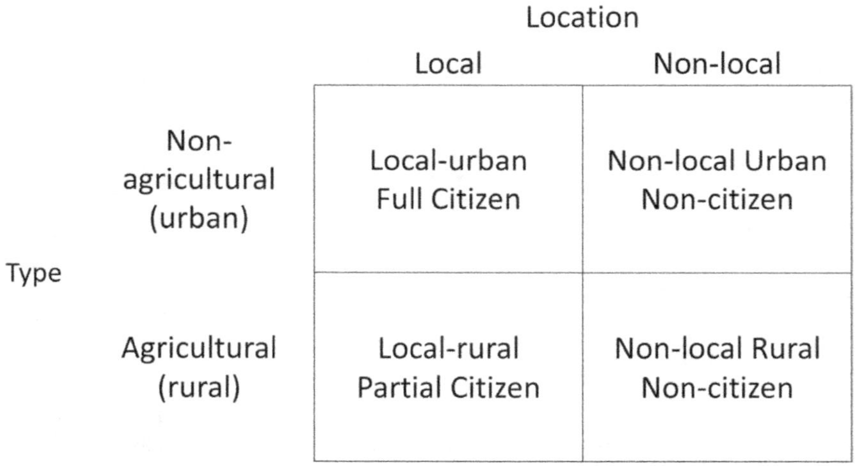

	Location	
	Local	Non-local
Non-agricultural (urban)	Local-urban Full Citizen	Non-local Urban Non-citizen
Agricultural (rural)	Local-rural Partial Citizen	Non-local Rural Non-citizen

Type (row label for the two Type rows)

FIGURE 1.2. Membership categories in Chinese citizenship regimes before reform. Appendix A has more details on definitions.

professional skills to transfer their family members (Ministry of Public Security, Ministry of Food, and National Bureau of Personnel 1980). Family reunification naturalization granted *hukou* and thus grain rations for skilled cadres' family members, allowing skilled cadres to move more easily.

At the national level, conflicting interests from provincial representatives stymied most reforms targeting institutional deconstruction of the *hukou* system. Migrant-receiving areas benefited from greater labor mobility but also from continued local citizenship, because migrant workers would return home to access welfare services such as medical and old-age care. Migrant-sending areas, however, suffered a greater burden of social welfare spending without the benefit of productive labor, other than through remittances. These competing interests stalled larger pushes for deconstructing the *hukou*. For example, those wanting reform encouraged the rollout of the national identification card system (身份证), hoping it would replace *hukou* altogether and create a much more flexible labor market. But conservative voices subverted this reform by attaching the ID card system to *hukou* registration rather than replacing it (Interview 11141001).[27]

Greater reform happened locally through policy experimentation, both official and unofficial.[28] Local officials often give new policies a trial run before provincial or national adoption. Official experimentation, or higher-level governments directing local governments to try new policies, included allowing more naturalizations in special economic zones, where development-driven demand for labor outpaced centrally mandated quotas limiting how many people could naturalize in a year (Ministry of Public Security 1992a). In 1995, the central government authorized experiments in a few counties to allow permanent migrants to naturalize locally by obtaining a *hukou* (Ministry of Construction 1995). The program expanded in 1997 to more counties in more provinces (Ministry of Public Security 1997a; State Council 1997). Local governments, both municipalities and provinces, experimented with new forms of intermediate institutions: identities that allowed some access to local citizenship but kept populations separate. For example, in 1986, Anhui Province implemented a green card system that entitled holders to legal residency but limited access to welfare programs. Shanghai and Shenzhen implemented blue-print *hukou*s in 1993 for migrants who could make financial investments locally. But blue-print *hukou* lacked full rights entitlements of local urban *hukou*.

38 *Chapter 1*

While the Mao era saw the formation of internal citizenship with clear lines of membership, rights, and responsibilities, the reform period marked the early development of internal citizenship regimes, or naturalizations that allowed mobility across citizenship membership categories. During the early reform period, three pathways to local citizenship dominated: work-unit-based transfers, family reunification, and education-based transfers (Ministry of Public Security, Ministry of Personnel, and Ministry of Labor 1994; Ministry of Public Security, Ministry of Finance, and People's Bank of China 1994; Ministry of Public Security, Ministry of Food, and National Bureau of Personnel 1980). Most frequently, these naturalizations were called rural-to-urban transfer (农转非) programs. Individuals with local rural *hukou* could naturalize into the local urban *hukou* if they were approved through one of the three naturalization channels. Central authorities strictly controlled the number of rural-to-urban naturalizations during the 1980s and 1990s through quotas that ranged from 1 percent to 2 percent of the local population, and central policies emphasized limiting naturalization to the specific categories of work-unit- and family-based transfers (Chan and Buckingham 2008; Ministry of Public Security 1977, 1989).

As *hukou* policy shifted away from extreme local membership to encouraging migration and naturalizations, the central government continued to deploy enforcement mechanisms for membership policies. In the first decade of reform, the central government issued multiple notices cracking down on the illegal sale of *hukou* (Ministry of Public Security 1992b; Ministry of Public Security, Ministry of Finance, and People's Bank of China 1994; State Council 1988, 1989). Any local government found to be advancing reform too quickly by permitting too many naturalizations was forced to rescind citizenship status for the new arrivals. For example, local officials in Beijing, eager to advance industrialization, dramatically increased the number of *hukou*s granted to migrant workers in the mid- to late-1980s. In response to what it saw as dangerous local innovation through unauthorized *hukou* transfers, the central government rescinded millions of the recently granted Beijing *hukou*s (Wang 2005).

To ensure that loosening migration controls did not fully undermine local membership regulations, the Office of Custody and Repatriation enforced membership restrictions. From 1982 until 2003, Custody and Repatriation Centers (收容遣送站) detained and repatriated unwanted migrants (State Council 1982). Migrants without permanent residence, employment,

The Institutional Evolution of China's Local Citizenship   39

or a permit to live in the city—the three-withouts persons (三无人)—were detained, questioned, and repatriated to the countryside. Under the pretext of keeping vagrants and beggars out of the city, migrants without *hukou*, or without their paperwork in hand, were routinely rounded up, detained, and forcibly sent back to rural areas after their families paid heavy fines. An estimated 3.2 million migrants were detained in 2000 alone. Reports of arbitrary detention, extralegal ransom, detainee mistreatment, and unexplained deaths of those in custody plagued the system until the centers officially closed in 2003 because of excessive abuse.[29]

LOCALIZING URBAN CITIZENSHIP RIGHTS PROVISION

The dismantling of the centrally planned economy also meant deconstructing the central provision of many socioeconomic rights. Although citizenship rights entitlements depended on local registration in the Mao period, the central government's planning commission held responsibility for socioeconomic provision. Central redistribution flowed through the *hukou* system, and *hukou* defined who received what redistribution. But following a wave of economic and fiscal decentralization, the central government tasked local governments with providing a larger proportion of expenditures, including for social welfare. In 1980, local-government expenditures made up 45 percent of all government expenditure. By 1990, that proportion grew to 67 percent (NBS, *China Statistical Yearbook* 2019).

The local state, facing fewer resources and growing responsibilities, backed away from the full suite of citizenship rights offered to urban workers, weakening the relative value of holding local urban *hukou*. Health care expenditures, for example, shifted from the state to the individual, and the individual share of all health expenditures grew from 21 percent in 1980 to 59 percent in 1999 (National Health Commission 2019).[30] Urban employees no longer enjoyed full cradle-to-grave support, and the state employed fewer people as the state-owned economy reformed.[31] The dismantling of the command economy reduced the value of urban citizenship rights but did not dissolve them. Local governments continued providing urban *hukou* holders more and better-funded citizenship rights than rural *hukou* holders and excluded those with nonlocal *hukou* when facing financial shortfalls.[32]

The 1980s and 1990s also saw the rise of local political rights as local congressional, neighborhood committee, and village elections proliferated. Although individual political rights remain underdeveloped, local-level

40   *Chapter 1*

reforms provided greater participation rights to local citizens.[33] These political rights, like socioeconomic redistribution, are reserved for local *hukou* holders. Migrant workers can vote in their local elections at home via proxies, but only a small percentage do.

The localization of rights provision made local membership even more consequential. Previously, when redistribution occurred through central planning, the biggest division between populations was urban versus rural, because the central planning committee designed nationally coordinated welfare programs based on the urban-rural dual economy. But decentralizing rights provision undermined the value of national, unifying identities such as urban worker and elevated the importance of local membership. Local governments varied in the generosity of their redistribution of socioeconomic welfare benefits, fundamentally reshaping local citizenship's value in terms of access to rights.[34]

DECENTRALIZED REFORM AND LOCAL CITIZENSHIP REGIMES

Decentralization of membership regulations and, specifically, the decentralization of control over naturalization policies followed the decentralization of citizenship rights provision. The decentralized reform era began in 2001, when the Ministry of Public Security announced the removal of central-government quotas for naturalizations and devolved control over rural-to-urban transfer policies to local governments (Ministry of Public Security 2001). Until this point, local naturalizations had occurred through a two-step process. First, the central government transferred agricultural *hukou* to nonagricultural *hukou* to ensure the command economy's implementation. Then, the local government managed the geographic naturalization from nonlocal to local. After 2001, the central government no longer considered rural-to-urban transfers a matter of central planning, meaning local governments gained control over a unified naturalization process.[35] This policy triggered a decade of reform below the national level. Local policy regulation proliferated, and so did diversity in *hukou* policies, especially in who qualified to naturalize locally. Local citizenship regimes now dictated who could and who could not become a local urban citizen with rights entitlements.

Locally Manipulated Membership

Since decentralization in 2001, the bureaucratic process of local naturalization allowed local governments greater authority over *hukou* transfers.

Figure 1.3 presents the multistage process of changing *hukou*. Applicants must first prepare the requisite materials for the specific type of transfer they seek. Once an application starts, applicants must complete all necessary documentation by a strict deadline and the local security bureau has a fifteen-day window to respond to the application. The application for local *hukou* status goes through three levels of government: the township via the local police station (派出所), the county, and the municipality. The municipality is the highest level of government to approve transfers. Once the application is approved, applicants are given a relocation permit (准迁证) for the new location. With this permit, they return to their original *hukou* location to apply for a migration permit (迁移证), which allows them to leave their previous location and cancels their old *hukou*. The migrant then takes the relocation permit, migration permit, and higher-level government approvals to the local police station of the new location to receive a new *hukou*.

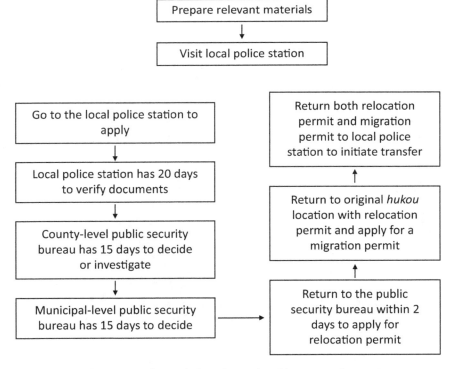

FIGURE 1.3. The steps to change *hukou*. *Source:* A public security bureau in an eastern municipality.

Decentralization reforms triggered policy proliferation at all levels of China's subnational government hierarchy (figure 1.4), and local governments wrote eligibility requirements for who could gain local *hukou*. Eager to signal alignment with the center, multiple provinces announced significant reforms to *hukou* management. Restructuring naturalization away from the multistage process of traditional rural-to-urban transfer was often interpreted as canceling the distinction between agricultural and nonagricultural *hukou* by fully naturalizing all local rural *hukou* holders into local urban status. By 2005, eleven provinces announced moves toward a unified *hukou* system that distinguished only between locals and nonlocals.[36] But although the headlines declared a full canceling of *hukou*, provincial policies and their implementation were much more circumspect. No province fully or even significantly dissolved the agricultural-nonagricultural distinction in *hukou* registrations. Nor did provinces fully integrate rural and migrant workers into social welfare systems. Instead, significant policy shifts began below the provincial level.

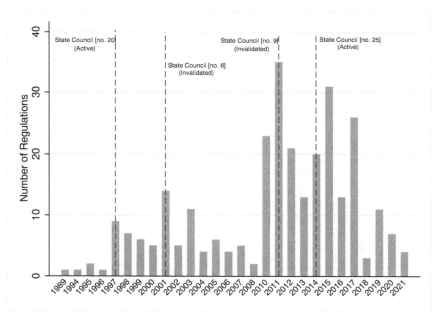

FIGURE 1.4. Number of provincial-level policies related to *hukou* management, by year. *Source:* Author's policy database, collected from Peking University Law database and provincial-level government web pages.

In *hukou* policies, provinces acted as microcosms of the national reform. Each province and the four directly administered municipalities managed both migrant-sending and migrant-receiving areas, urban and rural areas, and large and small cities. One *hukou* policy for an entire province rarely made sense. Instead, provincial governments coordinated *hukou* policies but delegated policy specifics to the municipalities below them (Interviews 11141102, 44120801, 44120804).[37] Provincial officials directed municipal and county leaders to draft *hukou* policies in line with the local context, mirroring the center's directed approach to *hukou* reform. The result was significant variation below the provincial level.

Some local experimentation occurred in nationally designated policy experimentation zones, which were explicitly directed to reform their policies by trying new policy formulations as test cases for potential national policies. But nationally designated experimental status created highly varied outcomes. As Wallace (2014) notes, *reform* at times meant no significant changes in naturalizations but, rather, new forms of managing the system. Other experiments made significant progress in reforming local membership policies but still fell short of widespread reform.

The city of Chengdu illustrates the evolution of local policy experimentation. Chengdu, the capital of Sichuan Province, gained official central approval for *hukou* policy experimentation in 2003. Locally, *hukou* reform as an essential element of social welfare reform began in 1997. Municipal welfare bureaus, including the local health bureau, pushed a program of integrating services, diminishing the differences between agricultural and nonagricultural services (Interview 51131101). This equalization would make *hukou* reform easier by putting local migrants from Chengdu's countryside and local urban residents on the same playing field and ensuring that more naturalizations would not overrun the city's services (Interview 51131102). In 2003, the city greatly expanded *hukou* naturalizations. The nonagricultural population was 37 percent of the city's population in 2003 and over 50 percent in 2005 (Sichuan Bureau of Statistics 2020). These trends, however, were limited to Chengdu. Other Sichuan municipalities failed to take up reform, even though Sichuan was an early mover, announcing plans to operate a unified *hukou* system in 2004. The effects of policy reform show up in the proportion of the nonagricultural population in Chengdu compared with Sichuan as a whole (figure 1.5). In Sichuan, the growth rate in the nonagricultural population jumped from 2.9 percent in 2003 to

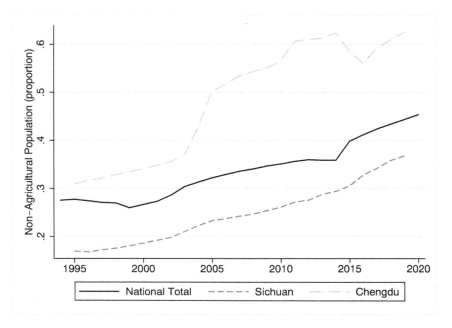

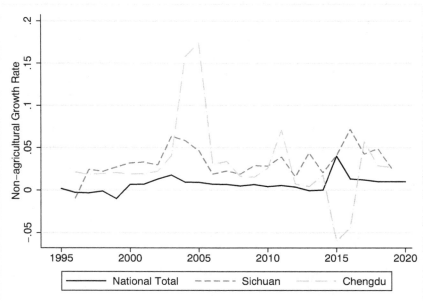

FIGURE 1.5. Nonagricultural population in Sichuan and Chengdu, 1995–2020, proportion of total population (*top*) and growth rate (*bottom*). *Source:* Various reports from provincial-level public security bureaus until 2013, Chan (2021) for 2014–2020. Sichuan Bureau of Statistics.

The Institutional Evolution of China's Local Citizenship   45

6.3 percent in 2004 but returned to a growth rate of 1.9 percent by 2006 (Sichuan Bureau of Statistics 2020). Although provincial governments may have announced big reforms, most of the work was done well below the provincial level. Even Chengdu's significant reforms, while making significant progress, could not fully integrate agricultural and nonagricultural populations seventeen years after reform was implemented.

Local variation also occurred outside formally designated national experiments. In Guangdong Province, for example, municipalities took many different directions with *hukou* experimentation, all centering on manipulating membership rules that dictated local naturalization. In one Guangdong municipality in 2009, for example, provincial leaders directed the municipal government to advance reform. Instead of outlining the details of policies to be implemented, the provincial government instructed the municipality to design new *hukou* naturalization policies that would "solve the city's problems" related to labor and migration (Interview 44120804). After consulting with economic planners, the municipal government centered *hukou* reform on education. They piloted programs that would allow migrant children who completed elementary and middle school in the municipality to gain *hukou* and remove naturalization quotas for migrants with college education, regardless of where the migrants came from (Interview 44120804). Another municipality in Guangdong tied *hukou* reform to health care by reducing barriers to the city's health clinics. The reform targeted the integration of local and intraprovincial migrants into a unified health system while restricting access by interprovincial migrants and not fundamentally altering membership through naturalization (Interview 44120806). In yet another city, the municipality introduced a points system that awarded migrants points based on their financial resources and human capital indicators like higher education. Once migrants reached a certain threshold, they were eligible to transfer. This points system would become a standard policy in more than twenty cities five years later (Interview 44141111).

Other cities succeeded in fully integrating local agricultural *hukou* holders into nonagricultural status, creating one local, unified *hukou* within the municipality. Altogether, eight cities, four of which are in Guangdong, fully integrated their populations in the early reform period.[38] None of these cities with successful unified *hukou* systems are in the provinces that announced reforms to cancel the *hukou*, indicating that provincial announcements only weakly signal local variation.

46   Chapter 1

Local policy experimentation in the decentralized reform era highlighted the dynamic nature of citizenship membership policies. No longer directly controlled by the central government, new opportunities arose, from both top-down influences and bottom-up initiatives. Although the fundamentals of local membership did not change, the locus of control did. Decentralization of *hukou* transfers resulted in the development of internal citizenship regimes, whereby citizenship rights and membership were not only locally defined but also locally controlled, with significant variation across space.

Rise of Rural Citizenship

The decentralized reform era also marked the rise of rural citizenship. Central-government policy during the Hu Jintao administration (2002–2012) aimed to break down barriers to social welfare systems and reinvest in equalizing policies, such as universal health insurance (policy implemented in 2009), education reforms (2007), and pension reforms (2009 and 2011). Previously, such services either lagged behind urban services or simply did not exist. For example, before health insurance reforms in 2009, there were no specific insurance programs to cover rural residents. State-managed health insurance programs covered government employees and formal urban employees, aligning specifically with urban *hukou* holders. This unequal coverage was the legacy of the *danwei* system and unequal citizenship of the Mao era. Social welfare reforms under the Hu administration created new programs for previously excluded populations and established richer—although still underfunded—rural rights of redistribution.

These reforms, however, did not dismantle the underlying inequalities created by the *hukou* system by integrating populations. Instead, they reinforced *hukou* divisions by building social welfare programs segregated and defined by *hukou* status and location. For example, when residence-based health insurance rolled out across the country in the first decade of the twenty-first century, two distinct programs emerged, one for urban registrants and one for rural registrants (Liu, Vortherms, and Hong 2017). Even urban nonlocal migrants faced difficulty using urban services across locations, because rights provisions were tied to *hukou* type and location. For example, one urban worker without local *hukou* in southern China could be reimbursed for only 25 percent of a hospital bill for surgery because their health insurance was in a different province (Interview 44150707). With local *hukou*, the bill would have been fully covered. Similarly, pension programs initially had strict geographic limitations and benefits were not portable across geographic lines (Zhang and Li 2018).

One undeniably important rural right that grew in importance during the decentralized reform era was rural land use rights. Local nonagricultural *hukou* holders were entitled to land use rights redistribution through their local villages.[39] Although the system of land use rights existed throughout the reform era, this right became more valuable during the decentralized reform period because of intertwined land reforms and the push for urbanization.[40] The decentralized reform period coincided with state-managed land markets that compensated agricultural *hukou* holders when the state took or developed land. These reforms increased the value of citizenship rights associated with agricultural *hukou*. As land values skyrocketed in the very first years of the 2000s, so too did the value of this rural right (Zhan 2017).

New-Type Urbanization Reforms: Accelerating Local Reforms

Rumors of the *hukou*'s institutional demise began circulating in early 2014, as state-controlled media reported reforms to urbanization processes. By the end of the year, two interrelated reforms with clear high-level backing addressed how urbanization processes occurred across the country. The 2014 New-Type Urbanization Plan and the "Opinion on Further Promotion of *Hukou* Reform" signaled a new attention on nationally coordinating *hukou* policies. These reforms tried to shift from urbanization driven by space and capital to people-centered urbanization. Official reform rhetoric reimagined local citizenship regimes as more fluid processes with fewer barriers to local naturalization and emphasized the need to detach citizenship rights from local membership. In the years immediately following reform, however, these adjustments remained only partially implemented, and variation continued at the local level.

The 2014 reform included both adjustments to programs already in place and policy innovation in *hukou* management (table 1.2). Together, the two national policies created significant space for local governments to adapt and adjust policy: policy adjustments signaled institutional continuation with more regularized naturalizations and policy innovations would dismantle some institutions' restrictions, fundamentally changing the *hukou*. The overlap of these dual motivations—continuation and reform—with the

48 *Chapter 1*

TABLE 1.2.
Key elements of the 2014 *Hukou* reform

Basic Principles
• Adherence to activeness, steadiness, regularization and orderliness
• Adherence to Putting People First and respecting the will of the masses of the people
• Adherence to adjusting measures to local conditions and differential treatment
• Adherence to overall planning of support service, and provision of basic guarantee
Readjustment of Policies on Residence Migration
• Full-scale lift of restrictions on settlement in towns approved by provincial-level governments and in small cities
• Orderly lift of restrictions on settlement in medium-sized cities
• Rational determination of conditions for settlement in large cities
• Strict control over the size of population in extra-large cities
• Effective solution of key issues in residence migration
Innovating Population Management
• Establishment of a unified household registration system for both urban and rural areas
• Establishment of the residence permit system
• Perfection of the population information management system
Practical Protection of the Legitimate Rights and Interests of Agriculture Migrants and Other Groups of the Permanent Resident Population
• Improvement of the rural property rights system
• Enlargement of the coverage of basic public service
• Strengthening of guarantee of financial resources for basic public service
Practical Strengthening of Organization and Leadership
• Prompt implementation of policy measures
• Actively doing a good job of publicity and guidance

NOTE: *Settlement* is the central-government term for local nationalization.
SOURCE: State Council (2014c; official translation).

policy's basic principles of local adaptation yields continued space for internal citizenship regimes below the national level.

Membership and Rights in the 2014 Reform

New-type urbanization called for two related innovations in the *hukou* system, one specific to local citizenship membership and one specific to local citizenship rights. The first substantive section of the 2014 reform attempts to formalize local naturalization by city size.[41] Towns and small cities should allow all migrants to change their *hukou* without restriction. Although this central policy of removing local naturalization restrictions gained significant attention in the media, it is largely a continuation of central policy initiatives since the 1990s.[42] The central government has always encouraged more open naturalization policies in these peripheral small urban spaces while protecting and restricting larger urban areas.

With full enactment of loosened naturalization policies based on city size, the new *hukou* system would resemble the early forms of the *propiska*, its institutional cousin from the Soviet Union. In the early years of migration control in the Soviet Union, household registration and internal passports were provided only to large cities of strategic importance. Those living outside the controlled areas did not have access but were also not tied down to one location and employment as the all-encompassing *hukou* did at the time.[43] If fully implemented, the *hukou* would grow to resemble the modern-day household registration in Central Asia, where living and working in large capital cities requires household registration.[44]

More innovative than the central push for small cities to remove naturalization restriction, however, was the call to integrate agricultural and nonagricultural *hukou* registrations to create a unified *hukou* system (城乡统一的户口登记制度). Although some localities had already begun this process, as discussed earlier, the 2014 reform marks an attempt to build a "new-type *hukou* system," or a *hukou* type that no longer segregated within one city but in which locality still mattered (State Council 2014c). The establishment of a registration system separate from inherited agricultural and nonagricultural systems marks a significant shift in membership regulations but not a complete dissolution of them. This reform featured a simplification of local citizenship groups but did not undermine the geographically defined distinction between local and nonlocal populations.

The 2014 reform also emphasized the imperative to restructure citizenship rights through two key pathways: integrating urban and rural services and providing migrants with urban services. First, integrating nonagricultural and agricultural *hukou* holders into one unified local *hukou* system necessitates an integration of welfare and redistributive rights entitlements. By granting unified local *hukou* to previously second-class rural *hukou* holders, the local government opens the door to urban services. Membership integration necessitates rights integration. Second, for nonlocals who moved

50   Chapter 1

across urban jurisdictions, the 2014 reform proposed a residence permit system. Holding a residence permit should entitle migrants to basic government services.[45] This policy innovation significantly shifted the consequences of local membership, if implemented rigorously.

Nearly overnight "new-type urbanization" became a buzzword in the media and across government reports.[46] Official newspapers covered a speech by then-premier, Li Keqiang, calling for people-centered reform. The 2014 reforms were a clear signal to lower-level governments to realign *hukou* policies to create a more flexible system of naturalizations but within a managed system that did not overwhelm larger urban cores. Managed reform was the most consistent theme across the *hukou* reform and the broader new-type urbanization policies. Naturalizations should focus on the "stock" of migrants (优先解决存量) long settled in cities without local citizenship (State Council 2014c). Encouraging *hukou* naturalizations for long-term migrants is an essential part of reform but does not deconstruct the system.[47] Yet the 2014 reforms explicitly carved out autonomy for local management of the system. Rather than overriding local-government policies, central reform enshrined local-government discretion in *hukou* policy-making specifics.

In sum, the 2014 reforms created a potential shift in the *hukou* system, whereby lines of exclusion between agricultural and nonagricultural *hukou* holders would fade while lines between local and nonlocals would remain but weaken. But reform-undermining strategies remained inherent in the formal policy through the need for local adaptation. This strategy allowed significant local variation, limiting the potential progress of reform.

Evidence of Reform Outcomes

The 2014 reform created an opportunity to redesign China's local citizenship regimes, but outcomes depended on local-government implementation. The two primary observable implications of significant *hukou* reform would be a declining floating population and a significant expansion of urban welfare enrollments. The first few years after the 2014 reform provide evidence that naturalizations increased. The floating population leveled off and even declined briefly until 2020, when it shot up, most likely because migration outpaced naturalizations (figure 1.1) (Chan 2021). As reported in annual migrant labor reports, there were 274 million agricultural migrant workers (农民工) without local *hukou* in 2014 and 291 million in 2019 (NBS, *Migrant Monitoring Report,* 2014, 2019). Because their intent was to resolve the situation for local stocks of migrants who had long lived in the city, policy makers did not direct policy change to manage circular migrants—those who go back and forth between home and their migration destination—and the growing population of new migrants. This provides incentives for short-term institutional adjustments but fewer long-term incentives to create sustaining policies for future migrants.

The second observable implication of *hukou* reforms would be welfare enrollments. If the 2014 reforms displaced old *hukou* policies by decoupling *hukou* from welfare, welfare services previously separated by *hukou* residence—health and pensions—should be integrated and urban welfare programs of unemployment, workers' compensation, and maternity insurance should have marked increases in enrollment. After the 2014 reforms, however, only the health insurance program experienced a significant increase in enrollments (figure 1.6).[48] Although integrating the residence-based insurance programs increased, no wave of long-term residents gaining access to most programs occurred. National education

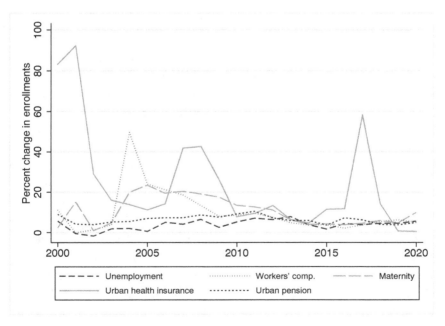

FIGURE 1.6. Enrollment in urban welfare programs. *Source:* NBS, *China Statistical Yearbook*, 2010, 2019.

statistics suggest some progress in enrolling children in schools: enrollment numbers have increased since 2014 compared with declining numbers in the preceding five years (NBS, *China Statistical Yearbook,* 2019).[49] But access to these programs is not equal. Emerging evidence suggests that manipulation of both citizenship rights and local membership regulations continues to privilege wealthy migrants over poorer migrants, especially in accessing schools (Friedman 2022a). These indicators present a mixed picture of *hukou* reform but above all else point to the continuation of local citizenship through local membership restrictions and differentiated access to local rights.

Discussion

The *hukou* system developed from an imperial tool for control and extraction to a citizenship institution that also redistributed socioeconomic rights. The devolution of citizenship rights provision and local membership rules—of who was and who could become eligible for citizenship rights—gave way to local citizenship regimes. Local policy variation proliferated, creating highly varied access to citizenship rights across the country.

This system of subnational citizenship moves beyond an unequal welfare state framework because of membership institutions. Local governments not only provide the bulk of citizenship rights but also control rules of membership, of *who* is entitled to these rights. This creates a quintessential case of multilevel citizenship (Vortherms 2021). In multilevel citizenship, belonging to the local state defines access to citizenship rights. Common in federal systems, multilevel citizenship creates a hierarchy of belonging (Maas 2017).[50] A person is a citizen of both the nation and the locality. Where local governments have stronger exclusionary powers in membership and provide more rights, such as in China, local citizenship matters more (Kovacheva et al. 2012). As the historical evolution of the *hukou* outlined here demonstrates, the *hukou* created multiple levels of citizenship in China across multiple eras, but the importance of local citizenship grew over time. The localized connection between socioeconomic rights entitlements and particularistic membership defined by *hukou* created the internal citizenship regimes that allow the state to disaggregate hierarchies of belonging and entitlement to citizenship rights while excluding many more.

The *hukou* is a highly institutionalized case of authoritarian citizenship in which socioeconomic redistribution dominates citizenship rights, but access to those rights is highly particularistic. Only those deemed important for inclusion gain access. Subnational particularism, defining membership in citizens, has been dominated by urban versus rural divisions, with local versus non-local distinctions rising in importance.

TWO

Manipulating Citizenship: Rights and Membership in Authoritarian Citizenship

News of a landmark *hukou* reform began circulating in Beijing in late 2013, months before the State Council announced the New-Type Urbanization Plan in March of 2014. With the formal policy announcement, Li Keqiang, then premier of China, emphasized the need for a "people-centered" approach to urbanization (Li 2014). Previous urbanization policies focused on building roads and high-rises left many people out of the process. Rural residents kicked off their land and the millions who moved into the newly built high-rises were not automatically included in formal urban citizenship through the *hukou* system. Urbanizing China's people, at least bureaucratically, would require dismantling at least some of the exclusion inherent in China's local citizenship institutions.

Many heralded the 2014 urbanization reforms as the beginning of the end of segregation across China's cities, declaring the pseudo-caste-like system that determined the fate of hundreds of millions of migrant workers to be over. As one academic asked me in the fall of 2014, "Didn't the government just cancel the *hukou* system?" (Interview 11141106). This was a common theme in many interviews immediately following the 2014 *hukou* reform. Local policy initiatives to reform *hukou* took off. The annual growth of the rural migrant worker population (农民工) decreased from 2.9 percent in 2013 to 1.3 percent in 2015 and 0.6 percent in 2018, according to the annual Migrant Monitoring Survey (NBS, *Migrant Monitoring Report* 2014, 2020), signaling some success at naturalizing these internal migrants into the local citizenry.

54

Manipulating Citizenship: Rights and Membership in Authoritarian Citizenship 55

Yet close watchers remained skeptical of systemwide dismantling of the *hukou*. The institution had been declared dead before, such as when national-level reform merely decentralized control over some policy elements (Chan and Buckingham 2008). Even if implemented in its ideal form, many doubted the ability of the 2014 reform to deconstruct the *hukou* institution fully (Chan 2014). In many places, bureaucrats permitted little change in their own municipalities while assuming other places reformed significantly. As a migration specialist said five years after *hukou* reform was announced, "Reforms are superficial. The localities will still find a way to use the system unless the system is completely abolished from above" (Interview 31191205). Seven years later, there was little evidence that reform fully dismantled barriers. An ever-growing floating population—those without local citizenship rights—outstripped reform advances with a record-breaking 376 million internal migrants identified in the 2020 census (Chan 2021; NBS 2021a), leaving even more migrants out of local citizenship than before.

Understanding the mixed impacts of the 2014 reforms requires answering two interrelated questions: Why would a government with powerful tools of exclusion expand access to socioeconomic rights? When autocratic systems expand redistribution, whom do they choose to include?

Drawing on over a thousand official policy documents and semistructured interviews with local policy bureaucrats and migration and urban planning experts from four different levels of government bureaucracy, this chapter lays out two motivations for manipulating access to citizenship: security and economic incentives. At multiple levels of government, policy makers balance the exclusion-driven incentives for security with an inclusion-driven need for economic development. Central-government-level leaders focus on security and stability to support regime longevity, which encourages the system's continuation, rather than a full dismantling of the *hukou*. Economic incentives drove devolution of *hukou* policy reform. As a labor allocation tool, *hukou* policy control relocated to the local level when economic development policies decentralized and proliferated. Local governments, especially at the municipal level,[1] used inclusion in local citizenship as a tool to attract development-supporting labor. The needs of local development policies dictated who was a desirable migrant targeted for local naturalization, resulting in local policy variation driven by local development strategies.

56   Chapter 2

Systemic Inclusion and Exclusion

Citizenship institutions provide tools to strategically manipulate who gets what from the state. Both rights and membership inherent in citizenship provide political leaders with opportunities to manipulate citizenship to their advantage, redistributing what they want to the people they want. They are not simply lines of inequality that give some people greater benefits than others but membership institutions—the rules that dictate who is entitled to autocratic redistribution—that are dynamic tools for both exclusion and inclusion.

Citizenship institutions, like other nominally democratic institutions, provide a mechanism for unequal distribution in nondemocracies.[2] Autocrats allow elections of varying quality and use legislatures to identify what and to whom redistribution occurs (Gandhi 2008; Magaloni 2006; Manion 2015; Schedler 2002). These institutions become tools to co-opt segments of society by integrating individuals and elites into state institutions (Gandhi and Lust-Okar 2009). They also operate as a mechanism through which redistribution occurs, credibly committing the autocrat to allocating resources to rent-seeking elites (Blaydes 2011). Citizenship membership institutions in particular allow autocratic leaders to create hierarchies of differentiated citizenship status with differing levels of redistribution. Privileged groups, defined in large part by their strategic importance to the autocrat, receive full redistribution, whereas those of lower importance to the state receive less.[3] Membership institutions crystalize these groups and impose a method of differentiation among the population.

Particularistic membership, in which not all within a polity are entitled to citizenship rights from the state, inherently limits redistribution and undermines entitlements to citizenship rights by excluding some groups from redistribution. But citizenship institutions also allow for strategic inclusion when autocratic leaders expand membership and increase access to citizenship rights. The question then becomes, when does the autocrat expand membership, granting previously excluded groups access to citizenship rights, and whom does the autocrat choose to include?

Exclusion and Stability: The Security Incentive

SECURITY IMPERATIVES FOR EXCLUSION

The security logic behind manipulating authoritarian citizenship begins in a place of exclusion. Autocratic leaders must redistribute benefits to some

Manipulating Citizenship: Rights and Membership in Authoritarian Citizenship 57

groups in society whose support is necessary to keep them in power. Autocratic leaders want to limit the number of people whose support they need to stay in power by cultivating an elite class through redistribution. Authoritarian citizenship institutions that formally delineate full citizens with entitlements to redistribution and second-class citizens and noncitizens with lesser or no entitlements limit the draw on state resources, a key to maintaining authoritarian longevity.[4] Limiting redistribution benefits nondemocratic rule by capturing rents that can then be used to ensure support from necessary groups in society. These regime insiders provide material and economic support necessary to prevent regime change.[5] By excluding other groups—those less instrumental to authoritarian survival—government officials benefit by saving resources and maintaining an elite, privileged status for populations important for regime survival. If an authoritarian leader redistributes too widely, it decreases the marginal benefit of supporting the autocrat and creates an opportunity for a challenger to win over supporters. This inherent inequality in redistribution through exclusion ensures that the elite class stays privileged and heads off potential challengers to the regime.

Security incentives primarily encouraged the restriction of redistribution by tying redistribution to *hukou* status and limiting the number and types of people eligible for local citizenship through *hukou* naturalization. By and large, government bureaucrats and the urban working class constituted the privileged class of insiders whose support the regime depended on for survival (Hong, Tseng, and Lin 2022). Supporting industrialization was essential for the young regime's survival, and the dual management system of keeping rural agricultural workers and urban industrial workers separate allowed segregation and limited redistribution (Chan and Wei 2019).

Because of the urban-centered industrialization policies of the Mao era, government bureaucrats and urban workers became the most important groups for redistribution. The state funneled resources and redistribution into urban centers to support industrialization while purposely neglecting the countryside.[6] To protect urban areas and ensure sufficient redistribution, migration controls strictly limited who could live and work in these areas of higher redistribution, thus restricting access to urban citizenship.

Internal migration became explicitly securitized with the presence of noncitizen ruralites in the city, who were seen as a threat to the regime. Blind migration, the movement of people outside socialist planning, threatened the state's ability to provide resources specifically meant to support central economic policies. Central planners used the phrase "blind migration" (盲流) because it sounds like "hooligan" or "rogue" (流氓), and they wanted to emphasize the social disruption caused by capitalist migration. As one interviewee joked with me, "Blind migrants are too rogue" (盲流者太流氓) (Interview 44140702). By limiting the movement of people, the state could prevent the wrong people—migrants not driven by socialist planning—from getting access to key areas. This exclusion made sure there were not too many people demanding more of the state than it could—or wanted to—provide. Even after economic reform shifted industrialization policy away from the Stalinist model, the *hukou* limited access to urban spaces considered sensitive. Purposeful reforms approved by the central government in the late 1990s in small and medium towns increased inclusion only when large, important urban areas were not nearby.[7]

The *hukou* creates exclusion by controlling not only the number of people who can gain access to redistribution but also the types of people excluded. Troublemakers, both general and specific, were often restricted from gaining full access to citizenship. For example, those with criminal backgrounds were regularly disallowed from changing their *hukou*, and those with even a suspicion of criminal activity faced greater barriers to entry to politically sensitive spaces, such as cities. The targeted population (重点人口)—those anticipated to be socially disruptive—are routinely tracked and excluded from local citizenship.[8] Ethnic minorities are often controlled by limitations on migration and local governments not wanting to integrate them. A *hukou* from a restive western region, for example, identifies an individual far from home as a potential threat in the eyes of a local official and marks the person as an outsider, facing significant discrimination.

Xiao Han's story illustrates the use of internal citizenship for security exclusion purposes. Xiao Han's family moved from central China to Xinjiang in China's northwest during the 1970s, in part to escape persecution during the Cultural Revolution.[9] When her father secured a job through a provincial work recruitment program, Xiao Han's family obtained Xinjiang *hukou*. Xinjiang Province is home to large ethnic minority populations, many of whom the Chinese government labels as violent extremists.[10] When she moved to China's coast for college in the first years of the 2000s, Xiao Han found her Xinjiang *hukou* created greater problems for her than she ever anticipated:

> Even though I am Han [the ethnic majority group in China], my Xinjiang *hukou* keeps me distinct. I have been denied at hotels when I try to register and they find out my *hukou* is Xinjiang. Even when I tell them my family is from Henan and they see I am Han, the formal *hukou* location is all that matters. . . . I was unable to change my *hukou* through my college program like my classmates were. If I could change my *hukou*, I could blend in, but without changing, I am always marked as different. (Interview 44150908)

By maintaining *hukou* institutions, the state benefits from a powerful tool of exclusion that helps provide stability and security, as defined by the regime. Reducing redistribution and preventing specific, unwanted populations from accessing government redistribution provides the state with significant tools for information collection and population control. As Xiao Han explains, without the *hukou*, it would have been much easier for her to integrate and leave that Xinjiang identity behind. But with it, both the state and society had significant power to identify her as the wrong type of person.

SECURITY IMPERATIVES FOR INCLUSION

Although security is a major driver of exclusion, it can create opportunities for inclusion. Greater inclusion in authoritarian redistribution can be used to shift groups or individuals into the privileged class to ensure security goals. Redistribution can co-opt different groups in society, preventing the rise of potential challengers.[11] Relatedly, redistribution can be used to repress potential regime challengers through surveillance.[12] As new challengers arise in society, the autocrat can extend redistribution to them, increasing inclusion in citizenship. Particularistic citizenship membership allows allocation of resources when politically expedient to potentially head off challenges. Greater inclusion in local citizenship arises, from the security perspective, when the state needs to coerce, co-opt, or repress different groups in society.

The state can expand inclusion for desirable groups in politically sensitive areas. For example, officials encouraged majority Han Chinese to move to western, minority-dominated areas of the country to increase integration of these regions and dilute the concentration of minorities (Hu and Hu 2011a; Hu and Hu 2011b; Toops 2004). Members of the Han majority group are seen as inherently supportive of the regime and the right type of people more than are ethnic minorities. Encouraging migration of Han

60   Chapter 2

populations to western regions, to shift the demographics of the potentially restive regions, involved enticing them with jobs and *hukou* transfers.

Expanding inclusion could also thwart security threats raised by labor activism. Many social protests in China relate to labor relations, including protests against unpaid wages and unfair working conditions, and migrant workers are major participants.[13] Urbanization, when workers move to highly concentrated industrial centers and often live in company dormitories with other migrant workers, increases the potential for collective action through protests.[14] Labor protests, especially those against unequal access to rights and those that condemn the state for not providing social protections, could challenge the regime.[15] Greater inclusion of migrant workers could reduce these pressures by providing access to government redistribution as social safety nets.

But it is unclear when migrant-driven protests elevate themselves to the level of threatening the regime. As Göbel (2021) argues, the majority of labor protests in the early to mid-2010s targeted private businesses, which would bear the cost of concessions rather than the state, and are less likely to face state repression. Similarly, many labor protests, although having ramifications for state legitimacy, lack a "formal political agenda working against the state" (Chan and Ngai 2009, 289). Although rising inequality was largely expected to greatly undermine Chinese Communist Party (CCP) legitimacy, public opinion studies show general acceptance of inequality (Whyte 2010). The dualism of migrant workers increasing social instability through protests but worker protests focusing on nonstate actors makes unclear under which circumstances greater inclusion in internal citizenship would be used to manage these threats.

Inclusion for Development: The Economic Incentive

The security incentive for both inclusion and exclusion is inherent in any discussion of authoritarian redistribution. But it is not the only driver of inclusion. Expanding citizenship membership can also support economic development. Nonrentier autocratic systems must ensure economic development for survival. Autocratic regimes desire economic development for two reasons: First, development funds the state to ensure sufficient resources for redistribution.[16] Without economic development, the state may not have sufficient resources to pay off supporters—either long-standing or newly included elite groups—to ensure regime longevity. Second, development itself acts as a form of socioeconomic redistribution. Improvements to economic well-being increase regime legitimacy by improving the quality of life for residents who benefit from higher incomes and improved services as a result.[17]

Membership in authoritarian citizenship can encourage economic development by cultivating a stronger labor force. Maintaining strict exclusion, in which very few people get access to socioeconomic rights, hurts development in the long run by interrupting labor markets and reducing human capital investment. Without socioeconomic rights, workers are likely less healthy and less educated, reducing labor productivity (Chen 2011). The *hukou* system's economically detrimental effects on citizens and noncitizens are well documented in existing economic research. Strict *hukou* controls increased inequality, institutionalized limits on intergenerational mobility, reduced the returns to education and human capital, and created labor market disequilibriums that hurt overall development goals. These forces undermined political stability by increasing the potential for social protest and hampering economic development.

Economic development encourages expanded access to government services and access to socioeconomic rights because governments can direct social welfare programs to specifically support economic policies. So-called productivist welfare states in East Asia use welfare and socioeconomic redistribution to support development (Holliday 2000). States invest in health care and education, for example, to encourage a productive labor force. And developmental states actively privilege some industries over others in the name of state-directed development.[18] China's market socialist system, although usually excluded from productivist theories because of its socialist policies, should be understood as a form of productivist state that directs government redistribution through welfare to support economic activity. Internal citizenship regimes help governments direct redistribution to support development policies.

The following sections lay out how inclusion in the *hukou* system—namely, to whom the state extends local citizenship rights—depended on the needs of development policies. Throughout the Mao era, the introduction of socioeconomic citizenship rights followed an economic logic and the central state dominated policy planning and maintained strict control over who was entitled to local citizenship. As economic policies decentralized,

62 *Chapter 2*

control over *hukou* policies also decentralized to allow strategic manipulation of internal citizenship regimes to achieve economic goals. Local governments sought development by pursuing capital from foreign sources, local resources, and central-government transfers. Each of these local development strategies created different labor needs and led to different levels and forms of openness: local governments extended local citizenship membership to some migrants but not others. Continued use of the *hukou* as an institution of labor allocation created selective inclusion, depending on local development strategies.

CENTRAL ECONOMIC PLANNING AND THE LOGIC OF LIMITED INCLUSIVITY

During the Mao era, the central state used redistribution to fuel economic policy by supporting workers' economic activity. In the early years of the command economy, when local citizenship institutions first developed, social services and redistribution specifically supported urban residents as socialist workers as laid out in the 1954 constitution.[19] Urban rights depended on worker status: workers in an urban work unit were entitled to social services, and others were not. Health care, pensions, and housing were all necessary for urban industrial workers to contribute to central planning objectives and thus were part of citizenship entitlements.

Because central authority dominated economic policy making, the central government maintained control over membership policies, aligning membership in local citizenship with labor needs for central planning. The central state explicitly tied redistribution to labor by establishing socioeconomic systems to provide for urban workers and not rural agricultural peasants establishing local citizenship as a means of ensuring appropriate labor allocation. Central planning dictated who could become a local urban citizen—who could shift from a rural have-not to an urban have—to allocate labor for central planning.[20] Economic policy set by the central government dictated inclusion. *Hukou* transfers were allowed only when central planners deployed cadres to new areas, when students crossed county lines to go to school, or for some family reunification purposes. Too much redistribution in the wrong places would undermine central planning.

Even family reunification, one of the most fundamental pathways to citizenship in jus sanguinis systems, was a potential challenge to government labor allocation. Before national rollout of *hukou* policies, planners in Shanghai expressed concern about allowing factory workers' families into

Manipulating Citizenship: Rights and Membership in Authoritarian Citizenship 63

the city. Workers were needed, but their family members were not. These "unproductive" populations would create unnecessary burdens on the system, undermining support for the urban workforce, and protection of local resources led to greater exclusion, preventing workers from bringing their families to the city with them (Cheng and Selden 1994).[21]

Central enforcement policed expanding membership by granting *hukou* "out of plan," or migration and *hukou* acquisition granted by local governments without central planning approval. During the Great Leap Forward (1958–1960), central economic policies identified steel production as a national priority. Local governments encouraged migration from rural areas to provide labor for fledgling steel production. But when faced with limited state grain rations and growing famine, more than twenty million of these newcomers were sent back to their original rural *hukou* location because of central-government directives (Banister 1987; Cheng and Selden 1997; Wang 2005). During the early years of the Cultural Revolution, peasant workers destroyed household registration records in protest of institutional barriers to equality, effectively becoming urban residents until forced repatriation returned them to the countryside a few years later (Wang 2005).

The shift from central economic planning to more mixed-market socialist policies during economic reform (post 1980) increased migration but did not fundamentally alter centrally dictated membership policies. Economic development drove highly limited access to socioeconomic rights in the Mao era, and changing development policies necessitated changes to *hukou* management. The late 1970s and early 1980s saw the gradual entrance of market forces into the economy. The introduction of market forces as a means of development in China encouraged increasing factor mobility, reducing state control on land, labor, and capital (Freeman and Kessler 2008). As market mechanisms increased economic development, incentives increased to reduce *hukou* restrictions so that labor markets could adapt more easily (Young 2013).

The central government allowed greater labor market mobility to meet market demands but did not demonstrably expand access to local citizenship, and internal migrants were not able to change their *hukou*. The center maintained strict quotas, limiting the annual number of people across the country who could change from rural to urban status. Rural-to-urban transfers were capped at 1.5 percent of the population to maintain "strict control"

64   *Chapter 2*

over the flow of people (Ministry of Public Security 1977; State Council 1989). Quotas were reserved for three types of transfers, or naturalization pathways: work transfers, school transfers, and those reuniting family. Targeted inclusion—limiting who could naturalize in the internal citizenship system—allowed the central government to use greater labor migration for development while still maintaining control over resource redistribution. The state, responsible for service provision, had few incentives to transfer rural workers to urban areas other than minor adjustments for economic development. Greater inclusion in local citizenship membership did not occur until responsibility for economic development policy decentralized to lower levels.

SHIFTING CITIZENSHIP DOWNWARD

In the 1980s and 1990s, central planning gave way to decentralized economic policies, triggering the decentralization of *hukou* policies. The central government, recognizing a need for greater local adaptation in development policies, gradually decentralized some economic policy-making authority to local governments. Local governments gained greater autonomy in managing the state sector and enterprises at the local level, allowing core central policies to adapt to local contextual needs.[22] Decentralization of development policies spurred the proliferation of local development models. Local development policies adapted to the interplay of domestic and international forces, local state corporatism, leadership choices, and existing economic structures.[23] With greater variation in development policies pursued at the local level, the central government needed to devolve control over the factors of production to allow local development policies to flourish. Previously managed by the central government, capital, land, and labor controls needed to be locally adaptable to support different paths to development. Capital reforms resulted in fiscal decentralization in the 1990s.[24] Local land management and markets developed in the 1990s and 2000s, allowing local governments to manage land resources (Zhu 2005). *Hukou* reforms allowed local governments to manage and manipulate local labor markets, completing the decentralization of control over the three factors of production: capital, land, and labor.

Central reforms in 2001 started major decentralization in *hukou* policies. The central government no longer dictated national quotas controlling how many people could naturalize locally and formally dissolved the central

Manipulating Citizenship: Rights and Membership in Authoritarian Citizenship 65

rural-to-urban transfer processes. Local governments gained control over deciding who could naturalize locally and over naturalization pathways to more easily source labor from rural areas (Ministry of Public Security 2001). Early reform policies encouraged the opening of naturalization pathways beyond those for government employees, college graduates, and family reunions (Ministry of Public Security 1994). But after the 2001 decentralization, local *hukou* policy experimentation that trialed new naturalization programs by county and municipal governments took off across the country (Interviews 44120804, 51131101).

Economic incentives catalyzed decentralization of *hukou* policies. The central government purposely decentralized control over citizenship membership to support localized development strategies. Although the central government granted greater flexibility to local governments in designing *hukou* policies, that should not be understood as the liberalization of the *hukou* marked by the central state relinquishing control. Instead, flexibility was the intention, similar to what Ang (2016) calls directed improvisation. This process led to significant variation in local citizenship regimes, not because of a principal-agent problem where lower-level governments ran amok with policy authority, but instead, because development policies at the local level vary in their economic incentives for openness. Who gains access to citizenship depends on trade-offs between security-driven exclusion and economically driven inclusion, balanced at three levels of government.

Balancing Security and Economics across Levels

Who gains access to citizenship through local membership depends on the balance between security and economic incentives. This section examines the three levels of government involved in *hukou* policy making and the evidence of security and economic incentives, especially around the 2014 national-level urbanization reform. Each level of government involved in policy making faced this calculation, but the balance between the two—security-driven exclusion and economically driven inclusion—varies by level of government. Ultimate adaptation of who was a desirable migrant for inclusion reflects the multilevel calculations of that balance because of China's nested bureaucracy. The central state, mostly concerned with regime longevity, established security considerations as a priority. The provincial

66   *Chapter 2*

level reflected security-driven exclusion promoted by the central state but encouraged the integration of populations within the province to develop the province's local labor market. Finally, the municipal level, where policy making and policy implementation converge, adapted the specifics of who gets included to support local economic development. Although security and economic incentives exist at all levels, the influence of local economic development grew the lower the bureaucratic level, driving variation in who got access to citizenship.

CENTRAL-STATE CALCULATIONS

Central-level policy-making processes and the resultant *hukou* policies evince both security and economic motivations. The dominance of the CCP and the Ministry of Public Security (MPS) in policy making indicates the priority of security incentives, but economic concerns eventually led to decentralization of *hukou* transfer policies.

Before 2014, security concerns encouraged conservative reforms from the central government. Since the 1990s, central policies targeted small and medium-sized cities for *hukou* reform. The motivation for reform in these limited contexts was not fiscal: often the smallest cities had the hardest time providing government services to their existing populations. Instead, small and medium-sized cities were the least risky places to trial reform because they were the least strategic economically and politically.[25] Expanding inclusion in local membership in the largest cities could potentially destabilize the major drivers of economic growth.

As reform advanced in the first years of the twenty-first century, national reforms aimed to maintain the system while controlling gradual reform. For example, after local governments gained control over local naturalization policies in 2001, central-government policies emphasized limiting reforms to not threaten social stability. The State Council condemned overly ambitious *hukou* reforms implemented locally:

> Some regions pursued rapid urbanization one-sidedly regardless of the actual circumstances of local economic and social development, and some other regions relaxed the conditions for permanent residence registration in cities without regard to city type or a city's comprehensive carrying capacity; and still some other regions violated the national policies without approval and impaired the people's vital interests.
>
> Preamble, official translation, State Council (2011a; since rescinded)

Manipulating Citizenship: Rights and Membership in Authoritarian Citizenship 67

All castigation of inappropriate reforms related to excessive reform rather than the lack of reform found across the country. Condemning localities for going too far was not matched with criticisms of laggard reforms, meaning the central government was more concerned about too much reform rather than too little. Central authorities primarily encouraged gradual reform that did not fundamentally dismantle the *hukou* system as a tool of social and economic control.

Security interests also dictated who would benefit from policy reform before and after the decentralized reform era. Central reforms gave highest priority to expanding local citizenship membership to migrants "well established" in the city, or those who had resided and worked in the city for many years. The 2014 urbanization reform iterated the need to resolve the stock of migrants (优先解决存量) (State Council 2014c, Sections 1.2 and 2.8). Policy specifics of whom to naturalize similarly granted *hukou* to migrants with established housing, jobs, and a longer track record of being in the city through social insurance payments (State Council 2014c, Sections 2.6 and 2.7). Even policies meant to be more progressive, such as the 2016 reforms to grant *hukou* to individuals without any *hukou* registration because they were born in violation of the one-child policy, specified this selectivity of prioritizing well-established migrants (State Council 2016). These long-term migrants were the easiest targets for integration, because they had already proved themselves able to integrate into local society and their local naturalization would be less likely to cause disruption.

The policy players involved in central reforms, especially the 2014 reform, reflected the concern of the conservative central state to maintain social stability. On June 6, 2014, in its third official meeting, the Comprehensively Deepening Reform leading small group (CDR) discussed what would become the State Council's 2014 national *hukou* reform (Reuters 2017; *People's Daily* 2014). President Xi Jinping spoke on the need for *hukou* reform with specific attention paid to ensuring local fit for policy reforms. Three years earlier, in 2011, under the administration of Hu Jintao and Wen Jiabao, the State Council had adopted a similar reform developed by the National Development and Reform Commission (NDRC). The 2014 reform canceled the 2011 reform, replacing it and, eventually, leading to more substantive reform.

The CDR's involvement in *hukou* reform above the NDRC signaled the Xi administration's desire to have CCP-led *hukou* reform without

68   *Chapter 2*

interministerial logjams. Xi Jinping created and chaired the CDR in 2013 as a party-led coordinating body—in contrast to the government-led NDRC—to accelerate policy reforms requiring significant cooperation across ministries.[26] Traditionally, the coordination of interministerial structural reforms fell to the NDRC. But since 2013, Xi has used the CDR to insert party authority over policy, accelerate reform, and stress specific policy areas (Grünberg and Brussee 2022). By elevating *hukou* reform to the party's coordinating body over the traditional, government-led structural reforms, the Xi administration signaled a desire to accelerate *hukou* reform. Promoting *hukou* reform to the CDR triggered far more local reforms than previous efforts. The 2014 reform saw three times as many local *hukou* policies in the following two years than the prior 2011 reform. This shift of *hukou* policy away from the NDRC reflects the decades of marginal *hukou* reform and the resulting excessive reform that the 2011 reform preamble, quoted earlier, refers to.

But this elevation of *hukou* reform to a party-led process was tempered by the CDR publishing only two policies on *hukou* reform, the first of which is the 2014 State Council reform and the second two years later regarding registering unregistered populations. For a complicated and consequential policy dependent on many ministries implementing fundamental institutional reform, this is relatively few, suggesting somewhat limited attention by the coordinating body. Instead of a strictly coordinated central initiative leading to the dismantling of the *hukou*, the 2014 reform emphasized continuing the *hukou* system and allowed local adjustment and reform, a strategic process that encouraged local variation by design rather than defect.[27]

Under the CDR reform, the MPS dominated *hukou* policy making. The MPS is responsible for the day-to-day operations of the *hukou* system, including recordkeeping, processing of transfers, and management of who is eligible for transferring their *hukou*. When national-level reforms specify the responsibility of different agencies in implementing reform, the MPS is always listed as the first responsible party, especially for the granting of *hukou* and management of urban-rural integration. The MPS is inherently a conservative force in *hukou* reform, managing the system of transfers while prioritizing social stability and the selectivity of transfers. For example, in 2016, the State Council announced reforms to grant *hukou* to the over one hundred million people who lacked any *hukou* at all, or "black

Manipulating Citizenship: Rights and Membership in Authoritarian Citizenship 69

hukous" (State Council 2016). In granting *hukou* to people previously excluded because of one-child policy violations or because of the administrative burdens that kept migrant children out of the *hukou* system, the reform instructed the MPS to target skilled migrants with higher levels of education or certified skill training for this "amnesty" (State Council 2016).[28]

The second key player at the national level is NDRC. As the government-side coordinating body, the NDRC had been a significant player in *hukou* reforms before the creation of the CDR (Interview 11141001). In 2014, the CDR tasked the NDRC with overseeing the coordination of new-type urbanization policies, of which *hukou* reform was a key component. The NDRC represented economic interests in structural reform tasked with overseeing the government-side operations of *hukou* reform. The launch of urbanization reform required the joint effort of fifteen ministries and departments, including the ministries of education, public security, civil affairs, finance, human resources and social security, land and resources, environmental protection, housing and urban-rural development, transportation, agriculture, and health and family planning, as well as the central organization department, the statistics bureau, and the People's Bank of China. The NDRC oversaw the interministerial meeting of the stakeholders involved in urbanization reform under the State Council (State Council 2014a). In the era of new-type urbanization, the NDRC looked to reform the system to be more dynamic and responsive to economic needs. In contrast to the conservative MPS, the NDRC wished to advance reforms in line with other economically driven structural reforms.

The shift of *hukou* reform responsibilities from the NDRC to the CDR and the dominance of the MPS shows the importance of security incentives for regime longevity. The CCP values regime longevity above all else, and *hukou* reform is essential for public security. From the center's perspective, the most desirable migrants to extend citizenship membership to were those who supported social stability. With a priority on security, the central government encourages the continuation of internal citizenship regimes, relaxation of membership policies in the least politically sensitive areas—namely, small and medium-sized cities—and targeting of permanent migrants for citizenship membership.

Within the CDR, then Vice-Premier Zhang Gaoli, the first vice-premier of the State Council and one of three original deputy heads of the CDR

(Xinhua News Agency 2013), oversaw *hukou* reform.[29] His leadership represented both economic and financial interests. Before becoming a vice-premier, Zhang had extensive experience at the provincial level, including in Guangdong, where he headed the Pearl River Delta Planning and Coordination leading small group, the agency responsible for coordinating economic development of one of China's most marketized economic regions (Guangdong Provincial Government 1994).[30] While deputy director of the CDR, Zhang also held a position in the Finance and Economic Affairs leading small group, bringing a fiscal perspective that may have tempered economic progressivism: financial concerns led to conservative reforms for fear of overdrawing fiscal resources, as discussed previously.

Economic interests were also represented centrally by the Ministry of Human Resources and Social Security (MHRSS), the successor to the Ministry of Personnel and the Ministry of Labor and Social Security.[31] Traditionally, national policy involving migrant workers originated in the Migrant Workers leading small group under the MHRSS, because migrant workers were labor resources previously controlled through the Ministries of Personnel and Labor. But the CDR leading small group taking over *hukou* policy indicated its importance for the broader urbanization agenda championed by Xi Jinping and Li Keqiang. The MHRSS acted as more of a supporting agency, and the Migrant Workers leading small group supported *hukou* reform but also worked to resolve fundamental migrant worker concerns, such as wage disputes and housing issues rather than structural reforms (State Council 2017). That the Migrant Worker leading small group did not spearhead *hukou* reform is not as surprising as it may seem. Once migrant workers change their *hukou*, they are no longer considered migrant workers and would not fall under the purview of the Migrant Worker leading small group. Instead, *hukou* reform became more fundamentally about structural urbanization reform that bridged the urban-rural dual management system, requiring the cross-ministerial coordination that the CDR leading small group provided.

The primary evidence of economic incentives at the central level was the continued call for local-level adaptation of central policies. If *hukou* reforms were to promote economic development, policies had to adapt to local economic conditions. This perspective pervades the 2014 central policy. Local governments were instructed to naturalize migrants with a "strong capacity of employment [and] who are adaptable to systemic transformation and upgrading of industries in urban areas and the environment of market competition" (State Council 2014c, Section 2.8), inherently a context-dependent calculation. Central policies instructed localities to reform *hukou* policies to specifically consider the local carrying capacity of the city to prevent excessive reform that might undermine economic development and fiscal resources. The central government decentralized *hukou* naturalization policies so that *hukou* policies could match local economic needs.

PROVINCIAL COORDINATION

In November 2014, then Vice-Premier Zhang Gaoli led a national teleconference overseen by the MPS that instructed local governments to advance *hukou* reform in line with national reform policies (State Council 2014b). State Council member and Minister of Public Security Guo Shengkun presided over the meeting, broadcast to representatives from every province- and prefecture-level unit. Relatively new to the central government, Guo began his career in the centrally managed China Nonferrous Metal Mining Group, and he became the first general manager of the Aluminum Corporation of China in 2000 (Li 2012). During the November broadcast, speakers from the MPS, NDRC, Ministry of Finance, Ministry of Land and Resources, and the Sichuan provincial government directed their counterparts in how to implement *hukou* reforms.

The Ministry of Finance spoke on adjusting local-government finances to self-fund the added costs of *hukou* transfers with more people entering urban welfare systems (Interview 11141102). National reforms after 2014 addressed self-funding local welfare programs. Local governments long used financial costs as an excuse to prevent *hukou* reform. Integrating more people into the urban welfare system increases demands on more generous urban welfare systems, although the actual concern of overdrawing urban coffers may be overblown (Zhang and Li 2016).

Representatives from the Sichuan government spoke of the *hukou* policy implemented in Chengdu, a national experimentation site for *hukou* reform since 2003. Chengdu's *hukou* reform began by integrating urban and rural welfare systems first, reducing the marginal cost of transferring a resident from agricultural to nonagricultural *hukou* status, to solve the financial problems of *hukou* reform (Interview 51131102). This reform ordering helped Sichuan province maintain a steady increase in urban-rural integration rates, unlike many provinces with stagnant rates of rural-to-urban transfers or occasional spikes of integration. Sichuan's inclusion in the formal tele-conference validated local officials' confidence that the reforms designed in Chengdu to integrate agricultural and nonagricultural *hukou* registrations would inevitably spread across the country. When asked the likelihood of policy spread from Chengdu to other areas of the country before national reform, one local official told me it was "not a question of if, but when" other municipalities would adopt Chengdu's policies because it was a "necessity" for economic reform and development (Interview 51131102).

The inclusion of both the Sichuan government and the Ministry of Land and Resources in the teleconference signaled the importance of urban-rural integration in *hukou* reforms. During the Mao era and beyond, the *hukou* system was an essential institution for the divided management of urban and rural spaces and economies. This dual management system meant that, after economic reform, the institutions that managed urban and rural spaces were divided across the two spaces. *Hukou* reforms could either integrate populations by breaking down these barriers or reinforce these divisions. *Hukou* reforms occurred with less resistance in Sichuan compared with the other national experimentation site, Chongqing, where *hukou* reforms focused on trading land for *hukou*, reinforcing the urban-rural divide rather than integrating across it.

Lessons from national rollout players display the center's emphasis on controlled reform and managing fiscal resources. The MPS's dominant role as host indicated the need to reform and decentralize within the boundaries of public security, and the Ministry of Finance's inclusion spotlighted the concern for local-government fiscal resources and ensuring sufficient redistribution throughout reform.

Provincial-level *hukou* policies reflect the security-driven conservatism seen in central-government policies but also expand and interpret economic incentives for inclusion. After the announcement of national policy reforms, provincial governments adapted and applied central directives to their provincial contexts. After the 2011 and 2014 national-level reforms, provinces responded by announcing their own policies. Between 2011 and 2012, for example, twenty-two provinces announced new *hukou* policies. Between 2014 and 2015, another twenty-seven issued policy directives.[32]

Provinces adapted central *hukou* policies on the basis of local contexts; coordinated policies across municipalities, often redefining *local* to the provincial level; and encouraged municipal governments to further adapt

Manipulating Citizenship: Rights and Membership in Authoritarian Citizenship 73

their policies for local economic contexts. Provinces acted as microcosms of the national reform. Each province manages migrant-sending and migrant-receiving areas, urban and rural areas, large and small cities. One *hukou* policy for an entire province rarely made sense. Instead, provincial governments coordinated *hukou* policies but delegated policy specifics to the municipalities below them (Interviews 11141102, 44120801, 44120804).[33] Provincial officials directed municipal and county leaders to draft *hukou* policies in line with the local context, mirroring the center's directed approach to *hukou* reform. The result was significant variation below the provincial level.

Emphasizing coordinated control, provincial policies largely reflected the language and intent of central-government policies with some slight deviations. For example, the 2014 urbanization reform stated that cities with urban centers with more than 5 million people should restrict membership and those under 5 million should expand naturalizations. Harbin, the capital of Heilongjiang Province, with a population that held steady around 4.73 million for nearly a decade, should have expanded *hukou* naturalizations (Heilongjiang Ministry of Public Security 2017). But the Heilongjiang provincial policy announced that Harbin should be considered a megacity because of its importance within the province and should therefore strictly control *hukou* transfers (Heilongjiang Provincial Government 2014) rather than opening migration as the central policy would dictate.[34]

Provincial policies largely repeated central-government policy initiatives and provided more detail on how implementation may occur below the national level, at times creating more limitations than the spirit of central policies. For example, central reforms called for a new residency program that allowed migrant workers to use local services while employed in the city. Most provincial policies announced after 2014 posit that residency systems should be built and that migrants should earn points toward accessing welfare services.[35] Instead of automatic access to education and old-age care, greater access is earned through a migrant's human capital and length of stay in the city. Wealthy migrants and those with higher education are likely to gain the best access to welfare systems, whereas those without will remain without local citizenship.

Still a policy-making rather than policy-implementing level of government, provincial governments coordinated municipalities below them. Without direct implementation power, provinces mostly tried to protect

74 *Chapter 2*

the largest, most economically important areas from migration pressures while shifting naturalizations to smaller and less desirable urban centers, just as the central government had. Similarly, provincial officials encouraged small cities to adopt open membership policies to take pressure off larger, more economically vital areas. Although not formally reflected in its policy, a smaller municipality in the Pearl River Delta—one of the largest manufacturing hubs in China—began opening more pathways to naturalization after provincial-level officials told them to "take the pressure off" Guangzhou, the provincial capital (Interview 44120804).

Economic incentives drove two common attributes at the provincial level: redefining local citizenship at the provincial level and further decentralization of *hukou* policies. The central government coordinates for the entire country, and provinces coordinate across municipalities. Intraprovincial migrants, compared with interprovincial migrants, become insiders from the perspective of the province, and provincial-level policies encouraged including these populations in local citizenship. To the provincial government, all people within the province are its citizens and local labor force, making them logical targets for inclusion. For example, in Guangdong Province, the tech center of Shenzhen was encouraged to integrate nonlocal migrants, but the rest of the municipalities were directed to put their intramunicipal rural migrant workers first and broader Guangdong migrants second, ignoring non-Guangdong migrants. As one municipal-level bureaucrat said, "Provincial leaders wanted us to prioritize Guangdong migrants, that with enough reform, we will switch to a Guangdong *hukou*, dissolving municipal lines" (Interview 44150903). Other provinces, such as Jiangxi and Fujian, made similar moves to redefine local at the provincial level to emphasize the provincial labor market. The same bureaucrat, in a more pessimistic view, also stated that although province-wide unification was the goal, "as long as municipalities implement the policies, municipal lines will still be strong" (Interview 44150903).

All in all, *hukou* reform at the provincial level reflected the central government's emphasis on security-driven conservative reform. After the central government's decentralization conference, provinces' reforms largely mirrored the language of central reforms, encouraged municipalities to integrate their urban and rural areas, redefining local to create more cohesive welfare and migration systems within the province, but largely ignored broader issues of cross-provincial migrants.

MUNICIPAL-LEVEL INTERESTS

Annual reviews for political promotion motivate municipal officials to provide both security and economic outcomes. Whereas regime longevity motivates the central government, local officials strive for career advancement. Annual job performance reviews of municipal mayors and party secretaries—the highest-ranking party official at every level of government—signal alignment with central policies and report provision of social stability, and economic outcomes, including local gross domestic product growth and revenue collection.[36] While these standards affect all local officials, the importance of economic performance increases at lower levels of bureaucracy (Landry, Lü, and Duan 2017). The *hukou* system interacts with all three of these performance objectives.

In the late 2010s, when greater central attention fell on *hukou* reform at the local level, municipal governments, like their provincial government, published hundreds of local policies on *hukou* reform. Between 2011 and 2020, 246 of 333 municipalities published over six hundred policies on *hukou* reform.[37] Although many of these policies followed boilerplate language similar to provincial and central policies, the proliferation of policies showed local-government alignment with the center.

The security incentives that dominate the central level also influence exclusionary policies at the local level. Municipal governments see migrants as a potential drain on local resources for redistribution, and all levels of government regularly cast migrants as socially disruptive, bringing higher crime rates and destabilizing local communities.[38] Security-driven exclusion also stems from protecting local financial resources. Municipal governments maintain final fiscal responsibility for socioeconomic programs.[39] Greater inclusion by expanding membership could undermine the municipal government's ability to provide redistribution.

Moreover, both exclusion and inclusion of migrants in the *hukou* system can lead to social protests, the primary conduit of public opinion influencing policy making and a significant threat to local social stability. Migrants themselves influencing policy making rarely came up in discussions other than officials' paternalistic expectations of what would be good for migrant workers. Formally, public opinion could be incorporated through public hearings, but research shows that migrant workers may not join public hearings because of lower political consciousness and efficacy (Chen, Lu, and Xu 2015; Ergenc 2014). Migrant workers may

76 *Chapter 2*

be more prone to labor protests, influencing public opinion and local policy making.

Public opinion also works against reform, because local residents see integrative reforms as a draw on resources meant for them, especially in the realm of education. Greater generosity to excluded populations, such as expanding school enrollment to *hukou* holders from poorer regions, leads to backlash from local citizens. For example, parents of local urban children protested across nine cities when a larger university quota for rural students was announced in 2016 (Yang 2016). Social protests such as these undermine local officials' political interests, because mayors whose cities experience significant social protests are rarely promoted.[40]

Institutionally, local public security bureaus remained responsible for designing, coordinating, and implementing reform, often through the local leading small group on *hukou* reform. Local public security bureaus run the day-to-day operations of the *hukou* system and also represent conservative interests in systemic reforms, prioritizing social stability over other interests. Additionally, local public security offices and police stations benefit from the *hukou* system not only as a generator of resources and employment—local police stations host *hukou*-specific employees responsible for maintaining and managing *hukou* records and investigate migrants living locally without permits—but also as a source of corrupt rent seeking. Local officers accept bribes to secure local *hukou* for migrants who do not qualify for a local *hukou* transfer or for individuals who want multiple *hukou*s to purchase multiple homes (Feng 2013; Fu 2018).[41] In a three-year campaign to crack down on corruption in the *hukou* system, authorities rescinded 3.1 million duplicate *hukou* registrations, corrected 11 million records with false information, and prosecuted 249 police officers and 702 others for their involvement in creating fake IDs and *hukou* (Xinhua News Agency 2017).

In most cities, public security bureau representatives oversee a local leading small group on *hukou* reform to coordinate work across different bureaus. The units involved span public security, finance, rural and urban development, and social welfare bureaus and commissions (table 2.1). These units compose the core of almost all local leading small groups, and the public security bureau both leads substantive reforms on *hukou* transfer regulations and oversees the other units. Other local bureaus involved often included the legal affairs office, the statistics bureau, local and national tax offices, information and propaganda offices, and ethnic affairs offices.

Manipulating Citizenship: Rights and Membership in Authoritarian Citizenship 77

TABLE 2.1.

Composition of local leading small groups, core units

Unit	Responsibility
Public security bureau	Oversee reforms, design and implement new transfer systems, build a unified local *hukou* system, strengthen information gathering systems, strengthen the resident permit system as a prerequisite for *hukou* transfer.
Land	Reform titling systems to allow rural-to-urban migrants to retain land use rights, create a more accessible system for relinquishing land use rights for rural-to-urban migrants.
Construction	Create a mechanism to link construction indicators with the number of agricultural migrants settling in cities, ensure sufficient housing for rural-to-urban transfers.
Rural affairs, rural development commissions	Ensure land use rights for locally transferred migrants, improve rural land transfer mechanisms, promote property rights of transferred migrants to rural collective enterprises.
Human resources and social security	Identify requirements for employable migrants based on the city's need.
Development and reform commissions	Expand the coverage of basic public services in urban areas, assist the public security bureau's new transfer system.
Finance	Ensure local resources for the incorporation of newly transferred *hukou* holders to enjoy social benefits.
Civil affairs	Reform social welfare systems integrated across urban and rural populations to align with a unified *hukou* system.
Education	Ensure sufficient school planning for incorporation of the children of newly transferred *hukou* holders.
Health and family planning	Provide migrants the same family planning restrictions as locals within a given time frame of *hukou* transfer.
Housing	Integrate rural migrants who have settled in the city into urban housing systems.

Despite the local level tying in many more economic and rural players, the public security bureau continued to dominate, often explicitly overseeing the work of other bureaus, such as in Handan, Hebei Province. The Handan municipal government released a twenty-five-point work plan on *hukou* reform (Handan Municipal Government 2015). The local public security bureau oversaw the first nine tasks related to *hukou* transfers, and other agencies provided support services and rural reform related to the consequences of *hukou* reform.

The public security bureau took on the task of reforming the means of transferring migrant workers' *hukou*, while the other structural reforms fell to the land bureau and rural development as well as social welfare bureaus.

Hukou policies of the first years of the 2000s greatly benefited real estate developers and rural development firms. As municipal governments expanded the city, ruralites were moved off their land, which was then developed and transferred to large agribusinesses, benefiting rural development offices and local-government coffers (Zhan 2017). But central pressure in 2014 curbed this financial incentive by reforming land use rights: migrants who transfer their *hukou* were to retain their land. This additional land reform in conjunction with *hukou* reform undermined the benefits of reform for local governments and rural industrial interests, creating fewer incentives for significant reform. Rural development offices and the local land bureaus were tasked with creating better mechanisms for migrants to voluntarily relinquish their land use rights, creating some benefit of land transfers but fewer than the land-grab era of the early 2000s. Local social welfare bureaus also faced significant structural reform. Previous welfare programs including education, health, pensions, and housing were all managed separately under different urban and rural administrations.[42] Integrating the rural countryside would mean an integration of rural and urban welfare programs and, primarily, an expansion of urban services to a larger population.

Economically, the municipal government stood to benefit the most from economically driven *hukou* reform. Local economic development is a key determinant of local-leader political advancement. Additionally, local economic development creates opportunities for local rent seeking even for less politically motivated local leaders. Because of the location-specific benefits of economic development, the municipal-level government is best positioned to gain when *hukou* reform supports economic activity.

But exactly how reform helps the local economy and the interests of local economic actors varies. State-owned firms and key industries benefited from conservative loosening of *hukou* policies. *Hukou* naturalizations began as a means of allocating labor across the state-owned economy: local governments distributed *hukou* transfer quotas to firms to allocate labor according to central production plans. After reform, state-owned firms and industries identified by the local government as areas for heightened local investment benefited from these quotas (Liu and Shi 2020; Interview 11141101). Local governments, directed by their economic planning offices and human resources and social security bureaus, targeted specific industries, often referred to as key industries, for preferential policies. Lower tax rates, greater government investment, and *hukou* transfer quotas are all policies that target given industries to spur growth.[43] Large manufacturing operations that relied on migrant workers for low-wage positions also benefited from marginal reforms. Maintaining strict *hukou* divisions allowed large manufacturers to suppress wages of their nonlocal employees.

This system advantaged connected firms that were able to recruit workers by providing *hukou* as a form of benefits that other firms not granted *hukou* transfer ability could not guarantee.[44] Expanded quotas benefited these privileged local economic actors but broader reform that opened up *hukou* transfers could undermine them. Instead of pushing for more universally open reforms, firms primarily used industrial associations to lobby for key industry status or used local relationships to lobby for increased *hukou* quotas for their firms specifically (Interviews 11150306, 11171205).

Small, private firms not part of key industries often saw no way they could benefit from targeted *hukou* reform through high-skilled recruitment. When asked if his firm ever petitioned the local government for more *hukou* transfers, a small-factory owner explained that the firm was out of the system (制度之外), meaning the *hukou* transfer system was not meant for firms like theirs (Interview 11150306). Similarly, when a firm fell out of favor with the local government, either because of changing local-government development or soured personal relations, the firm could lose access to quotas (Interview 11140701). These firms benefited most from a broad, open policy with greater flexibility in transfers but had little influence in local policy.

Manipulating Local Membership for Development

Local leaders had to balance both inclusionary and exclusionary pressures. The initial introduction of market forces and relaxation of migration controls did not directly increase the need for labor inclusion in local citizenship. Local economies needing labor for new factories benefited from the suddenly mobile workforce created by the floating population. In fact, exclusion, rather than inclusion, logically followed from the great migrations of the 1990s and early 2000s. With high levels of inequality across the country, rural migrant workers moved for higher wages and greater economic opportunities, even when doing so undermined their access to citizenship rights. Local governments benefited greatly, because internal migrants who did not receive local citizenship fueled local economic activity but did not

80   *Chapter 2*

draw on government services, saving local governments from paying long-term social welfare provisions.

There is an important distinction between welcoming migrants into a city and formally granting them citizenship rights. When migrants are excluded from local citizenship, they move and work with economic cycles. When the economy is booming, they flock to cities. In times of economic downturn, migrants without *hukou* and no access to government services are more likely to return to the countryside or try their luck in another city. This transient movement can prevent excessive burdens on cities in times of economic lulls. The local government wants to extend formal local citizenship by granting *hukou* only when the internal migrant will benefit the local economy in the long run. Once internal migrants naturalize into the local *hukou* system, they are more likely to remain in the city permanently because they would be unable to access citizenship rights elsewhere. In other words, the local government wants to target economically desirable migrants for long-term inclusion through naturalization.

LOCAL NATURALIZATION CONTROLS

Local governments practice strategic inclusion by manipulating the naturalization pathways that dictate who can become a local citizen and access citizenship rights. Changing *hukou* to naturalize in a new location—transfer *hukou* (转户口, 入户)—requires qualifying for a highly restrictive transfer program in a new city and navigating a complicated bureaucratic process. It involves three levels of government, both in the new location and in the home location; can require over a hundred documents; and stipulates canceling the old status (Interviews 44140703, 44150701).

Local naturalization regulations define and delineate both the number and the type of people eligible to obtain local urban *hukou*. The early years of the twenty-first century saw a significant rise in local governments writing and rewriting the eligibility requirements defining who could and could not transfer their *hukou* registration to become a naturalized local citizen.

Local naturalization pathways purposely mimic international immigration regimes by creating inclusion and exclusion categories. To create their *hukou* policies, local officials studied how countries managed immigration pathways (Interview 11141001). Each municipality publishes naturalization pathways, or methods for entering registration (入户办法), for would-be naturalizers. Naturalizations have four main pathways: high-skilled labor, long-term resident, family reunion, and investment.[45] Access to these pathways varies across cities, and quotas limit the number of naturalizations per pathway. By making some pathways easy and some pathways more difficult, the local government can strategically manipulate who has access to local citizenship and who does not.

LOCAL DEVELOPMENT AND INCLUSIVE MEMBERSHIP

By setting local naturalization policies, municipal governments strategically targeted certain types of internal migrants for inclusion while excluding others. The *hukou* and control over local naturalization pathways provided a tool to selectively open doors to desirable migrants, defined by local development strategy. Different types of migrants benefited different types of economic development and, consequently, different social and economic players. Three categories of local development strategies benefit from different types of migrants: outward-oriented, bottom-up, and top-down development.

Outward-oriented development engages with foreign economies for local development. Economic activities for foreign production directly benefit from high-skilled workers. Dependent on the influx of foreign capital, outward-oriented development creates more opportunities for technology transfer and less wage competition than does domestically oriented development. Globalization encourages greater investment in human capital (Ansell 2008), and the fastest way to develop human capital in the local labor market is to naturalize those who already have higher education and technical skills.[46] High-skilled naturalizations—allowing those with college degrees and technical skills to change their *hukou*—are particularly lucrative when the local economy hosts foreign production. Increasing the human capital of a local economy encourages new foreign contracts, because foreign firms are much less willing to go into markets that do not already have a sufficiently large pool of high-skilled labor (Interview 11171203). And naturalizing high-skilled workers is an investment in the city's future development, even after contracts with foreign firms end, because naturalized high-skilled workers remain in the city, working for other companies with their gained experience and knowledge (Interview 44140502). High-skilled internal migrants who lack local citizenship are more likely to return home when foreign contracts end. Thus, naturalization can encourage permanent settlement of these migrants for the benefit of local development.

82 *Chapter 2*

The targeting of high-skilled workers benefited firms with existing connections to the local government. High-skilled transfer pathways, as discussed in the next chapter, relied largely on firm-based quotas. The local government and its human resources bureau determined the number of transfers to grant and the distribution of these quotas to firms. Morphing from the explicit labor allocation of the Mao era, high-skilled transfers largely benefit state-owned enterprises and firms with good relationships with the local government.

Not all localities have the benefit of a foreign-driven economy. In *bottom-up development*, when local development depends on agricultural upgrading and cultivating a stable working class, desirable migrants are defined, not by skill level, but by where they come from. Bottom-up development detaches rural labor from the land and creates a pool of labor local governments can draw on to support development, regardless of skill level. Recognizing the need for broader recruitment of a working class, a smaller municipality in Guangdong implemented a program of *hukou* through education, which qualified children of migrants for naturalization after they completed middle school locally. The program targeted local migrants, who were more likely to bring their children with them to the urban center, compared with nonlocal migrants, who were more likely to leave their children in the countryside. The city developed this program because large manufacturing firms complained that worker turnover was high but that allowing children to naturalize would make their parents more likely to stay in the city (Interview 44131201).

Bottom-up development also relies heavily on leveraging land resources for development. In early twenty-first-century development programs, local governments prioritized the urbanization of land and capital by expanding cities through fixed-assets investments (Jaros 2019). This form of urbanization was highly lucrative for local governments, which captured rents from the sale and development of rural land and represented another form of extraction from the countryside to support urban industrialization (Chan and Wei 2019; Rithmire 2015; Whiting 2011). Many local governments began offering *hukou* to rural residents facing land taking as compensation for losing their land and to incorporate them into the urban center as a justification for usurping their land use rights (Cai 2016; Interviews 51131105, 34150305, 44120802). Cash-strapped inland municipalities offered land-for-*hukou* exchanges where rural residents could voluntarily give up their farmland and homestead land to naturalize in the city (Interview 51131105). These bottom-up processes, focusing on the divisions between urban and rural citizens within one municipality, targeted migrants very different from those targeted by outward-driven development policies.

Rural management offices and property developers benefit from bottom-up-development *hukou* reform, although to mixed degrees compared with previous eras. Because bottom-up development transfers local rural residents rather than targeting skilled migrants from both local and nonlocal populations, it potentially frees up rural land for development. Villages benefit when a rural resident relinquishes land use rights because the village gains land to redistribute to remaining residents or repurpose for small enterprises. Local governments, property developers, and the construction bureau benefit from suburban land relinquished for *hukou*. State and economic rural land interests captured fewer land resources after 2014 because of central pressure to reduce rural land taking, but a reformed *hukou* transfer system that encouraged rural and urban integration would create more possibilities for voluntary relinquishment of rural land.

Finally, some municipalities depend on central-government support for development. *Top-down development* strategies are often found in impoverished regions where other development strategies have failed to take root. Without robust local economic activities, these locations remained relatively closed off, with little incentive for expanding access to local citizenship. The primary incentive for inclusion in top-down development strategies is to meet central objectives. In officially designated rural poverty counties, central and provincial governments direct poverty alleviation policies, including resettlement (Central Committee 2000, 2005; State Council 2001). Relocation involves moving villagers from the poorest villages to larger villages or nearby urban centers. This strategy moves them closer to economic activity and government services, and—most importantly for local officials—reduces the number of impoverished villages and people. Full relocation, including formal naturalization, allows local governments to show progress in reaching centrally mandated poverty relief policies.

These development strategies—outward oriented, bottom up, and top down—are not mutually exclusive: local leaders may employ more than one at the same time. They may promote one over the other, but they can be, and often are, implemented simultaneously. A city negotiating a contract with a foreign firm may also expand its suburbs to develop its local area.

84   *Chapter 2*

Pursuing multiple pathways means naturalization policies will be the most open to the most people.

Discussion

Internal citizenship regimes in China allowed a flexible system of inclusion and exclusion from the government's perspective, one manipulated to ensure continued economic growth while ensuring social stability. The balance between limiting and granting access shows the interaction of economic and security logics in expanding access to government redistribution. Internal citizenship regimes allow the autocrat to identify and limit access to privileged status and thus access to redistribution. But redistribution also depends on ensuring economic development. Greater inclusion in local citizenship, or granting more internal migrants access to citizenship rights, can support economic development by developing and supporting the local labor market.

Both security and economic logics can dictate who gets access to citizenship rights through naturalization in the *hukou* system. Overall, security incentives support greater exclusion and restrictions, and only new challengers to the stability gain access. Economic incentives provide broader motivations for granting more *hukou*s as a means of enriching labor. These trade-offs between security and economics occur at multiple levels of the bureaucracy and the greatest variation comes from economic incentives at the local level. After control over economic development strategies relocated below the central level in the 1990s and 2000s, local governments adapted *hukou* policies to naturalize internal migrants who benefit local development. As a downstream effect of economic policies, this fragmented system of particularistic membership leads to significant variation in access to citizenship rights and experiences of citizenship within China.

The next chapter details local naturalization regimes as tools of targeted inclusion. It explores the different pathways to local citizenship, whom the pathways target, and how these pathways vary across China's municipalities, providing a national picture of variation in access to citizenship rights.

THREE

Internal Citizenship Regimes: Pathways of Local Naturalization

"It's easier to get an American green card than change your *hukou*," I was told dozens of times when speaking with people who had tried, successfully and unsuccessfully, to change their *hukou*. Bottlenecked access to *hukou*, with significant limitations on eligibility and shifting requirements, has been the standard for decades.[1] How does one become a local citizen? What are the rules that dictate who is and is not allowed to claim local-government services and permanent citizenship membership? In this chapter, I identify the policy tools local governments use to regulate local citizen membership. Put simply, who is considered a citizen and who can become one?

I focus on the rules dictating who is eligible for local *hukou*, and thus local citizenship membership, because they are the key tools of citizenship manipulation in China. The formal policies defining who is and is not allowed to be a citizen provide the legal framework for inclusion and exclusion. This chapter assesses the types of citizenship policies functioning in China's cities, allying internationally comparative logic and methodologies to the subnational context in nondemocratic China. Like national citizenship, the *hukou* system is one of jus sanguinis—a blood-based rule—initial registration rests not on place of birth but on location of parental registration. *Hukou* rights are exclusive, meaning it is illegal to be registered in more than one place and no dual citizenship is allowed. Anyone transferring registration location or type, between urban and rural, must relinquish previous registration and the rights associated with it. Local governments control these naturalization pathways—sets of policies that allow some migrants pathways to local citizenship while excluding others.

86   *Chapter 3*

This chapter distinguishes between permit and notification systems used to register populations around the world. It then turns to China's internal citizenship regimes and outlines how individuals acquire *hukou*: citizenship acquisition. *Hukou* naturalization policies mirror, quite explicitly, international naturalization pathways. Bureaucrats of all ranks mentioned to me how they defined local policies after learning from international immigration regimes (Interviews 11141001, 44120804), highlighting the importance of this framework in understanding policies that structure citizenship. I collected *hukou* policies and regulations from 317 of China's 333 municipalities to derive an index of citizenship-acquisition policy openness and subindexes of naturalization policies depending on whom they target: family reunification, high-skilled labor, long-term residents, or investors. I argue municipalities' sets of naturalization regimes form three distinct groups—selective, moderate, and open. I then use estimates of the net number of people who naturalize locally to show distinct patterns across the country with significant distributional consequences.

Permit versus Notification Systems

Countries around the world require individuals to register with the state, but not all forms of registration rise to the level of citizenship. The two main types of registration systems, notification and permit systems, are differentiated by the role of the state. In notification systems, residents must simply notify local officials when they change addresses, whereas in permit systems, migrants must apply for permission to change addresses or registration (Rubins 1998). An example of an extreme case of a notification system is the United States, which requires registration with the state of residence only if an internal migrant owns a car. New residents who own and operate a car must register with the local Department of Motor Vehicles when they change addresses, but they are often not required to carry address information as proof of identification. In the more regulated Germany, those who change addresses are required to register with the local government and obtain a local registration (*Anmeldebestätigung*, confirmation of registration) within two weeks of moving, which serves as proof of address for all official business. The German state does not, except in extreme circumstances, deny the registration of a new resident or change of address. Although anyone with much DMV experience in the United States might testify that it is not always easy to notify the government of a change of address, anyone with proper paperwork is eligible.

These notification-based registration systems are fundamentally different from permit-based systems. Under a permit system, local officials have the power to deny access to registration (Rubins 1998). Permit systems, like the Soviet *propiska*, Chinese *hukou*, or Vietnamese *ho khau*, require filing paperwork, as in notification systems, but also obtaining government approval, making movement within these countries more akin to international migration than internal migration. When migrants are required to obtain government approval to relocate, the state maintains significant control over who moves where.

China's *hukou* system is a typical permit-based system. Individuals must seek permission to register newborn children and to legally transfer from one location or type to another, and permission can be withheld. A change of status involves eligibility, review, and selection, dictated by the local government. Every transfer requires asking for permission and approval from both the old and the new local governments, which have the power of denial. The local government's power to restrict status is a defining feature of a permit-based system. By controlling who is and is not allowed to become a local resident, permit-based systems institutionalized state control over membership. The local state grants or denies privileged status. Not only does the local state decide who is eligible to gain citizenship status; it also decides the administrative burdens, or barriers, placed on naturalization, including how clear and streamlined or onerous and challenging the process is.[2]

When access to this status restricts migration flows or provision of government services, the local state's rules of membership operate similarly to international citizenship regimes. The more government services depends on holding a particular status, the more important local citizenship becomes relative to national-level citizenship.

Local Citizenship Acquisition

BIRTHRIGHT CITIZENSHIP

In China, local citizenship, like national-level citizenship, is based on jus sanguinis principles. Entitlement to a *hukou* is a right provided by the 1958 *Hukou* Registration Regulation. The primary means of obtaining a *hukou* is

88   *Chapter 3*

through birthright citizenship. Before 1998, all newborn children were registered with their local public safety bureau and given the same registration status and location as their mother, creating a matrilineal hereditary caste-like social order.[3] After national regulation change in 1998, children could follow either their mother or father (State Council 1998). According to a 2002 survey, 80 percent of urban *hukou* holders had the same *hukou* they obtained at birth.[4]

Administrative barriers can hinder access to initial citizenship acquisition. Municipal governments place administrative burdens on parents, requiring paperwork ranging from both parents' *hukou*s and identity cards (身份证) to parents' marriage certificates, to family planning certificates showing the child was born within family planning policies. Additional burdens fall on nontraditional families. For example, 10 percent of cities require certification of no other registration, proving the child is not registered elsewhere when parents each have a different *hukou*. There are also time limits to newborn registration. National regulations require children to be registered within a month of birth, but municipal limits vary between one month and eighteen years. Parents wishing to register their children after the deadline must pay additional fees (Interview 44140703).

Local officials use these administrative burdens to deny citizenship to newborns for technical and political reasons. Irregularities in paperwork can result in the denial of *hukou*, such as birth certificates without one mother and one father listed that many adopted children receive or even children born abroad to same-sex couples. Approximately thirteen million people lack any registration at all because they were denied *hukou* at birth. The vast majority of these "black *hukou*s" were born in violation of family planning policies or are children of migrants (Kennedy and Shi 2019; Vortherms 2019). Before policy reform began encouraging more births, those born in violation of birth-planning policies reflected poorly on local officials, who kept these out-of-plan children hidden to protect their reputations. At the time of the 2000 census, nearly 8 percent of children born to migrant mothers lacked *hukou*, compared with just over 1 percent of children born to nonmigrant mothers (Vortherms 2019). Migrant children were particularly susceptible to lacking *hukou* because of the subnational nature of the *hukou* system. To register a newborn, parents must apply for *hukou* in their *hukou* location, where migrant mothers are not living. Living in China without a *hukou* means living as a noncitizen without formal rights entitlements to an education, government-provided health care, or other government services.

LOCAL CITIZENSHIP NATURALIZATION

The other means of obtaining a *hukou* is through transfer—a local naturalization process. Transferring *hukou* requires a significant amount of bureaucratic effort. Like initial registration, transferring *hukou* is a multistep bureaucratic process that involves the township, county, and municipal governments and relatively few migrants are eligible. One internal report estimates the process requires more than 120 documents (Interviews 44140703, 44150701).[5]

Within the local public security bureaus, *hukou* officers manage the day-to-day tasks of issuing *hukou* for newborns, canceling *hukou* in the case of deaths, and changing addresses when people move within the city. This constitutes the vast majority of *hukou* changes in any given location (Interview 44150701). For transfers, *hukou* police officers catalog the paperwork the would-be resident brings in and issue the relocation and migration permits. *Hukou* detectives exert greater authority and control than *hukou* officers. They validate applications for transfer, know and apply local regulations related to transfers, and perform community policing. Traditionally, *hukou* detectives ensured the accuracy of records and addresses for everyone registered in their community. They also worked closely with other public security sections to identify migrants with insufficient paperwork and worked with the Custody and Repatriation Centers responsible for deporting unemployed migrants until these were restructured in 2003. After 2003, local neighborhood committees and local police stations took over monitoring and reporting individuals not properly registered with the state.

The multilevel bureaucratic process and significant paperwork burden of *hukou* transfers allow the state to formally gather information on the population and control who gains access to local citizenship. The administrative burdens inherent in *hukou* transfer processes are designed to create barriers to citizenship and to ensure that those granted citizenship are known entities to the state. As one *hukou* police officer put it when discussing the required paperwork, "How can I make a teacup with no clay? We must have records to work with first, before issuing *hukou*" (Interview 44150701). Through these bureaucratic barriers, local governments manipulate local citizenship policies to their benefit.

90 Chapter 3

Measuring Internal Naturalization Regimes

One of the most challenging aspects to understanding variation across the country in access to citizenship rights is measuring how difficult it is to become a local urban citizen. Formal policy of who can naturalize often varies from who, in practice, qualifies and is often even further from who does, in fact, naturalize.

To manage the gap between policy and its implementation and my desire to represent the *hukou* system as a whole, I collected a novel database of every way to localize naturally—to transfer one's *hukou*—in 317 of the 333 municipalities in 2016.[6] This database relies on information from local public security bureaus rather than more idealized, less reliable government press releases and media pronouncements. Instead of using formal policies announced at higher levels, this database centers the perspective of the individual. With the assistance of research assistants and a set of questions related to *hukou* acquisition, I collected data directly from public security bureau websites as if I were a would-be naturalizer. Public security bureau websites at the municipal level provide how-to guides and practical instructions and materials for applying for *hukou*. Information on these websites answered a set of questions I developed over months of semistructured interviews to capture the requirements, limitations, and administrative burdens present in all naturalization pathways at the local level. When the websites were insufficient for answering the questions, a research assistant called a randomly selected local public security bureau to inquire about the necessary qualifications, limitations, and documents necessary for each type of transfer offered locally. These naturalization pathways provide detailed information on how difficult it is to acquire *hukou* for individuals in practical ways that go beyond formal policy programs.

This study improves on previous studies that measured the relative openness of *hukou* policies in four key ways. First, I include all possible naturalization pathways instead of only employment or investment pathways, which are the primary focus of existing studies.[7] Second, I accounted for administrative burdens in my measure, similar to Zhang, Wang, and Lu (2019), including the amount of paperwork necessary to acquire *hukou*. I go beyond their number of attachments, however, and add qualitative measures of how difficult these attachments are to obtain as a better measure of how onerous the process is. Third, I expand the population on which the data are based by including 317 of the 333 municipalities.[8] This is particularly important because smaller cities are more likely to be left out of smaller samples, creating bias in the national-level picture of *hukou* acquisition. Finally, by pairing *hukou* policy with semistructured interviews, I add often-omitted dimensions of policy related to whom different policies target, an essential determinant of how naturalization approvals are processed.[9]

To measure the other dimension of openness—how many people are allowed to naturalize—I rely on government data of registered populations over time and natural growth to estimate local net naturalization rates. Migration data is often, although not always, considered an internal secret, and governments are not required to publish these data except in census years. Relying on any population data published by the government is questionable because local officials often manipulate their numbers (Chan 2007), so I used these data with caution.

Internal Naturalization Regimes

During the Mao era (1949–1978), the government allowed very few transfers. Almost all transfers were limited to military and government officials, and the *hukou* system was used to implement central planning (Cheng 1991). After decentralization of policy control in the late 1990s, some local governments increased the rate of *hukou* transfers. As *hukou* transfers increased, so too did the tools of local-government manipulation.

Each municipality operates an internal naturalization regime, or policies delineating who is entitled to apply for local naturalization. Naturalization policies, mirroring international immigration entry tracks, offer five tracks for local naturalization: family, high-skilled, residence, investment, and special categories.[10] Each track is further broken down into subcategories (table 3.1). By identifying these pathways to local citizenship, the local government legally defined who is and is not entitled to claim resources from the state, who is and is not eligible for redistribution. These naturalization regimes allow local governments to target certain groups for naturalization while excluding others. This section walks through each pathway to citizenship, how it relates to international models of immigration, and the constraints and administrative burdens that municipalities place on the bureaucratic process that create barriers to accessibility.

92 *Chapter 3*

TABLE 3.1.
Summary of four naturalization tracks, subcategories, and targeted populations

Entry track	Subcategory	Targeted population
Family	Newborn	Local rural
	Children	
	Spouses	
	Parents	
	Elderly	
	Care needing	
High skilled	Employment driven	All
	• Credential system	
	• College with work requirements	
	General pool	
	• Points systems	
	• College without work requirements	
Residence based	Land based	Local rural
	Family based	
	Work based	All[1]
	Residence-based	
Investment	Housing	Nonlocal
	Investment: individual	
	Investment: firm	

[1]Work-based and residence-based policies objectively do not distinguish between local and nonlocal populations. In practice, anecdotal evidence suggests that local rural populations are the primary beneficiaries.

FAMILY-BASED CITIZENSHIP

The most fundamental and common naturalization pathway is through family relations. Family-based citizenship acquisition occurs when individuals have a legal right to citizenship because of their kin-based relationship with a citizen. The primary determinant of citizenship around the world is through blood: children born to citizen parents are considered citizens. Parents, spouses, and children of citizens are often allowed to gain citizenship status on the grounds of blood-based rights. In Germany, for example, the Residency Act states that individuals with German citizenship, a temporary residency permit, or an unrestricted residency permit can sponsor a spouse, child, or parent for legal residency (German Residency Act, Part 6). In 2010,

Germany granted more than fifty thousand residence permits on grounds of family-based immigration in Germany (Heinemann and Lemke 2012). In the United States, parents, spouses, children, and siblings of US citizens can obtain permanent residence without being subject to country-specific quotas.[11] All localities within China have similar birth-based and family naturalization policies. In general, they are more restrictive than international immigration regulations, and formal policies for some family members, such as spousal transfers, were implemented across all municipalities only in 1998.

Limiting family-based transfers was one of the original goals of the *hukou* system. One of the first concerns of early *hukou* policy makers in the 1950s was keeping urban workers' families and dependents out of the urban areas, because they were seen as an unnecessary draw on state resources (Cheng and Selden 1997). To ease the separation of workers from their family and encourage dependent family members to stay in the countryside, the State Council issued the Provisional Regulations on Home Leave and Wages of Workers and Employees in 1957, guaranteeing home visits for employees with divided households (分居) (State Council 1957). It was not until the 1998 reform that specific provisions relating to children whose parents have different registration locations and elderly transfers were promulgated by the central government.

In 2016, there were five types of family-based transfers: parents registering children (子女投靠父母), spousal transfer (夫妻投靠), children registering parents (父母投靠子女) or elderly grandparents (老人入户), and children needing care (收养子女入户).[12] These policies defined family by spouse and parent relationships. Siblings, aunts, and uncles were almost universally excluded from family-based transfers.

Limits on family-based transfers depend on a variety of factors. Age limitations affect both child transfers and elderly transfers, and older children and younger adults are often excluded from eligibility. For example, 80 percent of municipalities limit child transfers by age, ranging from six to twenty-two. All older children age out of eligibility. Spousal transfer, or husbands or wives petitioning for their nonlocal, nonurban spouses to receive a transfer to their status, can also be limited through length and age requirements.[13] And marriage itself may not be sufficient qualification. Some cities require family planning certificates to prove the couple had not previously violated birth-planning policies or proof of stability such as proof of financial livelihood or homeownership.

94   *Chapter 3*

Family-based transfers target two general populations: the dependents of economically productive local citizens and elderly family members left behind in rural areas. By allowing children and spouses to transfer *hukou*, local governments encourage sponsors to put down roots in the city, regardless of where their family members come from. Allowing the elderly to transfer into a city might at first seem counterproductive in a system that views economic development as a priority. But allowing elderly transfers fulfills key social, political, and economic needs. Aging parents are often primary caregivers to their grandchildren, allowing the children's parents to productively participate in the economy. When parents transfer their *hukou* to their adult children's location, they join an established household with family support, reducing the likelihood they will depend on the state for social assistance. Finally, if the parents transfer their *hukou* from local rural to local urban, the local government could benefit by claiming the land they leave behind. This has led local governments to actively encourage some elderly parents in the countryside to join their children in the city (Interviews 32131101, 44120802).

HIGH-SKILLED NATURALIZATION

High-skilled migrants are a common target for local naturalizations. Educated migrants with technical skills raise the local pool of human capital without the government having to invest local resources. Municipalities in China studied the high-skilled immigration policies of Hong Kong, Canada, and Australia to devise naturalization pathways targeting desirable, high-skilled labor (Interview 11141001). Skill level can be quite subjective and specific to different industries, and so *hukou* policies use both education and professional rank or certification. Skilled workers with training and formal experience can apply for a professional rank or certification. These certifications are a hierarchy that disaggregates levels of technical skills.[14]

The resulting policies mirror international employer-selected and general-pool pathways to citizenship.[15] Employer-selected models allow naturalization of individuals who relocate at the request of an employer with a work contract in hand, like the US H-1B visa. These programs tie migration directly to the needs of firms. Early years of *hukou* implementation used employer-selected models begun when urban workplaces (*danwei*) needed to recruit employees (Solinger 1999). Almost every city had some version of these employer-selected models. The modern form of these transfers was

Internal Citizenship Regimes: Pathways of Local Naturalization 95

highly bureaucratic and varied according to the definition of high skilled. Local governments determined the number of workers they wanted to transfer into the city and then allocated quotas among firms on the basis of local economic development goals, industries targeted for greater administrative support, and firm market size and importance, as well as personal relations (Interviews 11140901, 11140501). Firms used these quotas to attract high-skilled labor or to promote existing employees who did not secure a *hukou* transfer at the time of employment. These quotas were mostly aimed at college graduates, including university graduates, most frequently within two years of graduation.[16]

An example of quotas in action is Beijing's foreign education quotas. The Beijing government formally provides *hukou* transfer quotas for foreign-educated citizens to key firms to attract skilled labor. The city government, in conjunction with the education bureau and economic planners, distributed the quotas across firms. Foreign-educated returnees who secured a job at one of these firms could apply for local Beijing urban *hukou*, considered one of the most valuable in the country. Beijing set aside 1,704 transfers in 2014 and distributed them to eighty-eight firms. Table 3.2 shows the top recipients of these quotas. Nearly all the local universities and larger technology firms, not only state-owned enterprises but also private and foreign-owned firms, benefit from this program.

Unlike employer-selected models, general-pool models do not require employment. Anyone who meets certain requirements of basic human capital accumulation and financial resources is eligible to apply for legal status, either citizenship or residency. These programs seek to raise the quality of the general-labor pool, which benefits the labor market but risks raising unemployment. Canada, Hong Kong, Australia, New Zealand, Denmark, the Czech Republic, and Singapore all allow outsiders to apply for citizenship or resident status on this basis (Papademetriou, Somerville, and Tanaka 2008).

There are two general-pool systems for internal migrants in China. The first is points policies (积分入户), piloted first in Zhongshan, Guangdong Province, in 2010. Applicants earn points based on their background, including education level, participation in social programs such as social insurance (社保), and participation in investment programs. Applicants lose points for "undesirable traits" (Interview 44120804). Shenzhen, a city in the southern Pearl River Delta, for example, gives points to those under age forty and subtracts points from those over forty. In Yunfu, Guangdong,

96 Chapter 3

TABLE 3.2.
Beijing's top quota-receiving firms, 2014

Firm/organization	Industry	Quota
Tsinghua University	Education	65
Lenovo	Technology	55
Sinopec	Natural resources	40
Industrial and Construction Bank of China	Finance	31
Renmin University	Education	30
Beihang University	Education	30
Peking University	Education	30
National Development Bank	Finance	25
Polytechnic University	Education	25
Minsheng Bank	Finance	20
China Construction Bank	Finance	20
National Center for Nanoscience and Technology	Research	20
China Agricultural University	Education	20
Beijing Normal University	Education	20
Peking University Medical School	Education	20

SOURCE: Ministry of Education (2014).

women who violated birth-planning regulations within the last five years are not allowed to apply through a points system. If a woman had a child out of wedlock and did not get married within sixty days of the child's birth, she loses fifty points. Local governments use the evaluation criteria for points programs to clearly demarcate desired and undesired populations.[17] Those with money, education, and established, formal employment are desired. Those who deviate from government policy, or in the case of Shenzhen, even suspected of committing a crime, are not.[18] Once individuals obtain a sufficient number of points, they are eligible to apply for a transfer.

Attaining sufficient points to apply does not guarantee naturalization, however. The local government still limits these transfers through quotas, and often unpublished requirements and limitations disqualify some applicants. Xiao, a masseur, for example, easily met Shenzhen's minimum threshold of 100 points, earning 140 points in 2015, after living and working in Shenzhen for twenty years. But his application, and numerous subsequent appeals, were all rejected because he was blind (Lianzhang Wang 2017).

Internal Citizenship Regimes: Pathways of Local Naturalization   97

These points programs are often touted as a means of integrating rural workers: many are titled "Peasant Worker Point-Based Transfer Program." In reality, most of the qualifications disproportionately benefit high-skilled labor, creating more barriers than opportunities for integration. Approximately 10 percent of cities were actively implementing or planning points systems, including all four directly administered municipalities—Kunming, Wuhan, Hangzhou, Guangzhou—and many smaller cities in Guangdong in 2016.[19]

The original purpose behind the points system was to institutionalize high-skilled worker recruitment and move away from the often-corrupt firm-based transfer program discussed earlier (Interview 11141101). A points transfer system makes transfer qualifications more transparent and keeps concrete regulations separate from local government relations with firms, in part by removing firm power and reducing potential protectionist policies. Cities have been resistant to it, however, because it removes *hukou* transfers as a local-government tool for rewarding firms with close relations (Interview 11141102). Most cities, including Beijing and Tianjin, implemented a points system while maintaining a separate work-based transfer system, continuing the quotas distributed to firms and reducing the power of the points program. Five cities—Shenzhen, Shenyang, Ningbo, Zhanjiang, and Haikou—completely converted to points systems for high-skilled recruitment.

The last high-skilled naturalization pathway, education-based transfers, falls under either employer-based or general-pool policy. Education-based transfers allow graduates (毕业生) to get local urban status. Before higher education reform in 2001, the state allocated jobs to college graduates, ensuring all graduates both a job and a local *hukou* because their labor was allocated by the state. While in school, a student's *hukou* transfers to the university as a group, or collective, *hukou* (集体户口). After graduation, the new graduates' assigned work unit provides local *hukou*, usually a collective *hukou* dependent on their continued employment at the work unit. Any students with a rural *hukou* who entered college and transferred their status to the university's collective *hukou* faced difficulties returning to rural status, and almost all college graduates become urban *hukou* holders after attaining their degree (Interview 11150302). During the 1990s, in the lead-up to significant higher education reform, the state backed away from its guaranteed employment allocation for college graduates. Without this state-driven job

98   *Chapter 3*

placement, cities adapted the system to retain and attract college-educated labor. Most cities allow students at local universities to transfer their *hukou* to local urban status if they find and maintain employment in a local firm, making this form of transfer an employment-based policy.

Education transfers also take a general-pool form when employment is not required. Some cities, approximately 30 percent, allow students to transfer their *hukou* status before finding a job (可先落户，后找工作; 先落户后择业), to build a larger high-skilled labor pool. Like a points program, these transfers develop the local labor market by adding to the general pool of high-skilled labor rather than matching students with employers. These programs are, therefore, more open than those that require secured employment.

High-skilled programs gain a lot of local media attention, especially because these programs are depicted as equalizers: transfers that do not require knowing someone in power. In reality, the majority of the Chinese population do not have the credentials necessary to avail themselves of the program. According to the National Bureau of Statistics, only 13 percent of the population has a college degree (NBS, *China Statistical Yearbook* 2016). Although high-skilled transfers are possible without a college degree, they are significantly less likely without it.

RESIDENCE-BASED TRANSFERS TO CITIZENSHIP

The most optimistic supporters of *hukou* reform emphasize the potential of the third naturalization pathway: residence based. Residence-based naturalization allows any permanent resident to naturalize locally. Stable-residence naturalization pathways most closely resemble international processes of naturalization from established residencies to full citizenship, such as a US green card holder becoming a US citizen. Piloted informally across China for decades, residence-based naturalizations became the crux of the 2014 State Council reforms. Ideally, anyone with proof of a stable (稳定) life in the city, including a work contract, housing, and history of paying into local social security accounts, would become eligible for *hukou* transfer. The national adoption of this policy was touted as the "end of the *hukou* system" (Interview 11141106). Academics and observers of national politics saw residence as the essential shift from a permit-based system to a notification-based system.

Residence-based programs, although growing in popularity, still restricted who could transfer *hukou*. Residency programs vary by how many requirements they list for proof of stability. Some cities require employment with a formal labor contract, which many internal migrants lack. In the 2013 China Household Income Project Survey, only 23 percent of migrants could qualify for a transfer that required a work contract. Residence programs can also require home ownership or payment into the local social insurance program, something very few informal or unemployed migrants do. Even white-collar workers who operate their own businesses might not qualify, such as Lao Li, who owned a chain of stores in southern China for more than fifteen years but paid for private insurance instead of paying into the public social insurance system (Interview 44160201). Other municipalities require residence-based transfers to have family in the urban core before they can qualify.

These residence-based programs follow old rural-to-urban transfer (农转非) policies that, although opening up transfers to low-skilled workers, required naturalizers to give up their land in exchange for local urban *hukou*. New policies building on old institutions is nothing new, but the tools of manipulation and control from the old institutions can subvert new policy aims. Two years after national reform encouraged all small and medium-sized towns to implement residence-based *hukou* policies, many programs continued to require migrants to relinquish their land or meet the other strict requirements of labor contracts and home ownership. All these pathways are limited by quotas, and although the policies suggest openness to all migrants, the often-unspoken rule in the years after national reform is that residence-based quotas were reserved for local rural populations naturalizing in the urban center, not for nonlocal migrants who crossed municipal or provincial boundaries (Interview 44120804).

INVESTMENT-BASED CITIZENSHIP

The final set of common naturalization pathways is through investment. Similar to international forms of investment citizenship, these programs provide direct capital transfers to governments and local markets. Under these programs, would-be citizens invest up front in domestic funds, directly paying the government or buying real estate in exchange for citizenship.[20] Approximately seventy countries provide at least one residence-based immigration channel through financial contributions (Surak 2016) and at least six have economic citizenship, in which financial investment grants outright citizenship, regardless of residency. The United States has an

100   Chapter 3

investment path to citizenship, which costs US$1.8 million.[21] Canada tri-aled multiple programs, including one that required investments of Can$2 billion in a venture capital fund and one in which immigrant investors paid Can$800,000 into a fund directly distributed to provincial and territorial governments.[22]

The early 1990s saw significant experimentation in purchasing of local *hukou*. Smaller cities and towns allowed outright purchase of local ur-ban *hukou*, and there was a "wild push" to commodify local urban *hukou* "to amass millions in hard, cold cash" (*Inside China Mainland* 1992, 76). In 1992, the price of *hukou* reportedly varied widely from RMB 4,150 to 150,000 (US$(2020)1,401 to $50,686) (*Inside China Mainland* 1992).

Piloted in 1992, the blue-print (蓝印) *hukou*—named for the blue ink used—became popular after 1994 in the large cities of Shanghai, Guang-zhou, and Shenzhen.[23] With investments, often of over RMB 1 million, individuals could gain local blue-print *hukou* status. Although the program did see some success, it was slowly phased out because blue-print *hukou* had undesirable limitations. For example, holders of blue-print *hukou* did not have full access to social welfare programs and often faced difficul-ties transferring their family members (Chan 2009; Interviews 44150701, 44140703). As with a green card in the United States, residents with the blue-print *hukou* had full legal residence in the destination location, but this could be lost or rescinded (Chan 2004). But local governments saw the boon these programs could provide for local finances or markets. Af-ter the 1990s, investment programs morphed into a general investment program with three paths: housing investment, small-business investment, and firm-based taxes.

In the first path, individuals and firms purchase housing in exchange for local residency. In one southern city, the size of the house corresponds to the number of *hukou* transfers available. Lao Li, a white-collar migrant from the northeast and head of a three-person household, purchased an apartment to get his son a *hukou*. He and his wife wanted his son to complete the college entrance exam locally and, they hoped, go to college at the local university. The house met the size requirement for two people to change their *hukou* but not for all three of them (Interview 44160201).

In the second, individuals can make a one-time investment in a local firm or industry. Local governments define what investments in what in-dustries qualify for *hukou*, usually high-technology industries rather than manufacturing industries. These targeted investment programs allow the local state to funnel money into industries that support its development programs. In the third path, a firm that pays above a certain threshold of tax can petition for one of its employees to gain local *hukou*. Large firms qualify for more *hukou* transfers, but even small firms in cities with this naturalization pathway can qualify to sponsor their employees. In many cities, this firm-sponsored investment coincides with the high-skilled firm-recruitment process described earlier. For a firm to qualify, it must make the tax payments and hire city-defined high-skilled workers. Most cities have at least one of these programs that allow migrants with capital to naturalize locally.

OTHER FORMS OF NATURALIZATION

The last two forms of transfers, military and government assignments and rural returns, are significantly less common than the forms of transfers discussed earlier but deserve mentioning. Members of China's military, approximately 2.6 million soldiers, and individuals working in local governments are considered a special classification of *hukou* transfer. Military personnel transfer their *hukou* from individual to collective (集体) status and move according to military assignment. Leaving the military or transferring *hukou* from military collective to individual is subject to local regulations. In general, when leaving the military, individuals are eligible to return to their original *hukou* location. If they wish to register as an individual *hukou* in a location different from their hometown, local governments have separate regulations for military personnel, which may or may not allow permanent settlement. Often, military personnel based far from home marry into local status, receiving family transfers rather than military transfers (Interview 44140701). Government officials follow a similar process. As officials circulate from location to location, their *hukou* follows them but is considered collective rather than individual. Overall, the proportion of the population managed this way is small, given the relatively small number of people in the military—less than 1 percent of the total population. The relative ease of changing government and military *hukous* shows the need for the government to keep these populations included in the privileged class. It is also necessary for implementing China's unique cadre rotation system. The central communist party rotates local officials across different geographic units to encourage Chinese Communist Party (CCP) identity and discourage localism (Edin 2003). Rotation from one location to another requires formal

Chapter 3

legal rotation to ensure that local officials retain access to government services and privileged class status.

Becoming Rural

The previous sections dealt with either rural-to-urban transfers or urban-to-urban transfers. It is possible to transfer from urban-to-rural and from rural-to-rural, but these processes are uncommon and often challenging to complete. Migrants may want to become rural for a few reasons. First, rural status entitles individuals to land use rights, which are often difficult or impossible to obtain for urban registrants. Second, from 1984 until 2016 in many parts of the country, rural registrants with firstborn daughters were allowed a second child. According to many urban migrants I spoke with, rural status was particularly interesting because of the possibility of having two children.[24]

The chief ways of obtaining a rural *hukou* are through family-based transfers that follow the rules outlined earlier or through special graduate returnee programs. In family-based transfers, the would-be migrant must also obtain permission from local village authorities to join the village. This approval can be contentious because of land distribution. Village authorities regularly redistribute land within the village, adjusting how much and what land different families have land use rights over. If the village distributes land based on the number of people in the household rather than by households, outsiders coming in means smaller individual allotments and local village leaders may not approve or accept transfer to the individual village. When this occurs, the migrant can still become local but may lack access to land use rights (Interview 44120802).

Another way for becoming rural is as a graduate returnee. When enrolling in a university, *hukou* is transferred to the university's group status. Not all students do this, but most do (Interview 11140601). According to one urban migrant I spoke with in Beijing, she did not transfer her status to the university's group *hukou* because she was afraid of being cut off from her hometown, where she planned on returning after completing her training. Despite most of her friends and colleagues coveting the possibility of changing their *hukou* to Beijing, she was hesitant to give up her rural status because her hometown in Shandong did not have a formal process to allow students to return home after graduation (Interview 11141108).

Local officials have conflicting incentives: letting migrants into the rural area threatens land-redistribution resources but can improve education levels locally. Larger political processes and programs limit these types of transfers. The central government pushed urbanization initiatives in the early twenty-first century, and governments at the county and municipal levels in many provinces reformed their systems to encourage urbanization. Any formal transfer to rural areas works against this political goal.

Forced Naturalizations

The preceding naturalization pathways are voluntary procedures for transferring *hukou*. Other processes force local naturalization, however, and are related to administrative upgrading and, more controversially, land expropriation. Administrative upgrading occurs when a region designated as rural becomes an urban administrative unit, such as a village (乡) becoming an urban neighborhood (街道). In this upgrade, current residents may obtain urban *hukou* because the administrative unit changed from rural to urban. These nonvoluntary transfers are considered policy-based transfers, or government policy that directly affects *hukou*. The processes that allowed cities like Shenzhen to completely integrate their rural and urban populations by 2005 fall into this category.

Forced transfers also occur because of land expropriation. When cities expand into suburban and rural areas, they expropriate land from rural residents. When urban planners wish to expand urban development or build large infrastructure projects like roads and railways, they must convert agricultural land to urban construction land (Cai 2016). Doing so means taking rural land use rights from residents and providing compensation. In some cases, rural residents displaced from their land are directly offered local urban *hukou*. In other cases, they are relocated into urban spaces without *hukou* and they must follow one of the preceding naturalization pathways to qualify. The residence-based pathway is in part meant to address this. More on involuntary *hukou* conversion is in chapter 5.

QUOTAS FOR TRANSFERS

The final means of manipulating membership is the management of how many people can naturalize locally. Two cities could have similar policies but set dramatically different quotas (名额) for their deployment.[25] Guangzhou and Shenzhen, for example, both use a points system to

104   *Chapter 3*

recruit high-skilled labor. In 2014, Guangzhou admitted 6,000 applicants through the points stream, and Shenzhen granted between 160,000 and 200,000 points naturalizations.[26] Looking at only the formal eligibility requirements misses this variation in implementation. Ideally, I would have included quotas as a measure of formal policy openness, but these data are not publicly available.[27] Instead, I constructed three alternative measures to estimate the number of people who transfer their status: net estimates of total local urban naturalization, local rural-to-urban naturalization, and nonlocal naturalization. The net naturalization estimates are the growth of the local population not attributed to natural growth. Appendix B provides a detailed description of these data and their limitations. For example, these data include urban upgrading that grants entire villages urban *hukou* because of changes in the administrative system. This creates an upward bias in estimating *hukou* transfers through the naturalization pathways discussed earlier. These estimates should be seen as relative trends rather than absolute values.

Figure 3.1 depicts estimated net naturalizations over time across municipalities. The bolded line estimates the average proportion of nonlocal migrants naturalizing into the urban core, based on estimated local migrant stock. The thinner line estimates the number of rural residents naturalized per total local population. Net rural naturalizations remain stable across this period of decentralization. Peaks in rural naturalization occur in 2013 and 2015, likely in the lead-up to and in response to the 2014 State Council plans for urbanization. Nonlocal naturalization is less stable across time. Although experiencing a local peak in 2014, nonlocal naturalizations decrease over time.

Transfers in Action

The different pathways to local citizenship vary by city and time. Local governments rarely publish how many people change their *hukou* by the naturalization pathway they take. Instead, there is evidence of these transfer processes in nationally representative surveys. The China Household Income Project Survey asks respondents what years they changed their *hukou* and why, whether cadre and military, education, housing purchase, land expropriation, marriage, or other (NBS, *China Household Income Project Survey* 2013). Overall, local naturalizations increase over time and vary significantly

Internal Citizenship Regimes: Pathways of Local Naturalization 105

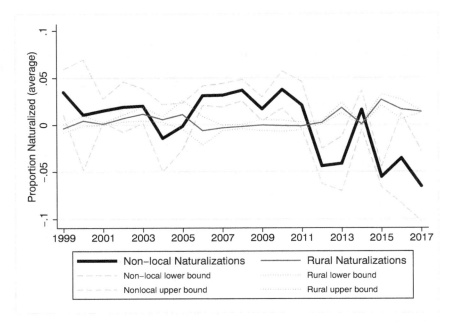

FIGURE 3.1. Estimated net naturalization rates across municipalities, nonlocal and rural populations. Solid lines present an average across municipalities. The dotted and dashed lines present 95% confidence intervals around the mean. Net naturalization estimated by the growth of the registered population is not attributable to natural growth. *Source:* Demographic Data of Counties and Cities in the People's Republic of China (Ministry of Public Security 1999–2013); the NBS Regional Economic Statistical Yearbook (1999–2014), NBS China City Statistical Yearbooks (1999–2014), and various provincial city and county yearbooks.

from one year to the next. Figure 3.2 presents unweighted sample averages of transfer types by decade of respondents' *hukou* change, roughly aligning with the naturalization pathways presented earlier.

The makeup of types of transfers varied over the years of reported transfer.[28] In the early Mao era, transfers were dominated by cadre and military transfers, and only a few education-based transfers were made and no investment-based transfers. This period marks the height of *hukou* as a central-government labor allocation system to manage *hukou* changes. Beginning in the late 1970s, cadre and military transfers declined in relative importance, going from an average 70 percent of all transfers in the 1970s to less than 30 percent in the 1980s. Education-based transfers averaged around

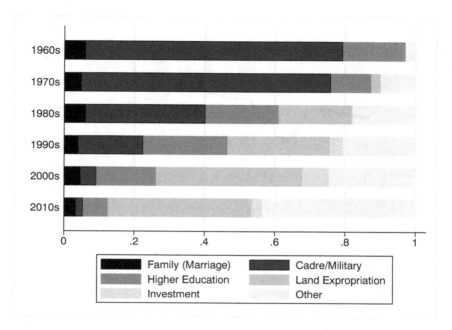

FIGURE 3.2. Rural-to-urban *hukou* transfers. Excludes rural-to-rural, urban-to-urban, or conversion to unified residence *hukou* because of survey questionnaire limitations. The 2010s include only 2010–2013. *Source:* NBS, *China Household Income Project Survey*, (2013).

24 percent of all transfers in the 1990s but began to decline after 2000. Investment programs, in which survey respondents naturalized *hukou* through the purchase of a house, began in the late 1980s and were more common in the first years of the 2000s, but they never reached more than 10 percent of the surveyed *hukou* changes. This pattern is contrary to much of the popular discourse on *hukou* transfers. A commonly held belief is that, in most of China's cities, housing purchase is an easy and acceptable pathway to local citizenship. The size of the population that makes a housing investment for citizenship, on the basis of this sample, is relatively small. Instead, the investment pathway for citizenship is more difficult than commonly thought by both the public and local policy bureaucrats (Interview 32131101).

Land expropriation jumped from 20 percent of transfers in the 1980s and 1990s to 40 percent of transfers in 2000 and 2010. This trend marks the rise of land-centered urbanization processes and the value of land to local governments during the decentralized reform period after 2001.

Marriage-based transfers are a low, steady proportion of *hukou* transfers. Work-based, low-skilled, and family transfers outside marriage fall into the other category, which represents slightly more than a quarter of transfers between 2000 and 2013.

Patterns of Policy

Before the next chapter explores the determinants of openness, this section identifies natural groupings of municipalities that implement similar policies through cluster analysis. Cluster analysis allows grouping municipalities by policies, creating a typology of municipalities that implement similar policy arrangements.[29]

To evaluate how policies vary across municipalities, I created a naturalization policy index for each municipality. The index uses principal component analysis on measures of the administrative burdens placed on each naturalization pathway. Essentially, the index measures how easy it is for migrants to qualify for local naturalization. The higher the index score, the easier it is to naturalize locally and the more open citizenship membership policies are. The different pathways to naturalization—family, high-skilled, residence, and investment—target different migrant populations and are thus kept separate.[30]

Municipalities fall into one of three clusters of naturalization regimes: selective, moderate, and open. Selective municipalities employ relatively closed policies. This is most representative of investment pathways to local citizenship. Selective municipalities either do not allow investment-based citizenship or set high minimum investment requirements (figure 3.3). The twenty-four municipalities that do not offer investment-based naturalization fall into this category. In the remaining twenty municipalities in this category, the average minimum investment amount was estimated at around RMB 800,000 (US$123,000). This is dramatically higher than the investment amounts required in other clusters—RMB 146,000 and 152,000 (US$22,500 and $23,400) in the moderate and open clusters, respectively. Selective municipalities have, on average, more closed high-skilled and family-based pathways than the other two clusters.

On the other end of the spectrum, open municipalities maintain open policies across all pathways. Open investment policies have the lowest required minimum investments. Distinct from the other two groups is the

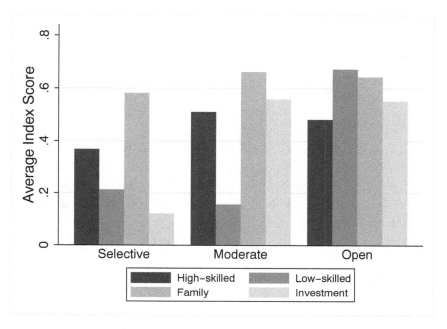

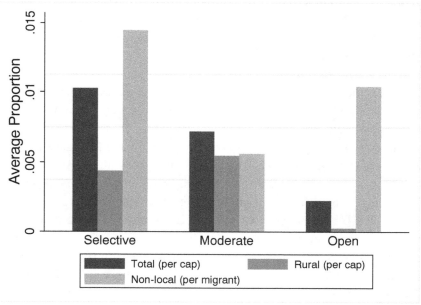

FIGURE 3.3. Policy openness index by cluster (*top*) and net naturalizations estimated as growth in the *hukou* population not attributable to natural growth (*bottom*). *Source:* Estimated from statistics from the National Bureau of Statistics and provincial statistics bureaus.

relative openness of residence-based programs. Residence-based programs in open municipalities are less likely to require family in the local urban area or require that residents explicitly relinquish land use rights. They are also likely to have the shortest minimum residence time and are less likely to require a formal labor contract as proof of local employment. These pathways are much easier to access in the open cluster than any other cluster.

Moderate municipalities fall between the selective and open municipalities. Moderate municipalities, like open municipalities, have more open investment policies but, like selective municipalities, relatively restrictive residence-based programs. High-skilled programs are the most open in moderate municipalities compared with the other two clusters.

All three clusters are found across China (figure 3.4). Open municipalities tend to occur in the central region: more central municipalities fall into the open cluster than do the other two regions, and this is statistically

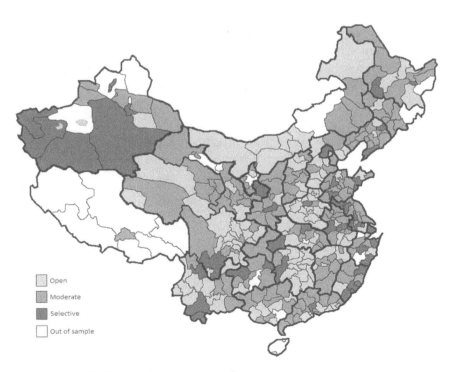

FIGURE 3.4. Distribution of clusters across China.

distinct.[31] Selective municipalities exist in every region, although not in every province. There are three clusters of selective municipalities: in Xinjiang, China's far northwestern province; the Fujian coast south of the Yangtze river delta and north of the Pearl River delta; and southern Jiangsu. Of the four directly administered municipalities, Beijing and Shanghai fall into the selective cluster, and Tianjin and Chongqing fall into the moderate cluster.

To identify whether these trends are systematic, I implemented a multinomial logit model predicting the probability a given municipality will fall into the selective, moderate, or open cluster. After controlling for municipal gross domestic product (GDP) and estimates of the local migrant stocks, I looked to see whether municipalities of different size or region are more likely to fall into one category or another.

Table 3.3 presents the predicted probability of a municipality falling into a cluster by region. Municipalities across different regions have equal probability of being in the selective cluster. This means eastern municipalities, those first to implement economic reform policies and often seen as the drivers of economic development, are no more or less likely to be selective than other regions. The same holds true for the moderate cluster. There is no significant variation in the probability of being in the moderate cluster. The open cluster, however, does have a regional bias. Eastern municipalities are less likely to fall into the open cluster, whereas central municipalities,

TABLE 3.3.
Predicted probability of being in a given cluster

By region	Selective	Moderate	Open
East	0.171	0.599	0.230
	(0.036)	(0.055)	(0.050)
Central	0.102	0.387	0.512
	(0.031)	(0.049)	(0.050)
West	0.170	0.481	0.349
	(0.039)	(0.051)	(0.049)
By size			
Small and medium	0.160	0.496	0.344
	(0.030)	(0.038)	(0.035)
Large and extralarge	0.133	0.452	0.415
	(0.030)	(0.052)	(0.052)

NOTE: Predicted probabilities of a municipality being in a given cluster are based on a multinomial logit model controlling for estimated migrant population and municipal GDP. Standard errors are in parentheses.

the senders of most internal migrants, are more likely to be open. Eastern and western municipalities are more likely to be in the moderate cluster than the open cluster, whereas central municipalities are equally likely to be in moderate or open clusters.

Table 3.3 also presents the predicted probabilities for size. Similar to region, size has no statistical correlation with the selective cluster. Small and medium-sized municipalities and large and extralarge municipalities are equally likely to be in the selective cluster. Large and extralarge municipalities are slightly more likely to be in the open cluster than small and medium-sized ones, although this correlation is just outside statistical significance (p = .107). This suggests that one of the primary alternative hypotheses, that the central government dictates local policy on the basis of size, is reversed. Small and medium-sized cities, meant to be the most open in central-government policies, are more likely to be in the moderate cluster than the open cluster.

Do more open policies correlate with larger naturalizations? On the basis of estimates of naturalization in the five years before the policy index, policy openness does not correlate with more naturalizations (figure 3.3). The estimated naturalization rates of rural and migrant populations by policy cluster is presented in figure 3.3. Selective municipalities have the highest naturalizations per total population, just above 1 percent. Open municipalities have the lowest rate, less than 0.2 percent of the total population. The aggregate number of naturalizations has an inverse relationship with relative policy openness. The other notable pattern is the populations targeted for naturalization. Both selective and moderate municipalities maintain around a 0.5 percent naturalization rate of their rural populations per year. Open municipalities, however, have a net naturalization rate of near zero. Nonlocal migrants, with approximately 0.5 percent naturalizing, have higher net naturalization rates in selective municipalities than in any other cluster, followed by open municipalities and then moderate municipalities.

These naturalization estimates should be interpreted with some caution. First, these estimates are of net naturalizations. Using available data, I cannot distinguish naturalization into and transfer out of a city, only net effect. The low number of rural naturalizations in open municipalities is likely due, in part, to large out-migration in these municipalities. This out-migration, however, is not being outpaced by local attempts to urbanize the population, an important balance to keep in mind. Second, population data

Chapter 3

is subject to manipulation. There is evidence of manipulation, of municipal governments overreporting rural-to-urban transfers at the peak of urbanization campaigns, for example, as discussed in appendix B. Third, these naturalization numbers consider both the availability of local naturalization and migrants' desire to naturalize, a factor discussed separately in the next chapter.

Discussion

Since the first years of the 2000s, local-government authority over *hukou* policy implementation grew and *hukou* naturalization pathways flourished. Local governments, especially at the municipal level, defined and manipulated the ways in which migrants could naturalize. Disaggregating local naturalization policies reveals that policy variation allows the local government to target certain groups for naturalization and that policy reforms create variation in naturalization policy openness. With decentralization, local governments could use the *hukou* system to complement other policy objectives, such as economic development. The remaining question is which governments implement which policies and how local conditions correlate with policy openness. The next chapter assesses the relationship between policy openness—how easy it is to get a *hukou*—and economic determinants of openness.

FOUR

Balancing Security and Development: Municipal Variation

As *hukou* policies developed over time, local governments gained tools to strategically manipulate their citizenry and labor markets. Controlling who was permanently included in the local polity allowed governments to deliberatively choose their people. How do multiple, often competing incentives over security and economic goals affect internal citizenship regimes and determine who is a desirable migrant? This chapter defines the correlates of internal citizenship regimes. Specifically, it identifies how local officials navigate the trade-offs in balancing security and economics, maintaining citizenship membership restrictions while strategically opening to migrants when economically prudent.

Local officials at the municipal level constantly juggle multiple demands. They often have both formulation and implementation power over policy but face pressure from above because provinces and the central government coordinate policy reform. But local officials also oversee county implementation below them. They must reform one policy while balancing its effects on other policies: allowing more *hukou* naturalizations while deepening coverage of welfare programs. Annual reviews from their supervising organization departments prompt local officials to provide social stability and public security while advancing economic development. An expansion of the local citizenry through more *hukou* naturalizations could undermine social per capita performance indicators that dictate local-official political advancement. But expanding access to citizenship can improve economic indicators by transforming the local labor market to support development.

113

114   *Chapter 4*

Migration and population management are deeply tied into public security and economic development, and both are considerations in *hukou* policy making. As a tool of exclusion, the *hukou* system provided local governments with a means of protecting local resources and limiting demands on the government. The narrative of socially destabilizing migration developed in the Mao era remained for security managers in cities well into the reform era. Localities responsible for welfare programs are fiscally chauvinistic, preferring to spend resources on local populations rather than nonlocal noncitizens. Local citizenship institutions like the *hukou* provide local officials with tools to limit and restrict citizenship, reducing redistribution.

Economic development, in contrast, provided a liberalizing force. Continued economic development was a policy imperative, both because the local government needed to make economic quotas set by the center, but also because the local authoritarian state depended on development to generate resources for redistribution. Local citizenship policies are downstream effects of local development policies. When development depended on more open citizenship regimes, naturalization liberalized, expanding who could become a citizen. But not all economic development is created equal and not all migrants are desirable for all development strategies. Variation in local economic development strategies changed who was considered a desirable migrant and targeted for naturalization. Local governments pursued *hukou* policies that supported economic development strategies.

In this chapter, I outline three stylized forms of development—outward-oriented, bottom-up, and top-down—and the type of migrants that supports each development strategy. Outward-oriented development occurs when local governments compete for capital and production from foreign industries. It encourages naturalization of high-skilled migrants, to supply foreign firms with needed labor and also to take advantage of spillover effects related to technology transfers. In contrast, when local governments pursue bottom-up development focused on local resources, there are no explicit incentives for targeting high-skilled migrants for naturalization. Instead, rural development processes dislodge local rural populations from the land, creating potential for mass protests but also a pool of labor to be reallocated to support local development. Finally, top-down development, driven by central-government development policies for poverty alleviation, creates little incentive to expand citizenship membership unless naturalizations help reach development goals charged to local governments.

This chapter draws on semistructured interviews and a cross-sectional analysis of *hukou* policy openness at the municipal level to demonstrate the conservative pull of security concerns and the liberalizing push of economic development in *hukou* policies. Building on the variation in *hukou* policies discussed in chapter 3, I show broader trends in both security and economic correlates with *hukou* policy. I implement ordinary least squares regressions on a policy index measuring the openness of *hukou* policy—how easy it is to change *hukou* status—in 2016 broken down by naturalization pathway. This analysis shows how different development policies targeted different populations for naturalization. I also present evidence from estimated net *hukou* naturalizations during the decade of decentralized reform to show how these forces of security and economics influenced policy outcomes during the decentralized period of *hukou* reform.[1] These methods show both the logic behind *hukou* reform and the broader trends in *hukou* policy changes leading up to and immediately after the start of the new-type urbanization era.

Security, Stability, and Fiscal Chauvinism

The three main functions of the *hukou* system are ensuring social stability and security, organizing labor, and distributing government-provided rights. Internal citizenship regimes provide social closure, excluding populations from redistribution as a means of control, a trend seen throughout the *hukou*'s historical development (Wang 2005). The fear of uncontrolled migration is not isolated to the central level but extends to the local level as well. As in international contexts, migrants are seen as socially disruptive and as a threat to social stability.[2] These concerns lead to conservative forces maintaining *hukou* restrictions when possible because the *hukou* allows local governments to exclude unwanted populations.

SOCIAL STABILITY AND SECURITY

The local control of desirable and undesirable people mirrors the national level. Threats to local stability stem from who and how many people migrate. Government officials involved with *hukou* policy formulation and implementation differentiated types of migrants to exclude undesirable migrants from local citizenship. Undesirable migrants were those without jobs, without family connections to the city, and from regions of the country

116   *Chapter 4*

charged by the central government as being hotbeds of secessionism, especially Xinjiang (Interview 44140702). Sometimes local governments are explicit that some migrants are undesirable and inferior. For years, Beijing's municipal government used the phrase "low-end population" (低端人口) to refer to the migrant population in the city. And this depiction is not isolated to the largest cities.

Those without jobs and family ties threaten social stability purely because they are socially detached. Lacking connections is affiliated with crime, especially petty theft. The single migrant, usually a young man in the imaginations of bureaucrats, has some amount of anonymity. The temporary nature of his sojourn means he can steal wallets and other property and then disappear into the countryside, hiding his crime from both family and the police. Locals, in contrast, are known entities, integrated into public surveillance and morally bound to be a positive, contributory member of their community (Interview 43150901, 44140701). Migrant neighborhoods are known as danger zones, and newcomers are advised that they should not walk there, not carry a bag, and never enter that neighborhood before Spring Festival because poor migrants rob a person right before they disappear by getting on a bus to go home for New Year celebrations. The unconnected migrant as a threat is echoed in national policy rhetoric too. Even updated reforms to the *hukou* in 2014 emphasized that a key "innovation" of a new *hukou* system would be the "perfection of the population information management system" (State Council 2014c, article 11) to track and monitor people.

Public security bureau and military officials are concerned about how many migrants move into a city. The migrant population in the city challenges public order, and problems grow exponentially with each added migrant. As one local military official told me, the migrant population was an inevitable problem that needed to be managed. Migrants bring chaos (混乱) and uncertainty to city districts, and it was the job of the local government to control the spread of chaos (Interview 44140701). Security concerns lead to the demonization of migrant workers and the "disruption to social stability" they bring with them (Interview 44140701), which is then used as an excuse for the government to wield significant power to make the city inhospitable via strategies such as demolishing housing and schools. Housing destruction occurs regularly across the country. An infamous example occurred in Beijing in 2017 when tens of thousands of migrant workers became homeless overnight during a thinly veiled fire safety campaign that led to demolition of predominantly migrant neighborhoods (Shepherd and Thomas 2017). "I was a lucky one," Xiao Wang, a white-collar migrant worker who was evicted in 2017 told me. "I had three days' notice to move out. And I've lived in other areas of the city before, so I had a network to rely on to find a new place" (Interview 11171201).

After the fire safety campaign in Beijing, not only were discussions of the campaign censored in social media but also nongovernmental organizations that popped up to provide temporary housing or even winter weather clothing to migrants were shut down by authorities, to force migrant workers out of the city. After some public discontent, the Beijing government rationalized its actions in terms of social stability and public safety, diminishing its expected role in caring for migrants because they were, in the end, not local citizens and their home governments were responsible for caring for them. The view of migrants as a threat to the city's urban core extended to fears of local-government legitimacy. Controlling the migrant population to prevent the spread of their destabilizing force—real or imagined—was an essential element of local-government legitimacy. Without peace and low crime rates, local officials would be seen as failing their people.

Security concerns are particularly pronounced in large cities and provincial capitals. All municipal government officials worry about stability in their urban centers, but large and capital cities have the added concern of provincial and central attention, because the higher-level governments coordinate development policies across cities. Provincial capitals and economic centers are more strategically important for the local and regional economy and government legitimacy. Top-tier cities are the most capable of naturalizing migrants because of greater financial resources but also more sensitive to possible political and social unrest, often leading to more conservative policies.[3] In earlier waves of *hukou* reform, experimental counties near strategically important cities pursued less progressive reforms than those further afield (Wallace 2014). Thus, more important cities should be more conservative because of the stakes at play than lower-tiered cities. Stricter family policies in big cities bring in needed labor while excluding less productive dependents. Stricter investment policies in economically active areas protect financial markets from greater competition and prevent bubbles in attractive real estate markets, which are much more likely to occur in top-tier cities than lower-ranked ones (Interview 11141102).

118   *Chapter 4*

The other common theme in conversations about security was ethnicity. The central government sees ethnic pluralism as a threat to social stability, and it strategically implements development plans to integrate minority regions and people (Clarke 2007). Development programs encouraged the migration of majority Han populations to minority regions, often found along the western edge of the country (Toops 2004). This strategy purposely dilutes the concentration of ethnic populations and is built on international models for integrating ethnic minorities. Hu and Hu (2011a) discuss the "melting pot" versus "hors d'oeuvre platter" models and in subsequent writing support, for example, the "organic . . . blending" of ethnicities through *hukou* transfers (Hu and Hu 2011b). Greater Han migration to ethnically diverse regions dilutes minority concentration, reducing or erasing the local culture altogether.

Migrant selectivity is the most important in these locations. In the same way security is most important in high-tier cities, it is a primary concern in areas with high minority concentrations. Local governments must balance both incentives—remain open to Han migrants from the east but prevent rural migration that leads to more minority concentration. This trade-off leads to higher selectivity.

FISCAL CHAUVINISM

Fiscal chauvinism occurs when governments favor locals for redistribution and is a common influence on immigration policies around the world. Governments can be chauvinistic about jobs when outsiders are seen as taking the jobs and lowering the wages of locals (Epenshade and Calhoun 1993; Malchow-Møller et al. 2008; Muste 2013; Shin 2017). Governments can also be protective of their own finite fiscal reserves and not want to include a foreign population in redistribution (Hanson, Scheve, and Slaughter 2007; Money 1999).

Local fiscal chauvinism derives from the fear that inclusion of outsiders will come at the expense of local populations: welfare is often seen as a zero-sum game (Citrin et al. 1997). In the absence of economic development, expanding the local population by granting citizenship to migrants inherently creates a larger burden on the local government for service provision. Newly minted citizens are entitled to government services and programs they were previously excluded from because of their noncitizen status. When expanding citizenship to include previously excluded groups, the government has two choices: expand fiscal provision of services and welfare to maintain per capita entitlements or face potential backlash from now decreased entitlements with the same budget covering more people. This choice creates incentives for local governments to be chauvinistic: the fewer people added to local citizenry, the less likely the government is to have to make this trade-off.

The local favoritism that pervades the Chinese system is, at least in part, due to the ration-based economy in the Mao and immediate post-Mao era. During the planned economy and the early reform eras, local governments limited resources allocated by higher-level governments. The distribution of these limited rations had to be carefully considered, even into the 1980s and early 1990s. Distribution of these resources to outsiders threatened the local government's ability to provide for its people, causing it to balk and restrict the provision of services to outsiders (Chan and Wang 2008; Solinger 1999). As the central state stepped back from service provision, the rationale for fiscal chauvinism shifted from distributing resources down the bureaucracy to limiting local-government budgetary obligations (Solinger 2014).

The need to protect local resources for locally entitled populations came from both the government itself and the general population. Local-government officials have long cited budgetary shortfalls as the primary reason they cannot liberalize the *hukou* system by allowing more and easier *hukou* transfers, even if third-party assessment suggests otherwise (Zhang and Li 2016; Interviews 11140601, 11140802, 32131101, 44120801, 51131101, 51131102).[4] When implementing reforms, some policy makers attempted to "guess [which migrants] had money" and would be less likely to depend on municipal resources as newly minted citizens when writing rules to allow *hukou* transfers (Interview 44120804). Exemplifying attitudes toward outsiders, another municipal official told me, "Those outsiders [外地人] have social welfare rights from other locations. Taking away food from our citizens to feed the citizens of other cities is not fair" (Interview 32131104).

Popular opinion of locals also drives fiscal chauvinism. In 2016, the Ministry of Education and the National Development and Reform Commission announced that universities in the wealthiest fourteen provinces would admit more students from poorer provinces and counties. The rationale was to help distribute education resources more evenly across the country, allowing greater access to higher education resources for students in provinces without nationally ranked universities, a standing concern for the education

120   *Chapter 4*

bureau (Interview 11141102). Even though universities are funded primarily through the central government, local residents saw access to local universities as a specific right of their city or region. In response to the eighty thousand new-student quota implemented in Hubei and Jiangsu Provinces, local parents took to the streets to protest (*Sina News* 2016). Carrying signs that read "Oppose External Transfers" (反对外调), "Oppose Reduction in Enrollment" (反对减招), and "Education Equity" (教育公平), parents were upset that resources they saw as designated for their children were being directed to others, unfairly disadvantaging their children (Yang 2016). The parents believed the resources of the system should be equally distributed, with each local citizen taken care of by that citizen's own local government, regardless of inequalities between local governments.

Economic development can overcome chauvinistic tendencies because it has the potential to expand the metaphorical pie. Development leads to greater government revenue and more resources, which makes it easier to include more people. But once people have physically moved to an area because of economic development incentives, the local government has no reason to expand citizenship: why provide entitlements when the city is already benefiting from a migrant's labor?

Local Economic Development Calculus

Municipalities in China, like most states, begin from a position of fiscal chauvinism when formulating development and inclusion policies. Economic development weakens the chauvinistic impulse because it increases the potential resources available to local governments by growing the economy. Development, and the associated flow of capital, increases incentives to allow migration. Development ensures a regular supply of resources used for both rents and redistribution. Inequality and limited markets disrupt this relationship between economic development and redistribution, potentially challenging the state's ability to strategically redistribute. Instead, development processes encourage the strategic opening of citizenship regimes when naturalization supports development. In this way, the *hukou* remains an institution for allocating labor resources, much like in the Mao era, but with adaptation relocated to the local level.

Economic development and the introduction of market forces increased the need for greater internal migration, but allowing migration and

Balancing Security and Development: Municipal Variation 121

encouraging permanent migration through local citizenship naturalization are two different questions. Without long-term incentives for inclusion, security incentives and exclusion prevail. Governments naturalize migrants—allowing them to change their *hukou*—if they benefit development in the long run. Development forces might encourage migration, but development strategies themselves encourage the naturalization of some of those migrants and not others. Formal membership institutions like the *hukou* allow the state to selectively naturalize desirable migrants. Who counts as desirable depends on the local development strategy. Labor needed for one form of development is not necessarily a priority for another. Outward-oriented development, or development based on foreign capital and new technologies, causes targeting of high-skilled workers for naturalization. Bottom-up development, or development under policies focused on developing local resources, especially in land and agriculture, leads to the naturalization of local rural residents over nonlocals, regardless of skill level. Top-down development combined with poverty alleviation measures dictated by higher-level governments encourages little naturalization unless it directly addresses central-government policy edicts.

Variation in Development Policies

ORIGINS

Economic development policies derive from a wide range of factors, some constant, some varying, including geography (Fan 1995a, 1995b), intergovernmental negotiations (Chung 2013, 2005; Jaros 2019), and political incentives and leadership in the public sector (Donaldson 2009).[5] The central government shaped initial development policies by controlling the level of economic openness in the early years of reform. Geography dictated the first stages of Reform and Opening Up in the 1980s. Special Economic Zones, where liberal economic policies engaging the outside world first trialed, dotted the southeast coast, taking advantage of seaports and proximity to Macau and Hong Kong. Even after decentralization of economic policy, the central government set the economic policy agenda. The central government influenced policy formation and implementation by publishing broad directives for new policy, creating political incentives for local officials to align policies with the center and distributing resources to encourage or reward local policy alignment with central directives. These early policies

122 Chapter 4

created a first-mover advantage for some regions to pursue outward-oriented development.

Decentralization in the 1990s and 2000s created opportunities for local autonomy and variation in policy (Montinola, Qian, and Weingast 1995). Although the central government maintained political power through personnel management—central authorities appoint political leaders at the local level—both implicit and explicit areas for local-government management of economic policies remained.[6] Provincial governments filter the central government's broad agenda, coordinating policies across municipalities to benefit the local, provincial market (Jaros 2019). Municipal and county governments have implementation power. Central directives are often vague about the level of implementation, allowing local governments to interpret and influence how policies are enacted on the ground (Ang 2016). Localities also often experiment with new policies not officially sanctioned by the central government, as officials attempt to solve local problems while pursuing career and material incentives (Heilmann 2008b). The central government relies on these bottom-up approaches to policy reform, which creates significant space in authority to implement policies locally (Heilmann, Shih, and Hofem 2013).

Finally, major economic players such as firms and business associations influence policy outcomes both directly and indirectly. They can directly lobby for favorable policies (Kennedy 2005), or foreign firms can create competition, inducing reform in the state sector (Gallagher 2011). Firms can petition for local-government policy by participating in and lobbying through official trade organizations (Interview 11140502; Dickson 2003; Shue 1994). Personal relationships between firms and local-government officials also matter for favorable policy outcomes: a falling out between a local official and a firm representative can result in punitive policies (Interview 11140701). But, by and large, governments want to encourage industrial growth and are more likely to work productively with economically important firms (Interviews 44150707, 44120804; Kennedy 2005).

The development policies that result from these negotiations are not mutually exclusive: local leaders may employ several at the same time. They may emphasize one over the other, but they can be implemented simultaneously. An interview with a policy bureaucrat in a southern city illustrates this point. He worked on a policy research team before his municipality implemented *hukou* reforms meant to formalize local naturalization and improve the efficiency of migrant management. The policy, dubbed *hukou* through education, allowed migrant children to become local residents after some years in local schools. I asked him why they wrote the policy that way. He answered,

> We tried to guess who had money [laughter]. We did not want to encourage migrants who would be dependent on us, the lower-quality [素质低] migrants. But really, the higher officials told us the problem—that turnover in factories was too high. We had firms coming in and not enough middle managers, line managers, to fill the factories, and it was hurting our foreign business. Those foreign firms preferred to go to [neighboring cities] where there are more college graduates and people with technical skills. . . . Also, this [policy] is what the government should do. If the people are living and working here, we should treat them as our citizens [公民]. That's the socialist road [社会主义道路]. (Interview 44120804)

This conversation was particularly telling for several reasons. First, it highlights the intersection of many different policy motivations, from the state as an actor with interests to the specific economic interests of foreign and domestic firms, to the state's perception of its ideological duties. This bureaucrat's candid recollection was rooted in fiscal chauvinism. Migrants are welcome if they do not need the government. Migrants who contribute to society are accepted but not those who detract from it and drain public coffers. Second, the order of the rationales he presented was also revealing; from the local government's basic assumption of good and bad migrants to the economic rationale, to the abstract. He shared candidly that the policy team tried to write the rules to let in only people with money, but as the conversation unfolded it was obvious that multiple demands and considerations weighed on the policy process.

For this reason, the following analysis of the correlates between naturalization regimes and development strategies are measured, not as exclusive categorizations, but on continuous lines; multiple development strategies could be occurring simultaneously.

THREE PATHWAYS TO DEVELOPMENT

This section walks through three nonmutually exclusive pathways to development and their relationship with labor demands. It draws on theoretical arguments, semistructured interviews, and local-government policy to highlight the mechanisms linking different sources of development and their incentives for labor management.

124   *Chapter 4*

Outward-Oriented Development

Securing foreign capital for development is the defining feature of outward-oriented development and provides the primary resource for economic advancement. Foreign capital encourages development by increasing scarce capital. It can also push development by directly encouraging economic reform through investment-friendly policies and by indirectly inducing competition.[7] After Reform and Opening Up in 1979, national policies and local incentives aligned, encouraging governments of all levels to secure foreign capital to drive development (Chen 2018).

Foreign capital further drove development of labor markets. When foreign capital enters local markets, it incentivizes governments to increase local human capital—the skills, training, and value of labor—through more open labor markets and higher wages, technology transfer, and competition across localities.[8] First, greater economic openness increases the return on human capital because workers can sell their labor outside the local market, to foreign firms. In autarky—a closed economy—investment in human capital decreases skilled wages of the whole system because it increases the supply of skilled labor without increasing demand. This increases labor competition and decreases potential wages, thus lowering incentives to invest in human capital development. In open economies, however, increased human capital does not challenge the existing wage rates and there is greater incentive to invest in human capital. High-skilled workers can sell their labor outside the local market, thus reducing competition among labor locally (Ansell 2008). This increases the returns on human capital and the value of skilled labor. To advance development in an open economy, especially one emerging from autarky as China is, openness to foreign capital increases incentives to develop local human capital and skilled labor. The fastest way to increase human capital is through incorporating high-skilled migrants. Naturalizing migrants with higher skill levels is an investment in local human capital without the waiting period.

Second, foreign investment often leads to higher demands for skilled labor and provides potential for technical upgrading (Acemoglu 2003; Feenstra and Hanson 1997; Kratou and Goaied 2016). High-skilled workers are needed to attract and retain foreign investment and production and also create long-run benefits. Foreign capital creates opportunities for technology transfer: the dissemination of higher production technology between people and firms. When a new firm enters a market, it trains local

Balancing Security and Development: Municipal Variation   125

employees. If those employees change firms or remain after the foreign firm leaves, they can apply knowledge they gained to a new context, advancing industry beyond the initial firm's contract. Although not all foreign technology transfers, more innovative markets with higher levels of human capital are more likely to capture technology benefits, especially in middle-income contexts (Berman and Machin 2000; Fu, Pietrobelli, and Soete 2011). If a government attracts foreign capital, it gets the benefit of that particular contract as well as economic advancement gained through technology transfer to domestic firms. This technology transfer occurs only if the labor market is sufficiently developed to implement the foreign technology.

For example, the government of Shenzhen, a city whose economy largely depends on high-technology firms, wants to encourage the permanent migration of high-skilled workers so that even after short-term contracts with foreign firms end, the high-skilled workers could open their own start-up company domestically, applying what they had learned while working for the foreign firm (Interview 44140502). This benefits Shenzhen in the short run, by developing human capital to fill the needs of foreign capital, but also in the long run, by taking full advantage of the externalities of that capital. Governments can improve the local labor market for such transactions by improving citizens' health and education in the long run or by encouraging permanent high-skilled labor migration for quicker returns. Maintaining a robust high-skilled labor market was one of the most important concerns for local development offices (Interview 44140502).

The final pathway connecting outward-oriented development and high-skilled labor recruitment is competition. Because foreign capital increases the need for high-skilled workers and skilled workers are relatively scarce, the introduction of foreign capital induces competition. As foreign enterprises enter a market, domestic firms compete for the same labor. This competition generates improved labor outcomes and market reforms in the state-owned sector (Gallagher 2011). Competition for high-skilled labor within the local market puts pressure on the local government to increase supply to ensure future investments.

Competition also occurs among localities. When foreign investors compare locations, access to needed labor is a leading factor. Municipalities may lose contracts if they do not have sufficient local labor, an especially challenging condition when trying to obtain high-skilled workers in places other than Beijing, Shanghai, and Shenzhen (Interview 11171203). Cities

126   *Chapter 4*

compete to attract and retain college graduates across provincial capitals, in a so-called war for workers (Xinhua News Agency 2018c). In Wuhan, a central provincial capital with dozens of colleges and universities, approximately two-thirds of its graduates have left the city (Xinhua News Agency 2018a). This out-migration of high-skilled workers is called "peacocks flying southeast" (孔雀东南飞) because many move to Shenzhen, which calls its high-skilled recruitment plan the Peacock Project (*People's Daily* 2018b). Some cities entice college graduates with subsidies and housing assistance, such as Changsha, which offers housing subsidies that increase with education (Changsha City Government 2017), or free rental housing as in Zhengzhou and the province of Hainan (Hainan Provincial Government 2018; Zhengzhou City Government 2018).

When city governments think they are losing the war for workers, they turn to *hukou* reform to catch up and stay competitive. A comparison of naturalizations in Chengdu and Xi'an illustrates this perceived competition. Chengdu was a first mover on *hukou* reforms, bundling policy experimentation in *hukou* transfer with social welfare reform beginning as early as 1997 with welfare reform and continuing in 2003 with *hukou* reform. The two combined efforts were an essential element of a development plan to attract foreign investment out of the southeast and into China's west, where local populations could supply both low- and high-skilled labor (Interview 51131101). This resulted in significant *hukou* transfers for not only the local rural population but also skilled workers from outside the province, actively encouraging them to settle in Chengdu, a strategy not always followed so early in *hukou* reform (Interview 51131102; figure 4.1, top panel).

Xi'an, compared with Chengdu, lagged on *hukou* reform. Unlike many other cities, it did not have an explosion of naturalizations after the 2011 central policy reform (figure 4.1, bottom panel). Xi'an fell behind in urbanization targets, set in 2008, naturalizing only 453,000 people between 2008 and 2016 (*People's Daily* 2018b), far short of the planned 510,000 per year. Media coverage highlighted the laggard nature of Xi'an's labor policies and how enticements, like the new high-speed rail and more innovative, exciting, and lucrative foreign jobs, moved graduates to Chengdu faster (Interview 11171205).

Foreign capital also draws low-skilled labor to a city: all firms need a mix of high- and low-skilled workers. Foreign invested factories not only need engineers to manage the factory floor but also line workers to produce goods. Because foreign investment increases multiple forms of labor migration, landing a contract can be a boon for the local government, but losing

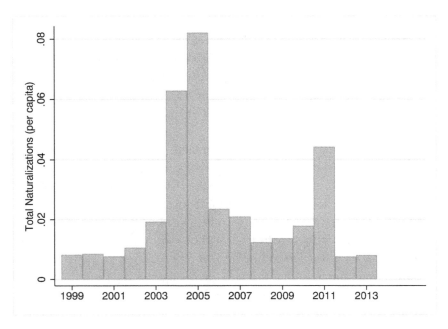
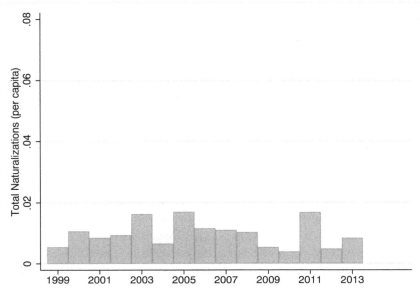

FIGURE 4.1. Estimated naturalizations per capita in Chengdu (*top*) and Xi'an (*bottom*). *Source:* Author's estimation of naturalization rates calculated as growth in the *hukou* population not attributable to natural growth. Population and natural growth from the National Bureau of Statistics.

128   *Chapter 4*

one can be a financial shock. In 2014, 70 out of 287 municipalities received less foreign direct investment (FDI) than in 2013 (NBS, *City Statistical Yearbook* 2013, 2014). If a foreign firm leaves a city, the local government prefers that the relatively abundant, now unemployed low-skilled workers also leave the city rather than remain and put a strain on local welfare resources (Interviews 51131101, 44120802). Local governments want only people who will have jobs in the long run.

These three mechanisms—more open labor markets and higher wages, technology transfer, and competition across localities—create incentives to encourage high-skilled migration and naturalization. High-skilled labor is some of the most desirable labor for local governments to chase. It is also relatively scarce, compared with nonskilled workers. But not every municipality can economically benefit from high-skilled workers. Higher levels of foreign capital and foreign technology prompt local governments to invest in developing human capital through greater naturalization of high-skilled workers. In municipalities that lack this catalyst, economic development may not overcome the conservative pull of fiscal chauvinism, and they may remain relatively closed. This is primarily true for naturalization policies that are separate from formal employment.

Foreign-oriented development policies, therefore, encourage the permanent integration of high-skilled labor but do not provide specific incentives for other types of migrant inclusion. The observable implication of this connection is that municipalities that host a larger foreign presence will provide more opportunities for high-skilled labor to transfer permanently. This is more likely to occur when foreign firms operate locally, because local operations bring in more advanced technology.

Bottom-Up Development

Bottom-up development concentrating on local sources and targets of capital investment, particularly in the agricultural sector (Fan 1995a), can also induce openness in naturalization policies. But unlike outward-oriented development, bottom-up development encourages the naturalization of local populations, less directly tied to skill level. Openness to low-skilled workers, especially those from the local countryside coevolved with land-centered urbanization.

Bottom-up development revolves around land-centered urbanization and its consequences for agricultural production. The wave of urbanization policies implemented in the early twenty-first century focused on the growth of urban centers and investment in fixed assets. Urbanization entailed building roads and bridges and expanding the physical footprint of cities, all of which depended on new forms of land management and greater government revenue for development projects. The most lucrative method to ensure both urbanization targets and local-government revenue was the conversion of rural land into urban construction land.[9]

Land, like labor and capital, was a factor of production managed by the state in the Mao era. The passage of the Land Management Law in 1986 created the first markets for land, making land a commodity to be traded, developed, and managed.[10] No full market exists in China, however, where farmers can sell their land use rights directly to another user or develop the land directly.[11] To convert rural agricultural land into urban developed land, the local government manages and orchestrates a cumbersome bureaucratic process. Local governments identified periurban areas with low population density or in geographically strategic locations to upgrade to urban spaces. Local governments relocated villagers to high rises or urban villages (城中村) where they were either separated from the plots they held land use rights for or compensated for relinquishing their land use rights altogether (Po 2012). Once the local government converted the land from agricultural land to construction land, it was auctioned off to developers, who paid much more for the land than the local government paid to dislodge peasants. The government thus benefited from both land sales and rent from newly converted construction land (Cai 2016). Local governments used their monopoly in the market to land fiscalization (土地财政) so that it generated fiscal revenue (Rithmire 2015; Whiting 2011)—the capital needed for development and a key policy target on local official evaluations. This process led to local fiscal dependence on land conversion[12] and rising land expropriation throughout the first decade of the 2000s.[13]

Land-upgrading policies and land-centered urbanization are inherently tied to *hukou* reform (Tao et al. 2011). Naturalization became another tool in the compensation toolbox to upgrade rural land (Zhan 2017). Local governments, given management of their *hukou* naturalization policies and quotas after 2001, used *hukou* as a form of compensation for land taking, adding to other forms of compensation such as financial payouts and government pensions (Cai 2016).[14] Land taking, especially when it involves physically moving a rural resident into suburban development regions, urbanizes people in everything except legal identity through *hukou* naturalization. Many local governments began offering *hukou* to rural residents, not just to incorporate them into the urban center, but also as a justification for taking their land use rights (Interviews 51131105, 34150305, 44120802). The shift to people-centered urbanization in the New-Type Urbanization Plan centers the need to not only upgrade rural areas around people but also integrate people into urban systems.

Another essential element of land-centered urbanization is increasing rural productivity through labor-replacing technology (Feng, Liu, and Qu 2019). Urbanization during the 1990s and 2000s drew millions of workers out of the agricultural sector. Throughout the early decades of the reform era, agricultural production remained a labor-intensive endeavor on small landholdings with little capital for investment in the primary industry. One of the main hurdles to increasing rural productivity has long been the lack of capital in the countryside (Yang et al. 2013). Mechanization requires greater capital investment than labor, an abundance of which traditionally characterized Chinese agricultural production.

Both national and local governments pursued policies to increase capital investment in the countryside. In 2004, the central government introduced subsidies for mechanized agricultural production and abolished highway tolls for agricultural machines. This move encouraged cross-regional machinery use and support services (Zhang, Yang, and Thomas 2017). Local governments went further by subsidizing storage facilities and covering mobile phone service costs for cross-regional service providers (Yang et al. 2013). By reducing the relatively high fixed costs of mechanization, these policies increased the supply of heavy machinery.

At the same time, rising wages catalyzed the mechanization of agriculture. More off-farm employment opportunities, higher wages, and removal of *hukou*-based migration restrictions pulled workers off the land and into cities. With greater financial resources, households turned to mechanization, because less labor was available for agricultural production and because efficiency had been gained from introducing machine-driven cultivation (Wang et al. 2016; Wang, Yamauchi, and Huang 2016). These bottom-up forces, combined with government support for rural upgrading increased use of heavy machinery over time. In 2000, approximately 974,500 large and medium-sized tractors operated in China, only a slight increase over the 740,000 operating in 1980. By 2014, there were more than 5,679,500 units across the countryside (NBS, *China Statistical Yearbook* 2019). The effectiveness of local-government policy to implement rural mechanization also varied over space, and only some agricultural regions could fully adapt to increase efficiency through agricultural mechanization.[15]

Land fiscalization with urbanization and the mechanization of agricultural production created incentives to naturalize rural populations. As rural areas developed, became more mechanized, and shrank, rural residents detached from the land, because their labor became superfluous and because urban areas expanded and consumed their land. Mechanization, a labor-replacing form of technological advancement, required fewer workers for the same level of production and dislodged rural residents from agricultural production. Displacement of rural workers from agricultural production created a labor surplus in rural areas that added little value to the local economy.

Rural mechanization created landless peasants (Sargeson 2013), or urbanized rural peasants (Chen 2011). These populations hold rural registration but lost land use rights as cities grew and agricultural production increased through bottom-up development. Landless peasants and rural underemployed became a separate category of second-class citizens potentially eligible for local naturalization. From the local-government perspective, they also became a potentially contentious population. Small- and large-scale protests over land confiscation rose in the first years of the 2000s and into the early 2010s (Chen 2020; Tang and Côté 2021). Although some negative elements of a local official's performance review can be negotiated, mass protests, especially those that require management from above the locality, remain black marks on local cadre evaluation (Leng and Zuo 2021). This potential for bad reviews led to better compensation for urbanized rural residents, including their inclusion into the local urban citizenry.

Beyond the market and political promotion logic, a fundamentally socialist logic pervades rural development and the transfer of *hukou*. On the one hand, state legitimacy still depends on the provision of socioeconomic protections and collective rights, underlined by equal access to government protections. When large segments of the population were uprooted from their rural connections as a direct result of government policy, the government had a moral obligation to provide for them. On the other hand, state planning, although not institutionalized as it was before economic reform, lingers in the state psyche. Local peasants are still local citizens and their

132   *Chapter 4*

labor is still a resource for government distribution. One local bureaucrat in southern China equated landless peasants to scattered uncooked grains of rice. Rather than sweeping them off the table as trash, it was the government's responsibility to make use of them, he said. He then smiled and repeated an axiom: every uneaten grain of rice will become a freckle on your face, implying a permanent mark of the failure to value the work of others (Interview 44120804).

Bottom-up development is characterized by local resources driving economic development and fiscal revenue. In the period of land-centered urbanization, much of the capital needed for development stemmed from the conversion and rental of land. Local governments captured fiscal revenue from land transfers but also created landless ruralites. As land taking and rural mechanization grew, so too did the need to incorporate these populations into the urban center, encouraging economic activity and discouraging social protest over urbanization. Rural labor continued to represent a resource to be managed and upgraded to productive ends, blending market and socialist motivations for development. Rather than dividing desirable and undesirable migrants by skill level, bottom-up processes divide migrants into local and nonlocal groups, and local rural populations are labor resources to be managed and nonlocal migrants are external to the development process.

Top-Down Development

Finally, some municipalities rely on development policy directed from above and achieve economic development targets primarily by using capital from the central government. China's central government collects taxes from all provinces and provides fiscal transfers to poorer provinces and cities. Development assisted by transfers from higher levels of government most often comes in the form of earmarked funds meant for specific development purposes, such as education and poverty relief.[16] Rural poverty counties (国家扶贫开发重点县) are officially designated under antipoverty initiatives to receive funding for infrastructure and social development, such as subsidized loans for industries and grants for education program development (Rogers 2014).

The central government drives top-down development policies, which do not rely on the same economic processes as outward-oriented or bottom-up development and are less controlled by local governments. Without the

Balancing Security and Development: Municipal Variation 133

underlying economic motivations of labor and land management, there are few incentives to integrate high- or low-skilled workers because the benefits of continued economic development are not guaranteed. Instead, permanent naturalization means an expansion of the entitled population without the economic benefits.

Because there are fewer native economic development drivers in poorer municipalities, economic development incentives cannot overcome chauvinistic tendencies, and these municipalities remain closed to migrants. Imagine a government that receives capital investment from the central government to reach a particular development target such as school enrollment. Expanding citizenship may challenge the government's ability to reach that target because of the expanded burden of all entitlements, such as unemployment or retirement benefits. Migrant children would also have to be included to reach the central government's target if they were naturalized locally with an open *hukou* policy. If, however, migrant children are kept out of schools, or at least out of official population numbers, it is easier to reach development goals defined by per capita measures.

Top-down development does interact with migration and *hukou* naturalization through poverty alleviation resettlement. Resettlement began with encouraging people to move for economic opportunities, but most relocations since 2000 moved people from villages that are inherently unsuitable for economic development because of disadvantageous geography or ecological degradation (Xue, Wang, and Xue 2013). Removing people from geographically defined regions also reduces the overall estimates of poverty because it reduces the number of people living in poverty by physically removing them from officially defined poverty regions. Poverty alleviation resettlement was part of multiple national development plans, including the Western Development Plan (Central Committee 2000), the Poverty Alleviation Plans (State Council 2001, 2011b), and the Building a New Socialist Countryside initiative (Central Committee 2005).[17]

In resettlement, the local-government officials in the poverty-stricken area and at the resettlement destination must coordinate to move and support residents (Merkle 2003). Villagers can be resettled to other rural areas by adding to an existing village or creating a new settlement village. Villagers can also be moved into urban areas, usually small towns (Yang, de Sherbinin, and Liu 2020). The central government prefers long-distance resettlement into cities because it is most likely to deliver the desired development

134 *Chapter 4*

outcomes in the long run and aligns with urbanization targets (Lo, Xue, and Wang 2016).

Urban resettlement destinations varied geographically and over time. Between 1998 and 2010, Linfen, a municipality in Shaanxi Province with five official poverty counties, relocated a total of 15,219 villagers, resettling 3 percent in urban areas (Xue, Wang, and Xue 2013). With the rise of urbanization goals, long-distance resettlement increased. A study in 2013 of thirty resettled villages in the provinces of Shanxi and Shaanxi found that approximately 35 percent of villagers had been resettled to urban areas (Lo, Xue, and Wang 2016). Not all those relocated for poverty alleviation, however, were integrated in the *hukou* system; resettlement does not guarantee a *hukou* transfer. Local governments continue to selectively naturalize resettlement populations. This push for inclusivity paired with selectively highlights the balance of security and economic incentives even with one development pathway. In a 2020 survey of 553 villagers resettled in urban areas, only 12 percent had changed their *hukou* to their destination location (Tang, Xu, and Qiu 2021).

Dependency on top-down financing for development goals increases incentives for local bureaucrats to direct resources in ways that benefit local governments (Huang 1999). This can mean using central-government funds strategically to meet specific development program goals, manipulating both policy implementation and indicators of policy outcomes for their political benefit. One of the fastest ways to improve statistics is to encourage out-migration, especially of potentially dependent populations, because it improves indicators measured per capita.[18] This is not inherently a miscarriage of policy, however. Top-down development provides capital to move people out of poverty and to integrate them into urban areas when market mechanisms fail to do so. Its impact, however, is dampened by economic and fiscal concerns.

Development and Policy Outcomes

Local officials must balance security and economic development— maintaining smaller populations to ensure redistribution, protecting local resources from outsiders while expanding the included class of citizens to ensure economic development. This section applies these logics to broader evidence beyond my semistructured interviews in specific cities. I use indicators of each force, security and economic, to identify correlations with policies dictating the openness of *hukou* naturalization. The first part of the section explains patterns in *hukou* naturalization pathways and the second addresses net naturalizations.

Figure 4.2 presents the geographic distribution of key economic variables related to the three development pathways of outward-oriented, bottom-up, and top-down development strategies. I use foreign-owned production output as a percentage of gross domestic product (GDP) as a proxy for outward-oriented development (figure 4.2, first panel) because it best captures the mechanism linking foreign production and skills; FDI or exports also captures the need for low-high-skilled workers. Foreign output means there is a greater chance of future economic benefit from permanently naturalizing skilled workers, making a clearer link with the mechanisms of outward-oriented inclusion than other possible measures. For bottom-up development, my proxy is the use of machinery in agricultural production (figure 4.2, second panel).[19] Mechanized rural production, not labor-enhancing tools such as fertilizer, acts as labor-replacing development, thus capturing the mechanism of dislodged labor. In localities where agricultural machine use is high, there should be higher rates of residence-based and family-based naturalizations, because these policies specifically target local rural populations. Finally, I use centrally defined poverty counties as a proxy for top-down development (figure 4.2, third panel). Municipalities with poverty counties in 2014, predominantly in China's western and central regions, face greater incentives to manipulate their rural and impoverished communities, creating incentives for their inclusion in urban areas as a means of reducing the number of people living in poverty.

To measure policy openness, I use the policy indexes described in chapter 3. The indexes are separated by naturalization pathway—high skilled, residence based, family, and investment—because development policies should target the types of migrants in line with development policies.[20] Each index measures how difficult it is for a migrant to qualify for that specific naturalization pathway. The most restrictive policies, for example, are when no pathways exist. These are scored as zeros in the database. The most open policies include those with the fewest paperwork requirements and the lowest bars for qualification. A detailed discussion of scoring is available in appendix B. These indexes reflect policies used by local public security bureaus to manage *hukou* naturalizations in 2016.

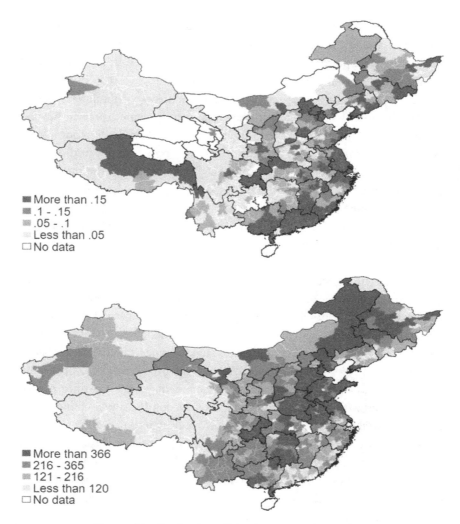

FIGURE 4.2. Geographic distribution of development policy indicators, 2014. Foreign firm production (*first*), agricultural machinery use (*second*), poverty counties (*third*). *Source:* Regional Economic Yearbooks, city yearbooks, government documents.

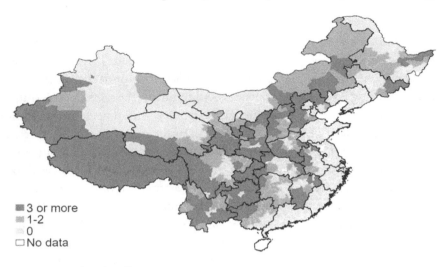

FIGURE 4.2. (*continued*)

TABLE 4.1.
Indicators and expected directions

Force	Indicators	Expected direction by policy indicator
Security	Minority counties	All: Closed (–)
	Top tier	All: Closed (–)
Development		
Outward oriented	Foreign output	High skilled: Open (+)
Bottom up	Machinery	Resident based, family: Open (+)
Top down	Poverty counties	Resident based, family: Open (+)

To identify correlations between security and economic indicators and *hukou* naturalization policies, I run ordinary least squares regressions in which the dependent variable is the normalized policy index openness and independent variables are five-year averages for the given security and economic variables, summarized in table 4.1.[21] A full results table is in appendix C.

SECURITY INCENTIVES

Two primary indicators of fiscal chauvinism are the relative importance of a given city and the size of its ethnic minority population. Larger and more economically important cities are more important to protect than smaller cities, reducing incentives for openness. Additionally, the state sees minority populations as creating fundamental instability, meaning municipalities with larger minority populations are at a greater risk of instability. These two indicators are correlated with family-based naturalizations but not with high-skilled or residence-based pathways (figure 4.3). The correlation between top-tier city and investment-based naturalization is just outside statistical significance. Municipalities with autonomous minority counties, meaning they have a higher proportion of ethnic minorities living in the local periphery, have stricter family pathways, making it more difficult to naturalize. This result supports the somewhat counterintuitive result of the

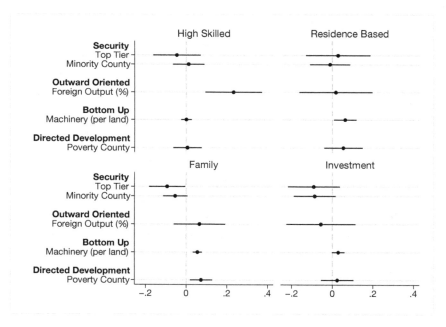

FIGURE 4.3. Marginal effects of development policy indicators on naturalization rates. Marginal effects estimated using ordinary least squares regressions, 95% confidence intervals. Controls include FDI per GDP, land price, migrant stock (quartiles), GDP, and regional indicators.

cluster analysis that municipalities in minority areas have stricter naturalization policies. Family-based policies would encourage more migration and naturalization of local minority populations rather than the more desirable Han migrants from other parts of the country.

OUTWARD-ORIENTED DEVELOPMENT

Outward-oriented development is positively and significantly correlated with openness to high-skilled naturalizations. The more important foreign-funded production is locally, the more accepted are high-skilled workers. Table 4.2 breaks the high-skilled index into the two primary forms of naturalization pathways: general pool, in which skilled workers gain local citizenship without a job, improving the general pool of labor, and employer selected, in which skilled workers are required to secure employment before naturalization. The table also has an additional indicator of outward orientation: the growth in foreign output proportion from 2009 to 2014. This indicator captures how local dependence on the foreign economy grew since the low point of the 2008 global financial crisis, an exogenous shock to local economic production.

Foreign production as a proportion of total local production and growth in foreign production are both correlated with more open high-skilled

TABLE 4.2.
Outward-oriented development and high-skilled indexes

		High skilled	
Variables	Total	General pool	Employer selected
Foreign output (proportion)	0.148***	0.126	0.130**
	(0.0565)	(0.0930)	(0.0560)
Foreign output (growth since 2009)	0.385***	0.738***	−0.0736
	(0.144)	(0.219)	(0.125)
FDI (per GDP)	0.499	1.178	−0.317
	(1.252)	(1.648)	(1.360)
Observations	246	246	246
R squared	0.126	0.133	0.067

NOTE: All models include controls for migrant stock quartile, region, and local GDP per capita.
*** $p < .01$, ** $p < .05$, * $p < .1$

140   Chapter 4

naturalization pathways. Foreign production is positively correlated with employer-selected pathways but not with general-pool policies. Municipalities with greater foreign production are more likely to open naturalization for high-skilled workers and are more likely to open pathways that do not depend on secured employment. The growth of foreign production is, in contrast, positively correlated with general-pool policies but not employer-selected policies.

Overall, employment-driven policies, such as firm-based and education transfers that require employment as a condition of naturalizing, are the least affected by the foreign economy. This is not fully unexpected. Employment-driven policies are the legacy of how *hukou* transfers used to operate. Before the central government pushed to institutionalize *hukou* transfers, the system was more ad hoc, and local governments rewarded some industries and firms deemed strategic or that had closer ties to the local government. Local state-owned enterprises benefited greatly from a near monopoly on transfer quotas (Interview 11140501).

To this day, *hukou* transfers processed through firm-based quotas dependent on employment are seen as disproportionately benefiting large, state-owned firms (Interview 11140501). This system could be related to market mechanisms, giving the largest quotas to firms with the highest need, but this would not be reflected in *hukou* policy openness. Because firm-based quotas are also a means for local governments to reward firms with which they have closer relationships, there is little incentive for local governments to change standards for development-based reasons. General-pool policies, however, are more directly tied to market-based processes and are more likely to benefit people who do not work for larger state-owned firms.

Other measures of foreign economy engagement, such as FDI, do not hold this trend. The simple flow of foreign capital has no impact on the openness of labor naturalization rules except the nonlabor-specific naturalization pathway of family. This null result is because FDI encourages migration but not necessarily naturalization, from the local-government's perspective.

BOTTOM-UP DEVELOPMENT

As agriculture becomes more mechanized, fewer workers are needed to tend to the fields (Chen et al. 2009). Machinery used in agricultural production is a capital investment that reduces the need for labor. Locations with heavier use of machinery in rural production are expected to have more open residence-based policies because more intensive machinery use makes labor redundant. Figure 4.3 shows just this relationship. Machinery use in rural production is positively correlated with openness to residence-based transfers and to those with family connections, the two naturalization pathways that target local populations. Municipalities that have higher mechanized agricultural production have the potential for greater labor surplus in rural areas. As rural labor detaches from production, municipalities have greater incentives to incorporate local rural populations into the urban core.[22]

Family-based transfers primarily target local populations, especially households divided between the urban center and the countryside. Lowering the barriers for family-based transfers encourages the naturalization of people who already have connections in the city center. These populations are safer targets for naturalization because local governments assume that their family members will care for them. Additionally, encouraging the transfer of older family members from rural registration to urban registration alleviates the financial burden on lower-level governments to take care of the aging population left in the countryside. A 2013 law requiring children to visit their aging parents was aimed, in part, at providing basic care for the elderly living separately from their children (National People's Congress 2013). By lowering the controls on *hukou* transfers when less labor is needed in the countryside, the local government can selectively encourage the types of transfer populations that are most strategic for local policy.

TOP-DOWN DEVELOPMENT

Local officials walk a fine line when managing *hukou* policies and poverty alleviation. On the one hand, integrating rural residents into urban centers draws villagers out of poverty. On the other hand, naturalizations tax the local government's provision of services for municipalities with poverty counties. This balance results in slightly more open naturalization policies and fewer overall naturalizations. Residence-based, family, and investment pathways are slightly more open in municipalities with at least one poverty county than those without poverty counties (figure 4.3).[23] The marginal effects are small compared with other determinants of policy, suggesting a relatively small increase in openness.

An interesting trend to note is that the high-skilled index is no more open or closed in municipalities with poverty counties. Although high-skilled labor is usually the poster child for naturalization, openness to naturalization is not always a given. Without a local economic market for high-skilled workers, there are few incentives to expand the local policy, leaving high-skilled pathways unaffected.

NET NATURALIZATIONS

Security and economic development forces encourage not only loosening naturalization pathways by expanding who is eligible but also expanding how many people are allowed to naturalize. Cities across the country put quotas on naturalization pathways, numbers that are unavailable apart from a select few cases. To estimate the impact of security and development policies on how many people are allowed, or the depth of openness, I estimate fixed-effects time series models on the net naturalized population calculated from growth in the city's urban population not attributed to natural growth.[24] Figure 4.4 presents key indicators for security and economic development strategies.

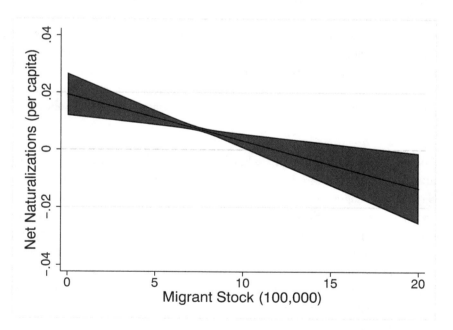

FIGURE 4.4. Marginal effects of security and development correlates of net naturalization rates. Security: migrant stock (*first*). Outward oriented: foreign output (*second*). Bottom up: machinery use in agriculture (*third*). Top down: poverty counties (*fourth*). Predictive margins are based on fixed-effects time-series data from 2005 until 2013. Models include time and municipal fixed effects, lagged dependent variable, economic controls, and indicators from other hypotheses in an aggregate model. See appendix B for full results.

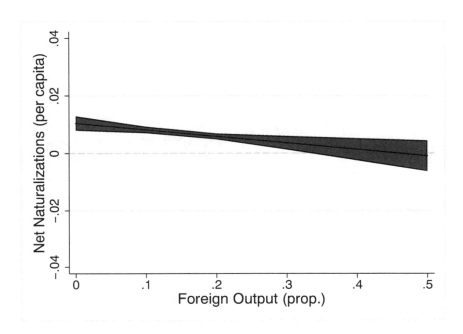

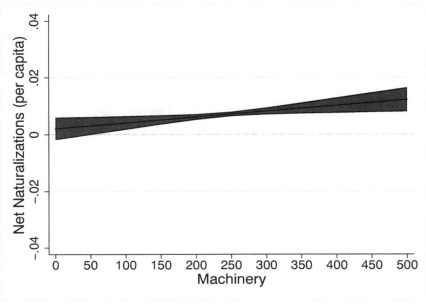

FIGURE 4.4. *(continued)*

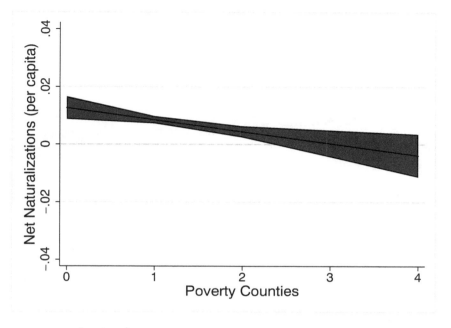

FIGURE 4.4. (*continued*)

From the perspective of security concerns, evidence is mixed of security management of net naturalizations. City tier is negatively correlated with naturalizations, meaning the largest, most important cities in the first tier naturalize more migrants than those in the bottom tiers. City tier is correlated with economic development and size of the migrant population, creating a mixed overall result in which economics dominates security concerns. Migrant stock is negatively correlated with net naturalizations (figure 4.4, first panel). The more migrants a city hosts, the smaller the proportion of migrants who naturalize. This relationship also holds with total number of naturalizations, not just naturalization rates. Cities with more migrants naturalize fewer migrants, absolute or relative. This result provides some support for the security hypothesis, that large influxes of migrants represent a security threat, encouraging local officials to maintain strict exclusionary policies.

Outward-oriented development affects both the numerator and the denominator in naturalization rates. On the one hand, outward-oriented development is correlated with city size, with the largest, most important municipalities securing the most foreign production. Migrants are more likely to flock to these cities, increasing the denominator in naturalization rates. On the other hand, outward-oriented development increases the need for selective naturalization of high-skilled workers, potentially at the expense of nonskilled workers. The second panel of figure 4.4 presents the predicted relationship between total naturalization rate per capita and two indicators of outward-oriented development. Foreign firm output as a percentage of total output is negatively correlated with naturalization rates. As foreign production increases, a smaller proportion of migrants and rural residents are naturalized relative to the total local population. FDI, however, has a very slight positive correlation with naturalization rate, but this relationship is about half the size of the foreign output correlation.[25]

This negative relationship between overall naturalization and foreign production adds to the hypothesis that outward-oriented development strategies need to be selective in their naturalizations. As foreign-driven development increases the need for labor, naturalization of just the most desirable populations, those with higher skill, brings the most economic return to the local government.

The bottom-up measure of machinery use in agricultural production is positively correlated with net naturalizations (figure 4.4, third panel). As a municipality employs more heavy machinery, naturalizations increase, all else being equal. In municipalities that pursue bottom-up development strategies, by industrializing rural areas and physically expanding the city and thus inducing greater dislocation of the rural population from the land, local governments are more likely to increase opportunities for rural residents to gain full urban citizenship.

Having a poverty county decreases both the rate and raw number of naturalizations in a given municipality. As the trend line for poverty counties in the fourth panel of figure 4.4 shows, having more poverty counties relative to the total number of counties in a municipality decreases naturalization. Most municipalities have one or two poverty counties out of six or seven county-level units, and this is where the strongest correlation lies. Although resettlement creates incentives to naturalize migrants, fiscal chauvinism in the face of poverty reduces incentives to naturalize overall. Local poverty counties are also likely correlated with higher out-migration. Poor and middle-income people are more likely to migrate than those with high

146   *Chapter 4*

income. This trend also decreases the denominator in the net naturalization calculation, adding to the negative correlation.

Discussion

Security and economic policies interact at the local level to drive variation in citizenship membership policies. Municipal governments were in a prime position to align *hukou* policies with economic development policies. This local adaptation of citizenship policies represents a continuation of *hukou* as a labor allocation tool: local governments use *hukou* to strategically manipulate their local labor market for economic gain.

This leads to variation in both the types of migrants they are willing to naturalize and the depth of that openness. Even though the central government pushes regulations based on size, policy openness does not appear to be correlated with city size. Similarly, minority autonomous areas appear to be comparable to nonautonomous areas. Regionally, there is little variation among high-skilled policies but significant variation in residence-based and investment policies. Demographics play a role in policy breadth but not necessarily in depth.

Outward-oriented development reduces barriers to high-skilled migrants when it increases the possibility of technology transfer. But foreign production decreases the depth of inclusion overall; foreign capital increases local naturalizations, and dependency on export industries decreases nonlocal naturalizations. The drive of foreign capital allows local governments to be more selective in which migrants can naturalize. Bottom-up development increases openness to low-skilled workers, specifically those from the local countryside whose land was appropriated, both through lower barriers and allowing more people to transfer. Municipalities more dependent on top-down development sources have lower restrictions for family transfers but naturalize fewer people.

Both the bottom-up analysis and the top-down analysis show how local governments strategically target different migrant groups. Those with family connections—chain migrants—are seen as the most ideal populations to naturalize, especially compared with migrants from outside the municipality. Research on the migration decision itself has long focused on the importance of networks for migration streams, but this analysis suggests that governments themselves can act strategically, viewing these family-based connections as a safety net, making chain migrants less risky than those without local connections.

This analysis also finds that the time horizon and sustainability of development gains matter for *hukou* policy openness. Many locally controlled development pathways are notoriously short lived. But evaluations under the Target Responsibility System (TRS, 目标责任制度) encourage local leaders to produce quick returns, and economic development strategies often focus on short-run gains. More temporary development drivers correlate with benefits of short-term labor. If a large construction or land development project requires a massive influx of labor but will not provide sustained employment, local governments have little reason to open citizenship through more relaxed naturalization policies. These trends have significant consequences for how development policies and local-government incentives evolve over time. As long as the system motivates local leaders to look for short-term gains, *hukou* reform is likely to be stymied.

FIVE

Voluntarism and the Naturalization Decision

In Guangdong Province, the hotbed of *hukou* policy proliferation, local governments jumped to provincial calls for *hukou* policy reforms early in the twenty-first century. While some cities experimented with naturalization pathways by developing the new, selective points system, one city quadrupled quotas for *hukou* transfers. This opening of the door to migrants was, in the minds of local officials, a signal to higher-ups in the party that they were serious about *hukou* reform and managed finances well enough to afford an influx of new citizens. The reform initially generated popular enthusiasm. Within a matter of months, the local government received enough applications to fill all the recently created naturalization quotas. But by the end of the year, 40 percent of those who had applied, qualified, and filed most of the paperwork necessary to naturalize locally chose not to complete *hukou* naturalization. The following year, the local government canceled the expanded quotas, embarrassed at overestimating demand for local urban status and baffled as to why migrants would reject the citizenship rights openly offered. One municipal official asked rhetorically, "The migrants are too uncivilized [太不文明]. Do they not understand?" (Interview 44141103). Observers outside the city and region were less surprised, pointing out that midsized and even large manufacturing-based cities were lower in quality than megacities like Beijing and Shanghai. In their view, even economically thriving middle-tier cities would never be desirable for migrants; "Who would want to live there?" (Interview 34150305). But perhaps most importantly, it shows the centrality of one variable ignored by local bureaucrats: individual demand for *hukou*.

148

Beyond variation in policy making and implementation, individual-level demand also influences policy outcomes. If barriers to *hukou* naturalization were fully removed, some migrants would jump to naturalize and others would resist. This resulting balance in demand encourages the persistence of the *hukou* system rather than its dismantling. In this chapter, I evaluate the variation in demand for *hukou* that creates the mixed picture of individual attitudes toward *hukou*. Building on research about policy processes and outcomes, this chapter argues that policies create space for voluntarism—individual agency to influence policy outcomes. I ask a seemingly simple question: Who wants in and why? Answering this question reveals the rise of citizenship relative to subjecthood and of individuals with agency, awareness of entitlements, and institutional complexity that can seem daunting to many.

One important guiding feature of current *hukou* policy since 2014 is voluntariness: individuals have the power to make their own settlement decisions. When public policy creates space for individuals to choose whether to participate or decline to participate, understanding policy outcomes depends on understanding individual actions. Both the rights that governments supply and individual demand for inclusion drive variation in access to and acceptance of citizenship rights. The implications of variation in demand have far-reaching consequences for the success of policy reform. Institutional reform and the liberalization of the *hukou* system in practice created more naturalization opportunities for migrants. Unless the state forces transfers, the success of new policies to create a new *hukou* system depends on whether migrants choose to naturalize locally.

In this chapter, I lay out the logic of voluntarism in social reform under autocracy. Drawing on semistructured interviews with policy makers and migrants themselves and on policy analysis, I highlight the dissonance among central policy initiatives, local incentives, and demand among migrants themselves. I argue that voluntarism creates space for individual agency and that variation in demand alters policy outcomes—how many people transfer their *hukou*. Not all migrants want to naturalize into the city where they live and work, whereas others jump at the chance. To illustrate this variation in demand and its drivers, I present two survey experiments from an original, randomly sampled survey of over nine hundred migrants in Beijing and Changsha showing significant variation in demand for *hukou*. Demand for *hukou* is high in Beijing; migrants are willing to pay on average

150   *Chapter 5*

RMB 114,000 (US$17,168) for local urban *hukou*. In Changsha, a much less desirable location, migrants were not willing to pay to obtain Changsha *hukou*, reflecting inherent variation in the value of *hukou* across the country. Additionally, each city sample has significant regional, household, and individual variation, illustrating a complicated demand structure even within the same city. This variation in demand for local citizenship means that if *hukou* reform is characterized by voluntarism, uptake by individuals will be highly varied, increasing inequality and perpetuating the institution.

Voluntarism, Coercion, and the People

Variation in subnational policy implementation plays a significant role in policy outcome variation, but policy implementation is not the only driver of variation in policy outcomes. Stopping the causal thread at implementation assumes that the affected individuals accept outcomes and take up new or reformed policies. But policy implementation regularly faces friction, whether an unpopular or a popular policy, and people have different preferences for policy uptake and compliance.

Researchers studying nondemocracies usually consider coercion the primary driver of individual-state relations. Without recourse to democratic institutions and individual legal protections, individuals are policy takers and have few options when choosing compliance behavior. Coercion is more likely when policies are particularly unpopular or seen as necessary for state survival. For example, the Chinese state used significant coercion to implement the unpopular one-child policy, which was framed as a national security issue (Banister 1987; Greenhalgh 2005). Institutional design can also increase the likelihood of coercive policy implementation, especially at the local level. Coercion is a tempting strategy when policy reform is seen as a matter of national security or regime legitimacy and when there is widespread agreement among central elite. In these important matters, the autocrat does not want to leave policy outcomes to chance. The Chinese central government, responsible for advancing economic interests, regards individuals as subjects to be managed by the center when policies are framed as essential for national interests (Feng, Cai, and Gu 2012). This provides little room for agency and noncompliance at the individual level.

For example, defining targets in policy implementation can increase coercion in efforts to hit a specific target (Hardee-Cleveland and Banister

Voluntarism and the Naturalization Decision 151

1988; Müller 2017). When local leaders have hard policy targets, such as growth in urbanization or budgetary revenue, they face perverse incentives to use coercion to meet those targets. In politically centralized polities, like China, even if coercion is not in the center's plan, it can be an unintended consequence of compliance goals.

But not all policies are implemented through coercion; some allow voluntary participation. Institutional voluntarism occurs when formal policies explicitly and consistently provide space for individuals to opt in to new policies. These policies allow individuals to exert agency and to interact with policy rather than simply be policy takers.

Voluntarism provides an alternative to socially unpopular coercion and offers a middle ground in policies with conflicting goals. Coercion can lead to popular protests, which threaten social stability and undermine regime legitimacy. Protests are one of the most common—and often considered only—options to influence policy or to push back against unpopular policies. Urbanization goals of the late 1990s and 2000s and subsequent protests exemplify coercive policy implementation. To urbanize China's land and secure greater revenue, local governments expropriated land from rural villages and collectives, converting it to urban construction land. This conversion earned local governments significant rental income; land sales alone represented on average 40 percent of municipalities' local revenue (Ministry of Land 2016). Villagers deemed many compensation packages offered to them insufficient, and their protests garnered significant attention (Guo 2001; Kan 2020; Sun 2019).

Voluntarism is a powerful tool when policy reform involves significant conflicting interests. By allowing voluntarism in policy uptake by individuals, partial institutional change occurs rather than institutional displacement. The center gets the glory for pushing a reform necessary for the good of the people, boosting its legitimacy. But when there are conflicting goals and conflicting interests, voluntarism waters down institutional reform by allowing impartial compliance: reforming but not too quickly.

In many ways, the introduction of voluntarism strategically removes the possibility for extreme policy change and makes mixed implementation most likely. If uptake is uneven, the new policy is implemented in areas where demand for it was the highest. Where there is resistance to reform, implementation falls short. Voluntarism also allows leaders to avoid blame by surrendering discretion to other actors (Li, Ni, and Wang 2021;

152   Chapter 5

Ran 2017; Weaver 1986). Policies with voluntarism allow officials to point to reform efforts and deflect blame for unmet goals but not have to fully overhaul an institution.

Voluntarism is an essential concept for understanding policy outcomes of reform to the *hukou* system. The *hukou* is a quintessential case of conflicting policy goals. As discussed throughout this book, *hukou* is a powerful tool for both social stability and economic advancement. Strict *hukou* policies help maintain social order, and looser *hukou* policies benefit a fluid labor market, human capital development, and reductions in inequality. Conflicting interests exist both down and across the bureaucratic hierarchy. Central, provincial, and municipal leaders all have different definitions of who their citizens are and who should be entitled to government services. Horizontal variation also pits some regions against each other: provinces that receive many migrants have different interests than provinces that send migrants.

While balancing these competing interests, central policy makers delegate formal authority to local officials to adapt policy, and voluntarism is used to temper reform. By using voluntary transfers as the standard, the central government reduces the potential for coercion by local governments, preventing potentially destabilizing protests. Additionally, voluntarism means that policy reform uptake will be uneven and inherently limiting, preventing a flood of migrants into urban welfare programs. In this way, voluntarism is a strategic design element of reform, allowing reform to occur but limiting its potential impact.

Voluntarism and Coercion in Hukou Policies

The *hukou* itself is a coercive institution. It places legal limits on where an individual has a legal right to exist. The history of *hukou* as an institution is littered with coercion: Its institutional roots are in the *baojia* system for taxation and conscription. The Custody and Repatriation Centers detained, extracted fees from, and forcibly removed migrant workers from cities until 2003. Thinly veiled urban restoration and safety campaigns destroyed migrant housing to force migrants out of cities. Governments of multiple levels use the *hukou* to control and manage people, their physical location, and their right to exist in a given space through coercion.

Because of the *hukou* system's history of coercion and control, it may be surprising to find space for voluntarism. But tension between national-level policy goals and conflicting interests at the local level led to the rise of voluntarism in national and local policies. Over the course of national reforms, voluntarism arose in a key element of *hukou* policy, naturalizations, allowing the benefits of voluntary engagement with policy change while maintaining the core institution itself.

EARLY *HUKOU* REFORMS AND COERCION IN NATURALIZATIONS

Early reforms to the *hukou* system continued the general trends of the Mao era in subjugating individuals to greater economic policy targets and depicting the general population as masses to be managed. In the 1997 "Opinion on Improving the Rural Household Registration Management System," the "masses" (群众) are mentioned only in relation to publicity and education to spread awareness of the *hukou* system and reforms (Ministry of Public Security 1997b). *Hukou* reform served national interests, and the government had a duty to inform the masses why reform to the system was to their benefit. In the Ministry of Public Security's following "Notice on Promoting the Reform of the Household Registration Management System in Small Towns," the masses are again invoked in the need to do "thought work" (群众的思想工作; State Council 1997, Article 7) and as a justification because *hukou* work is "in the vital interest of the masses" (关系到群众的切身利益; Article 8). In 2001 the first sign of voluntarism appeared in the goals section of the policy, as the "will of the masses" (群众的意愿) being one consideration when implementing *hukou* reform, alongside economic and social interests, and as local variation for avoiding policy simply following the "will of the chief" (长官意志), or a one-size-fits-all model (一刀切, or one knife cut, directly translated; Article 1). Under the policy's work requirements, the 2001 policy placed the onus for protecting the will of the people on the public security bureau, which was to ensure that those who wanted to naturalize and had the proper paperwork could transfer their status (Article 3, paragraph 2).

Following these two reforms, the early 2000s saw significant policy proliferation at the local level. The 1997 reforms and the 2001 reforms allowed local governments to directly manage which migrants could naturalize in the *hukou* system. For the first time, this became an approved tool for local governments to manage and manipulate their population. It also became a useful tool to secure economic development, coercing naturalization when it directly benefited development. With the newly acquired power to manipulate *hukou* policies, local governments began using *hukou* conversion to

154 *Chapter 5*

achieve other policy goals, in particular urbanization and revenue building, poverty alleviation, and residence reforms.

Local officials, eager to convert agricultural land into commercial development land because of fiscal and economic benefits, dislodged rural residents from their land. *Hukou,* and access to specific programs such as health insurance and urban pensions, were used as inducements to accept the land grab, although this often blurred into coercion (Cai 2016). Land confiscation led to forced conversion throughout the reform period. According to the 2013 China Household Income Project Survey, 41 percent of respondents who changed their *hukou* between 2000 and 2013 did so because of land conversion, compared with just 26 percent in the previous two decades (NBS, *China Household Income Project Survey* 2013). Access to *hukou* was not guaranteed with land expropriation, however. Of survey respondents who experienced land expropriation, less than 40 percent received *hukou* naturalization as compensation.

Similarly, to meet central-government targets on alleviating extreme poverty, local governments implemented poverty alleviation relocation (扶贫搬迁) in combination with *hukou* transfers. Local governments moved villagers from the poorest villages to areas with higher development and often forced the new residents to change their *hukou,* giving up any land use rights they had previously held (Yang, de Sherbinin, and Liu 2020). These policies, according to government information, created the potential for unbalanced development and overburdened urban areas while undermining rural development and harming the "vital interests" of the people (State Council 2011a). Wildly unpopular, these extractions caused protests and social disorder, further delegitimating government officials and government policies.

Forced naturalizations also occurred under the partial reforms of the resident *hukou* programs. Reforms implemented in several provinces, including Guangdong, Zhejiang, and Shanghai, attempted to create a unified *hukou* in the early 2010s, well before the national-level reform in 2014. Resident *hukou* (居民户口) removed the distinction between urban and rural residents but maintained the distinction of local and nonlocal residents, as discussed in chapter 1. These reforms followed the models of small-scale conversion of all rural residents to urban residents in the cities of Wuhai (completed in 2005), Shenzhen (2005), Zhuhai (2003), Shantou (2003), Foshan (2004), Jiayuguan (2011), and Karamay (2006). While some experimental locations were successful, many others failed or stalled out. Some experimental counties in

Zhejiang stalled out with fewer than a third of residents converted to the new status (Interview 34150305). In other locations, the conversion practically stripped rural residents of their land use rights while not fully extending urban rights to them (Guo 2010). The program was abandoned in some counties because of popular resistance to reform (Interview 32131103).

Coercion remains for populations essential for state functioning, such as government officials, military personnel, and employees of large state-owned enterprises. Instead of having individual-level registration, these individuals must register with their collective, a remnant of the *danwei* organization. When cadres are moved across jurisdictions, their registration is assigned to the new location and their hometown registration remains "closed." If they leave the state sector, they lose access to whichever city they currently live in and must return to their original status at birth (Interviews 44140701, 11160101). This collective control extends to the largest and most powerful state-owned enterprises. Employees at many state-owned enterprises must surrender their identification documents, including passports and *hukou*, as a condition of employment (Interviews 44141107, 11160101). This control is both a matter of resource allocation, by the state dispatching bureaucrats to key positions, and a means of protecting information and state assets in the most strategic industries. An employee of a large state-owned bank, for example, said he is not allowed to travel abroad without formal approval, lest he compromise state secrets or be a victim of foreign state targeting. "They hold your passport so you cannot travel without them knowing, and they take your *hukou* so you can't get a new passport," he explained (Interview 44141107).

THE RISE OF VOLUNTARISM

After a decade of local experimentation, the central government feared localized variation would "severely affect healthy and orderly urbanization in accordance with law; severely affect the stable and rapid development of the economy, as well as social harmony and stability; and directly affect the smooth implementation of the reform of the household registration system" (State Council 2011a). New reforms pushed for a more tempered, coordinated institutional change. The 2011 reform made the will of the masses one consideration in the development of new *hukou* policies. But unlike the 2001 decentralized reform, the 2011 reform emphasized the will of the farmers (农民意愿; Article 2) rather than the masses. Between 2001 and 2011 consideration of farmers' interests increased because they were the primary

156   Chapter 5

losers from the perverse incentives in *hukou* policy reform that promoted land-for-*hukou* exchanges. The policy also considered farmers when transferring their land use rights when they changed *hukou*. Article 6 targeted farmers who had already moved to cities in *hukou* reform, stating that naturalizations should not be coerced.

Voluntarism became a central tenant of the 2014 urbanization reform. The will of the people changed from one consideration among many to a core guiding principle (指导思想). The second guiding principle, the policy states, is

> Adherence to putting people first and respecting the will of the masses of the people: The will of both urban and rural residents to independently decide on their settlement shall be respected. The legitimate rights and interests of agriculture migrants and other groups of the permanent resident population shall be protected in accordance with law. No coercive approaches may be adopted in processing settlements.
>
> State Council (2014c, Article 2, paragraph 2; official government translation)

The centrality of voluntarism in the 2014 reform sets it apart from previous reforms. No longer is it one of many considerations for formulating a policy, nor is it limited to local rural migrants caught up in land taking. Instead, all individuals have the right to choose their settlement location. This level of voluntarism goes well beyond previous discussion of the people who are affected by the new policies.

The importance of voluntarism was also reflected below the national level. After the central 2014 reforms, thirty of the thirty-one provinces published their update of central priorities and outlined policy guidelines for municipalities below them, the actual writers and implementers of *hukou* policy.[1] Of the thirty provincial-level reforms published within two years of the central reform, nineteen provinces explicitly state *hukou* naturalization should be voluntary.[2] Liaoning Province goes so far as to say resettlement to alleviate poverty will not require *hukou* naturalization (Liaoning Provincial Government 2015).

Demand for Hukou

If voluntarism is a key element of policy implementation, understanding demand for *hukou* is essential for understanding policy outcomes—who and how many people naturalize when given the chance. Migrants with low demand will remain outsiders in the *hukou* system, perpetuating institutional

Voluntarism and the Naturalization Decision 157

inequalities. The fundamental question is, Why naturalize after migration? Who wants to become local, if given the chance?

MEASURING DEMAND

Before reforms in the late 1990s, national and local policies provided almost no pathways for local naturalizations, meaning demand for *hukou* was rarely studied. Because of institutional limits on naturalization, surveys regularly depicted migrants as one mass without options, equating the desire to migrate with the desire to naturalize. Many assumed migrants had consistent and high levels of demand for *hukou*. But demand for *hukou* changed as the differentials between urban and rural *hukou* changed over time (Chen and Fan 2016). Since 2016, a few nationally representative surveys began including questions on the intention to naturalize in the *hukou* system.[3] The first papers on settlement intention, defined as desire to naturalize locally, showed that, across the country, land use rights can decrease desire to naturalize among rural migrants (Gu et al. 2020) and that geographic features, such as distance from home, and household factors, such as family size and income, all decreased plans to naturalize for interprovincial migrants (Gu, Liu, and Shen 2020). Spatial analysis on the determinants of naturalization discovered significant variation across space, suggesting that the factors at play depended on destination city (Lao and Gu 2020).

Building on this literature and semistructured interviews, I add an additional measure of demand: willingness to pay (WTP) for *hukou*. For normal goods, such as those available at stores, economists use prices as a measure of demand. Higher prices are a proxy for higher demand, all else being equal. But *hukou* is not a normal good with a market price.

To estimate overall demand, I use a contingent valuation survey experiment to estimate the value of *hukou*. Through a randomly sampled survey of more than nine hundred migrants in Beijing and Changsha, I estimate WTP for local urban *hukou*. Contingent valuation surveys ask respondents if they would be willing to purchase a good at a certain price. The price offered varies randomly across a set of prices. The resulting data estimate a demand curve, showing demand for a nonmarket good. Commonly used to value public and nonmarket goods, contingent valuation provides a nuanced understanding of variation in demand. In the survey, respondents were asked if they would be willing to purchase *hukou* at a specified price, which varied across bid prices. Variation in prices in different cities demonstrates different levels of demand.

158 *Chapter 5*

I followed up the contingent valuation with a classic choice experiment in which respondents could choose to simply apply for local urban *hukou* at no cost but access to local rights varied with *hukou* transfer. This second experiment helps identify not only desire to change one's status but also what it is about *hukou*-related rights that motivates demand. Details of the survey design are in appendix B.

These valuation techniques show comparative demand and provide more information on overall demand than does a simple intention decision. Intention to transfer *hukou* or not depends on many factors, including whether people believe they can apply. Knowledge and understanding of the *hukou* system is relatively low—less than 1 percent of my survey respondents stated they have a full understanding of the system, and 11 percent said they did not understand the *hukou* system at all. An intention to change confounds whether respondents believe they are eligible to change. Responses to a simple settlement intention question asking whether respondents plan to change their *hukou* from those who do not want *hukou*, those who do not think they can obtain *hukou*, and those who would have to be forced to change their *hukou* could be pooled. Using a hypothetical valuation in which anyone can purchase *hukou* levels the playing field and removes the complication of eligibility.

WTP estimates have an added benefit of identifying and evaluating *negative* demand. What if people do not want to naturalize? When using contingent valuation techniques, the value of *hukou* can be positive or negative or indistinguishable from zero. Positive WTP signals high demand and identifies people who would naturalize, given the chance. Negative WTP represents no demand; even if given the chance, migrants would not want to naturalize. WTP indistinguishable from zero suggests a balance across positive and negative demand.

VARIATION IN DEMAND FOR *HUKOU*

The international naturalization literature provides a basic framework for understanding demand for *hukou*. International naturalization is often portrayed as a cost-benefit decision. Bureaucratic barriers to naturalization define the costs of naturalizing (Dronkers and Vink 2012). Giving up citizenship in one's home country is also a cost of naturalization because identity is inherently tied to citizenship status. And assimilation into a host society is also considered a cost; the harder the social assimilation through efforts such as language learning, the less likely migrants are to naturalize (Diehl and Blohm 2003; Yang 1994).[4]

Access to greater rights, including social, political, and economic, represent benefits of naturalization (Bevelander and DeVoretz 2008; FitzGerald and Cuesta-Leiva 1997; Jasso and Rosenzweig 1986; Kahanec and Tosun 2009; Nam and Kim 2012). Migrants may choose to naturalize to avoid discrimination and pass a new, privileged identity to their children (Logan, Oh, and Darrah 2012; Street 2014; Yang 1994).

Many of these characteristics are expected to hold for domestic naturalization as well. Migrants in cities relatively wealthier than their home cities would stand to gain more from naturalization and should have higher demand for *hukou*. Demand could also be influenced by the push and pull of rights, in which more existing rights diminish demand and more valuable rights associated with naturalization increase demand. Identity, household, and individual characteristics could also affect demand. The trends in international literature expected to apply in Chinese domestic migration are summarized in table 5.1. The following sections discuss each category in turn.

TABLE 5.1.
Correlates of naturalization

Factor	Expected effect on demand
1. Location effects	
Destination attractiveness	Increase
2. Rights	
Value of existing rights	Decrease
New rights	Increase
3. Identity	
Discrimination	Mixed
4. Household factors	
Children and dependents	Increase
5. Individual factors and experiences	
Challenges in the destination	Decrease
Income	Decrease
Time horizon	Increase
Age	Mixed

Destination Attractiveness

One of the most important determinants of demand for *hukou* is the overall attractiveness of the migrant's destination. When migrants move to wealthy areas, especially from relatively poor areas, they have more to gain from naturalization. Wealthier locations offer more benefits, such as economic opportunities, better rights, and generous welfare programs. A destination's prosperity is a proxy for quality of government services; wealthier areas have higher quality of services. Naturalization also opens economic opportunities migrants may otherwise be unable to access, such as jobs that require local citizenship.[5] The only way to secure these rights in the long run is to naturalize locally. Intangibly, local naturalization provides an identity of belonging to a more powerful place. Some people believe prestige is associated with belonging to one location, such as Beijing or Shanghai, over another.

Demand for local naturalization is expected to be higher for more economically advanced cities with the best-funded welfare systems. The experimental survey design provides an estimate of WTP for *hukou*, a hypothetical estimation of overall demand. Because Beijing is one of the wealthiest cities in the country, with some of the best local citizenship rights, demand in Beijing is expected to be higher than in Changsha, an inland city traditionally considered second tier. Aggregate demand in Beijing estimates an average WTP for *hukou* at RMB 114,013 (US$(2016)17,664). In Beijing, urban migrants have the highest WTP at RMB 176,186 (US$27,297), compared with the average for rural migrants at RMB 92,807 (US$14,379). Demand in Beijing is significantly higher than in Changsha.

In Changsha, however, aggregate demand is RMB –196,320 (–US$30,415). The negative WTP in Changsha means the average migrant in Changsha does not want to change *hukou* and would resist policies that forced a change. In Changsha, urban migrant WTP is indistinguishable from zero, and rural migrant WTP is RMB –261,664 (–US$40,540).[6]

This suggests urban migrants have higher demand for *hukou* than rural residents. This pattern of higher demand among urban-to-urban migrants than rural-to-urban holds across Beijing and Changsha. This may seem counterintuitive, because migrants from rural origins have more to gain from urban *hukou*. But fundamental differences in migration experience—such as distance and plan for permanency or the fundamental rights that *hukou* bestows and how migrants value those rights—could be an explanation.

I estimate the impact of sending-region traits by looking at the relative value of welfare benefits in respondents' hometowns compared with the destination. The more generous existing rights are, the less appealing *hukou* naturalization should be. This trend holds in Beijing, where migrants from cities with less well funded welfare programs and lower average wages have higher demand for *hukou* (figure 5.1, top panel). As a migrant's home municipality grows in development, the lower the migrant's probability of wanting to purchase *hukou* at the destination. But the relative wealth of a migrant's home city is uncorrelated with demand in Changsha.

Distance from home has a less obvious relationship with demand. Migrants who travel farther have already shown higher demand for access to a new city by bearing the cost of that move. But migrants close to home may find naturalizing easier because assimilation is easier when regional identities are strong. In Beijing, distance from home is not correlated with demand for *hukou*, suggesting Beijing identity outweighs physical or identity costs of moving (figure 5.1, bottom panel). In Changsha, however, migrants from closer regions have higher demand for *hukou* than those coming from farther afield.

The Push and Pull of Rights

The most practical and complicated question in the naturalization decision is the push and pull of rights. In the early years of *hukou* reform in the 1980s and 1990s, local urban *hukou* was invaluable to anyone wishing to survive in the city. The fundamental necessities of survival, including food and housing, depended on securing *hukou*. As reform advanced, however, the gap between urban and rural residents in their ability to access government services decreased (Chen and Fan 2016). Health care and pension reforms meant rural migrants could secure some government protections, even if they were not as full as those with local urban *hukou*. But official and unofficial barriers and limitations can prevent full access to rights without *hukou*. Some cities integrated migrants and rural residents into urban services, although these efforts remain spottily implemented (Huang 2020; Yang 2021). Because of the incomplete integration of urban and rural services, gaining local urban *hukou* in most cities means greater access to social, economic, and political rights, all of which increase the benefits of naturalization.[7]

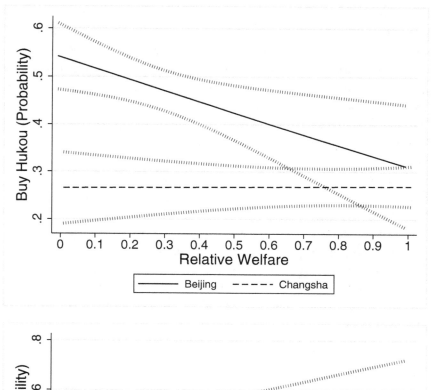
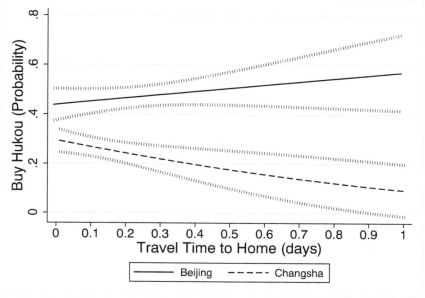

FIGURE 5.1. Impact of sending-region traits on predicted probability of buying *hukou* in Beijing and Changsha. Relative Welfare (*top*) and Distance (*bottom*) Appendix B has full results.

Education is one of the most talked about locally provided rights (Interviews 44120802, 32131102, 44140703, 44150701). Local urban *hukou* allows children to enroll in local schools and is still necessary to have when school quotas favor enrollment of local students, especially in higher education.[8] Local schools, from grade school to college, may discriminate against non-local students in many ways, such as enrollment quotas, required test scores, and attendance restricted to local students.[9] Because of these restrictions, migrant parents often leave their children behind in the countryside, where education is easier to access, albeit lower quality, than in urban areas.[10] More than sixty-eight million children were "left behind" (留守) in the countryside by at least one absent parent and nine million by two absent parents (UNICEF, China, and UNFPA 2017). Migrants who do bring their children pay steep fines when accessing government services, keeping their children from public schools, or sending them to illegal migrant schools that are often the target of government crackdowns (Interviews 11140501, 11141101). Even where local governments loosened social welfare programs to include migrants, those without local urban *hukou* still face barriers to accessing government services, such as extra paperwork or higher fees (Friedman 2022a; Wang and Zuo 1999; Wang 2012). Policy bureaucrats strongly assume that ensuring school access for children is a major motivation for changing *hukou*.

Pensions are another valuable right that intersects with *hukou*. Pension reform encouraged the integration of migrant workers into the urban pension program, but implementation has been spotty, especially among informal workers, predominantly migrants (Yang 2021). Additionally, transferability of pension programs is limited, and migrant workers often face barriers to accessing their full benefits. Although improvements have been made in the pension system, which now allow migrants to transfer pension benefits across municipalities, barriers remain. For example, only a portion of pension contributions are transferable and the system is underutilized (Zhang and Li 2018). Local urban *hukou* ensures local standards for payouts and allows migrants to retire where they live.

Land use rights are the most important rural right that might prevent individuals from becoming local (Andreas and Zhan 2016; Gu et al. 2020). Even with national reforms to the contrary, many local naturalization processes require migrants to relinquish their land use rights.[11] Land provides both employment and old-age care (Cai 2012). Working the land is a stable

164   *Chapter 5*

source of income, and agricultural workers too old to work can hire workers, providing old-age support. Land use rights can also be a financial asset. As cities expand, local governments take land from suburban villages for urban development. Financial compensation for land can be significant, increasing the value of retaining land use rights. Naturalization usually requires relinquishing land use rights, especially for nonlocal migrants. If migrants can retain their individual access to land use rights at home, they may be more willing to change their *hukou*. Many bureaucrats, policy makers, and academics I interviewed believed land would negate desire to change *hukou*.[12]

But evidence of the systematic impact of land on demand for *hukou* varies by context (Hu et al. 2011; Vortherms and Liu 2022). In some studies, family land use rights decreased demand for *hukou* and in others increased it, suggesting land use rights may be a signal of other migrant heterogeneity (Vortherms and Liu 2022).

To understand the pull of rights, I implemented a choice experiment in which respondents chose between government nationalization programs that offered different rights, including pensions and free education for children. Figure 5.2 presents the marginal effect access to education (first panel), pensions (second panel), and land (third panel) had on desire to change *hukou*. In Beijing, being able to enroll children in public schools for free increased desire for naturalization by 10 percent. Education had the biggest effect among nonlocal rural migrants, who were nearly 18 percent more likely to naturalize if naturalization came with free access to education (figure 5.2, first panel). Unlike in the Beijing sample, access to education did not increase demand for *hukou* in Changsha. Migrants were no more or less likely to naturalize if they had access to education.

Pensions, however, had a large and significant impact on the probability of naturalizing in both cities across all populations (figure 5.2, second panel). Getting access to a government pension increased naturalizations by 11 percent in Beijing and 6 percent in Changsha. Again, in Beijing, nonlocal rural residents were the most likely to be affected by access to pensions.

Keeping land use rights increased naturalization by 5 percent (figure 5.2, third panel). This did not vary across cities or by subsamples of respondents with and without land use rights at home. This effect is consistent across subpopulations and sample cities but is noticeably smaller than pensions, which had almost twice the marginal effect on naturalization in Beijing.

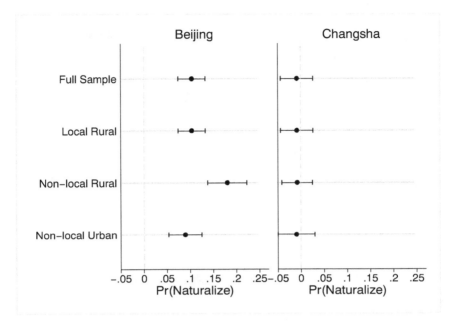
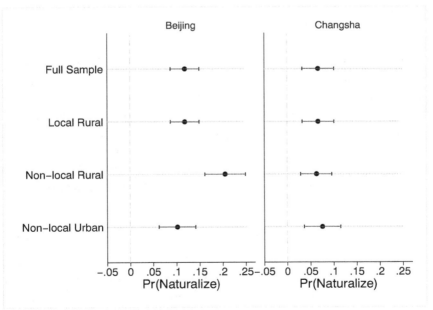

FIGURE 5.2. Marginal effect of new rights on probability of naturalizing, choice experiment. Education (*first*), pension (*second*), and land (*third*). Appendix B has full results.

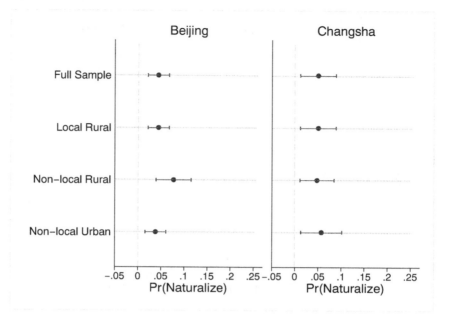

FIGURE 5.2. (*continued*)

But accessing new rights in the destination is not the only way rights affect demand. Because *hukou* is exclusive, transferring it requires relinquishing existing rights. Social and political rights are tied to *hukou* status, meaning changing status requires giving up existing government services and rights at home. This includes health insurance, housing assistance at home, and individual claims to family land use rights, which, in the vast majority of municipalities, are limited to local rural *hukou* holders.[13] If migrants prefer the rights provided by their current status, local naturalization is less appealing (Chen and Fan 2016).

In estimations of WTP, migrants in Beijing with land use rights were more likely to want to buy *hukou*. Being able to retain family land use rights increased the probability of purchasing a *hukou* by 15 percent (figure 5.3, first panel). One possible explanation is that land use rights are a proxy for household resources. Migrants with land use rights at home have greater long-term financial stability in their family, providing a more reliable exit route should they not succeed in Beijing, an expensive, competitive city

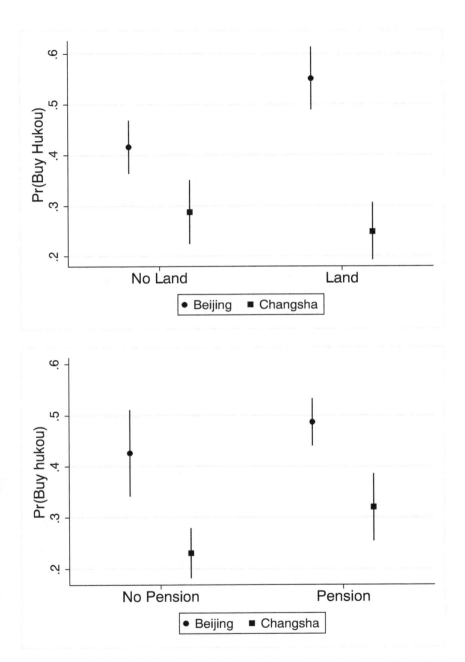

FIGURE 5.3. Predicted probability of buying *hukou* by existing rights. Impact of land (*first*), pension (*second*), and health care (*third*).

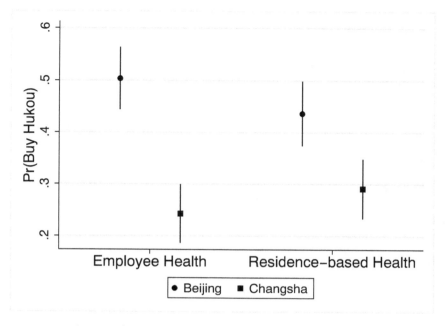

FIGURE 5.3. (*continued*)

with a track record of exclusionary policies toward migrants. Greater resources empower riskier choices, such as cutting off a retreat pathway by naturalizing. These results, consistent across two experimental questions, show the importance of context. Some citizenship, such as in Beijing, may be substantively different from citizenship in smaller cities.

On a similar front, migrants with access to pension and health care programs may be less willing to change *hukou* because the relative benefit of more welfare programs is lower. Similarly, they may not want to give up programs they already use, like the endowment effect in economics, in which an object owned is more valuable than one not owned. Through both mechanisms, existing access to welfare programs should decrease overall demand.

Already having access to a pension increased demand for *hukou* in Changsha by 7 percent ($p < .08$; figure 5.3, second panel). Pensions in Beijing, although having a positive coefficient, did not increase demand.[14] This is the opposite of the expected effect of existing rights influencing outcomes. But the finding is consistent with existing research suggesting that migrants find cities that offer welfare regardless of *hukou* status more attractive (Pizzi and Hu 2022). Because of universal health care, I could not estimate the effects of health insurance on demand. Instead, I compared employment-based health care, which is unrelated to *hukou*, and residence-based health care, which would have to change with naturalization. Having a residence-based health insurance plan that would have to be given up upon naturalization had no impact on demand in either city (figure 5.3, third panel).

Valuable Identities

Hukou is a signifier of identity, but identity can both increase and decrease demand for naturalization. Local urban *hukou* has long been synonymous with a privileged upper class (Cheng and Selden 1994; Solinger 1999). Within any city, a shift from rural to urban or from a fourth- or fifth-tier city to a first-tier city is associated with socioeconomic mobility. This is particularly true for the wealthiest cities, such as Beijing and Shanghai. Urban *hukou* confers higher social status that brings with it both economic and social benefits. These benefits from higher status include relationships and marriage (Yu Wang 2017). Romantic partners might look for either matching *hukou* or their partner to have a more desirable *hukou*, such as in Beijing or Shanghai. Although not always a deciding factor in choosing a romantic partner, a locally registered partner was highly desirable to many migrants in large cities because it ensured their ability to stay in the city, as well as the opportunity to buy property and raise a family (Interviews 44120804, 44120802). A Shanghai *hukou*, not a resident permit, signals a high-quality individual, as one auntie at the infamous Shanghai marriage market told me. "You'll find some people who say they don't care about *hukou*, but everyone does at least a little; they judge you by it. It is important if your child is not local" (Interview 31191205).[15] Local and urban status can also help in acquiring a better job in the state-owned sector and a more secure job regardless of sector.

In extreme cases, *hukou* status can legitimate claims to a place in the city and protect against government campaigns to remove migrants from their place of residence. These evictions occurred formally through actions by Custody and Repatriation Centers before 2003 and informally through urban upgrading and public safety campaigns.[16]

170   *Chapter 5*

But the potential new status is not the only identity that matters. Naturalizing requires leaving your old identity behind, at least formally.[17] Naturalizing in the new location also makes it difficult to return home. There is no national standard for a right of return to an original home municipality. Some statuses, especially rural *hukou*, have almost no formal processes for recovery once given up. Naturalized migrants can always physically return home, but they will be treated as foreigners and have no legitimate claims to government services and rights. For example, rural migrants who naturalize in the city cannot return to their village and participate in land redistribution. Village committees thus keep their populations small to increase redistribution of land and dividends from local enterprises. This prevents backflow into the rural areas when urbanization policies are implemented but also reduces incentives for migrants to formally naturalize because naturalization has more permanent consequences than migrating without naturalizing.

The fear of being cut off from home extends beyond rural residents. A theme in my conversations with migrants was the safety net of home. "Moving to a new place is scary for us Chinese. When you move you don't have connections [关系]." Using a *chengyu*, or Chinese idiom, one migrant equated changing *hukou* with "breaking the cauldrons and sinking the boats [破釜沉舟]," or cutting off the means of retreat (Interview 51131108). Many workers feared failure in the city. What if they lose their job or are mistreated by their bosses? Migrants who face wage arears are tempted to give up on legal proceedings because they have little to no support in the city (Interview 44120802). Changing *hukou* makes returning home more difficult because people have become migrants in their own city.

These intangible identity elements are captured in the aggregate WTP calculations presented in the preceding. Preference for a new status because of the identity it confers is part of the individual's cost-benefit decision.[18]

Discrimination

Because migrants often hold less socially valued identities, they may choose to naturalize to avoid discrimination (Logan, Oh, and Darrah 2012; Yang 1994). Significant wage, hiring, and contract discrimination still exists across *hukou* categories (Cheng et al. 2013; Gagnon, Xenogiani, and Xing 2014; Gravemeyer, Gries, and Xue 2010; Knight and Song 1999; Lee 2012;

Zhang, Nyland, and Zhu 2010; Zhang and Guo 2013). Migrant workers, especially rural migrant workers, are less likely to be self-employed, and they are less likely to secure a formal contract and get promoted than other workers. In a nationally representative sample surveyed in the 2013 China Household Income Project Survey, 46 percent of migrants had no formal employment contract and only 25 percent had a permanent labor contract (NBS, *China Household Income Project Survey* 2013). This lack of formal labor protections puts them in a weaker position for protecting economic and social rights. Many state-owned firms, known for stable jobs with good benefits, maintain quotas for locally registered employees (Yu and Chen 2012). Employers often see migrant workers as less reliable because, for example, they are restricted from accessing health care, a government service. One manager of a small firm explained that his secretary went on an extended leave of absence when her mother, who lived with her in the city, fell ill. They traveled back to their hometown for medical care because their health insurance reimbursement was lower outside their hometown. Because of this return home to access affordable health care, the secretary did not know when—or if—she would return to the city. The manager felt stuck, having found an otherwise reliable and capable worker for an essential job who ultimately disappeared on him; he said he would not hire a nonlocal for such an important job again (Interview 44150707). These concerns are particularly important for smaller firms and factories, as one Shandong factory owner told me, and many do not even consider nonlocal workers when hiring (Interview 11150301). This discrimination can increase the desirability of naturalization: a local status to get the best position in the job market.

Experiencing discrimination, however, can reduce demand for naturalization. Discrimination can make migrants feel less welcome in their host city. It can also prevent the accumulation of social capital and connections that make assimilation easier. This in turn can depress the desire to naturalize. In the contingent valuation survey, experiences with discrimination increased demand for *hukou* in the Changsha sample but not in the Beijing sample. Having experienced discrimination based on *hukou* in job hunting, housing, or romantic relationships increases the probability of buying a *hukou* by 15 percent ($p < .013$) in Changsha. This suggests that local naturalization may help overcome the problems that cause discrimination.

Chapter 5

Household Decisions

Like the migration decision, the naturalization decision is also a household decision.[19] Changing *hukou* impacts children's status as well. Parents may wish to naturalize so their children can have a more privileged status, a trend seen in international migration (Street 2014). In some cases, parents explicitly seek out naturalizations for their children. One internal migrant told me he bought a house in Guangdong so his son could take the local college entrance exam while he and his wife remained nonlocal (Interview 44160201).

But children are not always the direct reason. Huang et al. (2018) found that migrants who brought their children with them were more likely to plan on naturalizing than those who left their children in the countryside. These results suggest a complicated picture of migration, family location, and naturalization. In the contingent valuation survey, having children or having young or no children had no impact on the desire to buy *hukou*.

But children are not the only family members migrants could be considering in naturalization decisions. Household composition, specifically siblings, was the largest determinant of demand for *hukou* in Changsha, in desire to buy *hukou* for both the migrant and others. Migrants with older siblings are statistically less likely to purchase a *hukou*, and those with younger siblings are more likely to purchase *hukou*.[20] Those with younger siblings were no more or less likely to buy a *hukou* for themselves but were 12 percent more likely to buy a *hukou* for a family member. Younger children with at least one older sibling were 10 percent less likely to buy a *hukou* for themselves and 12 percent less likely to buy a *hukou* for a family member than those without older siblings.

These results provide context-specific support for a stylized interpretation of the Massey et al. (1993) argument of risk diversification. We see the expected pattern in birth order determinants of demand for *hukou*: commonly in China, older children provide more for their family than younger children. For migrants in Beijing, family structure does not affect demand for local naturalization. Older and younger siblings do not influence the naturalization decision, and having children is not correlated with demand for local *hukou* once age is controlled for.

Individual Factors

One broad determinant of naturalization is assimilation potential. Assimilation is largely defined by individual experience and traits. Assimilation potential, especially variation therein, should matter less for domestic than for international migration because of a shared national identity.

Long time horizons increase the benefits of assimilation, and long-term migrants are expected to have higher demand for it. This relationship holds in Beijing, where long-run migrants are more willing to buy *hukou*, but not in Changsha. Similarly, economic assimilation, and migrants' potential to take advantage of the economic benefits of their new city, is expected to be correlated with demand.

Migrants in Beijing who are unemployed and thus less assimilated economically are 16 percent less likely to want to naturalize locally. This correlation highlights the potential risks for migrants of staying in Beijing. With Beijing's higher levels of unemployment and high costs of living, a permanent transition to Beijing local citizenship could be risky for an unemployed migrant, cutting off an exit strategy.

Finally, some additional factors at the individual level matter in both Beijing and Changsha. In both cities, demographics play a small role. Middle-aged respondents were the least likely to want to change *hukou*, and younger and older respondents had higher demand. Other demographics, such as education and income, were not statistically significant.

The Limits of Voluntarism

As with other policies whose implementation diverges from formal policy, coercion occurs in multiple voluntary policies. In the early years of family planning, central officials claimed that the one-child policy should be implemented voluntarily (Hardee-Cleveland and Banister 1988), and formal policy merely states that individuals may choose the means of birth control and says nothing about uptake of the policy (Central Committee 1980). When fertility targets were used to evaluate their job performance, local officials used coercive measures alongside propaganda and education to ensure targets were met. Similarly, when rural health insurance rolled out, enrollment was meant to be voluntary, but informally, the Ministry of Health said that some involuntary enrollments were inevitable and should be tolerated (Müller 2017).

Formal voluntarism can be undermined, especially by local officials, when review criteria encourage coercion. In both the one-child policy and the rural health insurance cases, pressure on local governments to meet

174   Chapter 5

targets increased the use of coercion in policy implementation. In *hukou* implementation, these perverse incentives were seen before the inclusion of voluntarism, when naturalization was used in conjunction with land taking in the early 2000s. Urban upgrading, which reclassifies rural administrative units such as villages as urban neighborhoods and towns, may include coercive *hukou* transfers. This is especially true for reforms that unified urban and rural statuses. In these cases, *hukou* transfers are not individual choices. Transfers from nonlocal to local, however, remained voluntary. To promote urbanization, rural residents lost their land to urban upgrading in many localities and had their *hukou* transferred to urban status. But this transfer did not always occur with land taking (Cai 2016). Coercion is more likely if *hukou* transfers are included in the target responsibility system rubrics, the hard, quantifiable targets for local-government-official evaluations. As of 2016, *hukou* transfer targets were not included in these evaluations.

Discussion

Demand for *hukou* varies significantly, both across and within cities. The experimental survey presented in this chapter shows variation in demand between a top-tier city, Beijing, where demand is high, and a second-tier city, Changsha, where demand is low. But possibly more interesting is the variation within those populations for *hukou*. In Beijing, demand was highly motivated by access to rights, especially education. In Changsha, access to education had no effect on demand, but access to pensions increased demand. This result demonstrates variation in the quality of rights offered and migrants' valuation of these rights. Similarly, demand in Beijing appears to be largely driven by individual-level factors, whereas in Changsha, household-level factors matter more. This variation highlights the need to consider the interaction between heterogeneity in the migrant population and the local context.

Voluntarism is a purposeful choice in policy implementation in nondemocracies. Including voluntarism in *hukou* reform allows the Chinese central government to push for *hukou* reform where it is likely most popular while limiting reform where resistance is likely. Understanding the consequences of voluntarism is essential in understanding policy outcomes beyond variation in formal policy. Seemingly dramatic reforms can have superficial effects if voluntarism is not paired with inducement and can even reinforce institutional divisions. Because of this policy feature, observers should be cautious when interpreting policies from the center. Reform is most likely to be successful when naturalization policies target those who want it, including those in big cities, in younger and older age groups, and in the welfare system already. The 2014 reform aligns well with the last finding, that those integrated into services are more likely to want to naturalize, but it focuses on smaller cities, where demand is lower, rather than on larger cities. Formal policy variation combined with variation in demand suggests that national reform is likely to continue to divide the haves from the have-nots, and the most marginalized migrants will continue to remain outside the system. Choice in whether to transfer *hukou* leads to individuals selecting their bureaucratic identity, but it is also an inherent limit on the dissolution of the *hukou* system overall.

Conclusion: Beyond *Hukou*

> People are the principal part of promoting economic development.
> 人, 是推动经济发展的主体
>
> —Xi Jinping in 2013[1]

> Development is the first priority, talent is the first resource, innovation is
> the first driving force.
> 发展是第一要务, 人才是第一资源, 创新是第一动力
>
> —Xi Jinping in 2018[2]

Decades after the deconstruction of the centrally planned economy, government policies and regulations still treat labor as a resource to be managed and manipulated. In a speech to the Guangdong delegation of the Consultative Congress in 2018, Xi Jinping spoke of development through labor and technological innovation. Economic development of the twenty-first century, he said, should be driven by innovation, which cannot be achieved without using and developing human talent. Labor, like land and capital, is a resource to drive development. This view places labor as subservient to development: talent is a resource to be managed to achieve state-directed development ends.

This drive to manage economic development and use labor as a resource fuels China's internal citizenship regimes. China's *hukou* continues to be an essential tool for managing labor across the country, creating inclusion for those who contribute to development goals and exclusion for those who do not. The consequence of this system is varied citizenships within a single country, a stratified system of citizenship characterized by inclusion and exclusion. Remaining population controls that extended across different economic regimes in China allowed the state to maintain social security and advance economic development, reducing redistribution by systematically excluding large portions of the population from full membership in national citizenship. Similar incentives to ensure security while advancing development caused variation in local regulations on *hukou*. Some municipalities maintained strict regulations, granting very few *hukou* naturalizations, and others proactively integrated large portions of their migrant and rural populations.

This book argues that internally divisive institutions are characteristic of citizenship in authoritarian states, where citizenship institutions provide valuable tools to filter autocratic redistribution. Unlike universalistic, ideal-type democratic citizenship, citizenship in authoritarian contexts is particularistic: a tool to identify privileged groups who gain more from redistribution than excluded groups who receive less or very little. Autocratic leaders manipulate membership institutions, the rules defining who is included and who is excluded, to ensure that groups whose support the autocrat relies on for either security or economic development receive redistribution. Membership institutions create hierarchies within the broader population with varied experiences of citizenship. Rather than studying variation in citizenship across states or among people from different states, the study of authoritarian citizenship examines variation in citizenship within the state.

This conceptual framework, of understanding authoritarian citizenship defined by particularistic membership and socioeconomic rights, explains the experience of citizenship for China's 1.4 billion people. The state itself defines citizenship rights as socioeconomic, and individuals expect and feel entitled to improved socioeconomic status and welfare rights. Membership, however, is not created equal. Local governments strategically manipulate these membership rules to balance security incentives for exclusion with economic incentives for inclusion. This manipulation involves preventing local naturalizations to protect fiscal assets while targeting and encouraging naturalizations that benefit local economic development strategies. Because development strategies vary subnationally, so too do internal citizenship regimes. Citizens themselves demonstrate agency in how they interact with policies, choosing to naturalize or not, which creates additional variation in policy outcomes.

I draw on over a hundred semistructured interviews, more than a thousand government documents and media reports, and a survey of over nine hundred migrations to identify the defining features of Chinese citizenship and its variation. The Chinese *hukou* acts as a citizenship institution defining who is entitled to redistribution from the state. These subnational membership institutions developed in conjunction with state management of the economy (chapter 1). As an institution defining who is a member of the state and entitled to citizenship rights, the *hukou* became a tool to balance security interests with economic incentives for redistribution. Economic policies shifted direct control from the central government to local-level governments and citizenship policies shifted too. And variation in *hukou* policies resulted from the security-economics balance at multiple levels of government (chapter 2).

This decentralization led to internal citizenship regimes that defined and managed citizenship membership at the local level. Most *hukou* research is done in the biggest cities. In contrast, I identify the internal citizenship regimes in use across China in 2016 with a policy index of all the ways of naturalizing in the *hukou* system (chapter 3). I then explain variation in naturalization regimes by showing how security and social stability incentives increase fiscal chauvinism and local hesitance to allow naturalizations. Economic development, however, increases naturalization of specific groups, depending on the type of economic development strategy used locally (chapter 4). Finally, I bring the citizen back in by tracing the causes and consequences of voluntarism in *hukou* policies (chapter 5).

This book contributes to the study of citizenship in authoritarian contexts, the distribution of authoritarian welfare, and the consequences of economic development in China. It offers a framework for comparing citizenship across a spectrum of regime types and adds to the broader literature on authoritarian citizenship. Examining membership institutions inside one authoritarian state, it shows that, unlike its democratic counterpart, authoritarian citizenship is explicitly not universal. Authoritarian citizenship defines predominantly group-based rights selectively provided within a given country. Rather than creating a unifying and equalizing force, and far from the democratic ideal, authoritarian citizenship is a tool for division, exclusion, and selective redistribution. It is a tool by which autocrats implement the authoritarian bargain to redistribute just enough resources to stay in power, reinforcing their legitimacy. This book, and others in the growing field of authoritarian redistribution and welfare, adds to the discussion, refining how redistribution is used strategically to ensure regime stability. These books challenge notions of homogeneous masses repressed by the state and assert that subdivisions within populations are strategically crafted to ensure support while preventing excessive demands on public coffers.

The arguments in this book work in tandem with literature on the authoritarian welfare state. Citizenship and welfare are inextricably related, because welfare constitutes a large portion of socioeconomic rights in non-democratic contexts. Diverging from this literature, this book focuses on the membership institutions, those that dictate who is and is not entitled to rights. The citizenship framework helps structure inequalities inherent in the authoritarian welfare state and provides a helpful middle ground between the literature on the authoritarian welfare state and that on the authoritarian bargain for regime stability.

Both the conceptual framework and the empirical evidence presented here improve our understanding of systems of citizenship and market development in China. China's economy moved rapidly from the command economy of the Mao era to one of market socialism in the early decades of reform. Much scholarly attention focused on the different factors of production, land, labor, and capital, that were freed—or not—from government control. The emergent story of labor was one of dualism: the removal of migration restrictions created monumental change in how labor markets operated but the persistence of the system generated inequality. The arguments and evidence in this book complicate this narrative of two extremes. Economic development has had differential effects on labor markets and their evolution in China.

Beyond China

This book presents an in-depth case study of citizenship in one country. The broader argument, that authoritarian citizenship is particularistic and a tool for limiting redistribution, can apply beyond China. The purpose of this book is to encourage other researchers to identify the dynamics of citizenship manipulation in other authoritarian contexts to provide a more comparative understanding of citizenship. China is defined by a high level of institutionalization that uses location to divide the population but also by significant decentralized control. Other polities will vary on formality, lines of division, and level of control. Citizenship institutions can vary in their formality, with explicit formal exclusion or implicit informal institutions constructing membership. Different polities will have different divisions for

180 *Conclusion: Beyond* Hukou

included and excluded classes. The divisions in China discussed here are along location, but they could be by identity, such as religion or ethnicity. Finally, the level of manipulation can change, from local to national manipulation of inclusion and exclusion. In the next sections I introduce other possible cases for studying authoritarian citizenship. I divide the broader efforts into two categories: those with a direct comparison to China, or most likely cases, that operate formal subnational citizenship regimes and those with indirect comparison that use social identity to subdivide the population.

The most direct comparisons are states where local citizenship is highly institutionalized, such as the current and former socialist states of Central Asia, Vietnam, and Russia. Many socialist states used household registration systems to extend the reach of the state into the economy and to manage labor as a factor of production at the disposal of the state.

VIETNAM'S *HO KHAU*

The Vietnamese *ho khau* (household registration) is the most similar to China's *hukou*. Vietnamese *ho khau* was implemented in 1964 to maintain control over the population and intervene directly in the economy. The institution was based on Vietnam's existing institutions but also influenced by the Chinese use of *hukou* in its planned economy. Initially, the *ho khau* divided people along local-nonlocal lines and along a time spectrum of four categories of residence.[3] The government strictly regulated eligibility for changing registration status. Eligibility requirements for local naturalization largely centered on permanent residence and employment.[4] Local registration, as in China, was required for accessing citizenship rights, including government-provided services and housing, especially for education and health care for children.

As Vietnam's economy evolved, the *ho khau* reformed on a timeline strikingly similar to China's *hukou* reform (Hardy 2001). Major reforms in 1997 increased the mobility of labor. A 2006 reform reduced the categories of membership from four to two: permanent (permanent resident and resident of the same province) and temporary (long-term and short-term temporary residence). The Vietnamese *ho khau* has followed a pattern of decentralized control in the twenty-first century much like China's path. A regulation in 2013 formally decentralized control over *ho khau* regulations, and many city governments restricted access, creating internal citizenship regimes similar to China's (World Bank 2020). Eligibility for naturalization rests largely on possessing lawful housing, but local governments can define what constitutes eligible housing, such as minimum square footage (World Bank and Vietnam Academy of Social Sciences 2016). Although Vietnam has made significant progress in integrating services for migrant workers, those with temporary residence status confront barriers to accessing local citizenship rights, and temporary registrants cannot fully access education and health care or other government services such as registering motorcycles (World Bank Group and Vietnam Academy of Social Sciences 2016).

Manipulation of the *ho khau* system of local citizenship resembles that in China. The Vietnamese registration system not only developed out of specific institutional learning from China but its reform also allowed similar manipulation of inclusion, first from central authorities and then from local authorities. And yet there are important distinctions between the Chinese and Vietnamese local citizenship institutions, such as Vietnam's early distinction between local and nonlocal as a primary dividing line and its added element of time horizon as a source of institutional division. The *ho khau* has always allowed some flexibility, having temporary migration built into its original formulation, creating a more dynamic system than the Chinese system. Reforms to the *ho khau* also began deconstructing the link between local membership and local rights earlier than China's *hukou*, reducing the substantive differences between citizens and noncitizens (World Bank Group and Vietnam Academy of Social Sciences 2016). Future research should explore the ways in which the Vietnamese institution followed and yet deviated from the Chinese model.

SOVIET AND POST-SOVIET *PROPISKA*

The other set of direct comparisons is the Soviet Union's *propiska* system. Like the *hukou*, the Soviet *propiska* originated from imperial household registers and morphed into an institution of population control (Pipko and Pucciarelli 1985). Overlapping institutions of passports, *propiska*—the internal passport—and work register books created an encompassing system of information management to control the population (Matthews 1993). Eager to avoid the destabilizing forces of the proletarianization of the people through their movement from the countryside to the city, Soviet leaders locked peasants in the countryside by restricting access to housing and other government-managed services in cities. Much of *propiska* research focuses

182   *Conclusion: Beyond* Hukou

on the regulation of migration and movement within the Soviet Union as a tool of security and control. The system, however, was also the key institution for distribution of rights (Buckley 1995), creating internal citizenship regimes of inclusion and exclusion.

The *propiska*'s influence did not end with the collapse of the Soviet Union. Across the former Soviet republics, *propiska* institutions were dismantled, reformed, or continued, depending on local circumstances. In post-Soviet Russia, where the most significant *propiska* reforms occurred immediately after the collapse of the union (Matthews 1993), localized citizenship continues to this day. Just as the Chinese *hukou* and Vietnamese *ho khau* reforms did, Russia's decentralized reform strategy for the *propiska* moved authority from federal to regional governments. Varied and unequal citizenships within Russia proliferated (Blitz 2007; Rubins 1998).

The legacy of the *propiska* is particularly strong in Central Asia, where many newly formed states made only minor changes to the system after the collapse of the Soviet Union. Today's *propiska* in many central Asian states continues institutional exclusion that restricts access to citizenship rights, including political rights such as voting and socioeconomic rights including health care, education, housing, and employment (Tukmadiyeva 2016). The former Soviet states in Central Asia provide an excellent landscape for comparative study of changing local citizenship regimes, because states took different routes to reform or continue *propiska* (Turaeva-Hoehne 2011).

Internal migrants in Kyrgyzstan, for example, must overcome significant discrimination in accessing government services without registration. Access to the capital, Bishkek, is strictly limited by use of *propiska* as a prerequisite for housing, social welfare programs, and even employment. One report identifies "gross violations" of "unhindered access" to schools for children of migrants (Azimov and Azimov 2009, 21). A survey of migrants in Bishkek, the capital of Kyrgyzstan, found that 95 percent of migrant workers did not have labor contracts because their lack of registration prohibited employers from signing a contract with them (Nasritdinov 2008). The *propiska* continues in Bishkek and is the subject of institutional reform and evolution (Hatcher and Thieme 2015). In Uzbekistan, the *propiska* undermined national citizenship by creating local citizenship and belonging. This in turn increased the importance of subnational citizenship and regional rather than national identities (Hojaqizi

Conclusion: Beyond Hukou   183

2008). Kyrgyzstan and Uzbekistan are an interesting contrast of centrally led versus locally led manipulation of local citizenship: Kyrgyzstan remains a mostly central institution, and Uzbekistan experiences subnational manipulation.

In the Vietnamese *ho khau,* the Soviet *propiska,* and the Uzbek *propiska,* subnational citizenship is codified in legal structures to identify citizens, partial citizens, and noncitizens. Much of the literature on these comparative cases—the *propiska* in particular—examines how these institutions control migration.[5] But the consequences go beyond freedom of movement. Although the *propiska*'s impact on urbanization rates is debated, it had a significant impact on access to government services and redistribution (Buckley 1995).[6] Similarly, the *propiska*'s lasting impact in Central Asia lies in its consequences for access to citizenship rights. The confluence of localized membership and localized rights provision highlights the need to understand this institution as the evolution of local citizenship.

SOUTH AFRICAN BANTUSTANS

The most extreme form of subnational citizenship that overlapped location with identity occurred in apartheid South Africa. Under the apartheid regime, Black and Colored South Africans were stripped of their citizenship rights in white-controlled regions. Black South Africans were assigned a Bantustan, or homeland, far from the wealthy and fertile lands controlled by white colonists.[7] A full passport regime limited migration and created new, semicitizenship rights in Bantustans, which varied in level of independence from the South African government. Over decades of segregation and formal institutional exclusion, different identities, militaries, and politics developed within Bantustans (Egerö 1991). Institutionalized inequalities that result from the Bantustans continue to create subnational citizenship inequalities: the law "undermin[es] and bolster[s] the status of different parties," which "undermine[s] the legal status and citizenship rights of those condemned to the periphery" (Claassens 2014, 761). As Egerö (1991) argues, apartheid's Bantustans have received relatively little social science attention, in large part because of the colonialist influence over research and its attention on urban-led development (13). Using an authoritarian citizenship conceptual framework like this book's would allow comparison of this extreme case of subnational citizenship. It would also add the essential variables of race and identity to the discussion of inclusion and exclusion.

184　*Conclusion: Beyond* Hukou

MANIPULATING SOCIAL IDENTITY

The broader application of the conceptual framework from this work includes the extension of subnational citizenship to divisions based on identity. Identity politics is the natural companion to the study of formal institutions of inclusion and exclusion within one state. The form and manipulation of citizenship can also occur along identity lines when membership is dictated by identity groups and the state distributes rights to some social groups and not others. If subnational membership is dictated by identity, not by geographic division, the state has fewer means of manipulating membership but can still adjust the definition of the included versus the excluded by defining which identity groups count as full citizens. These practices exist even in developed democracies, where democratic citizens were white landholding men and other groups were excluded on the basis of race and class. Each of these divisions undermines the inclusivity of ideal-type democracy. The manipulation of who citizens are based on belonging to certain identity groups is neither new nor isolated to authoritarian contexts. Applying the idea of authoritarian manipulation of citizenship to identity-based citizenship blends much of the existing literature on citizenship as identity. The contribution of this book to the broader identity as citizenship is in the manipulation and mutability of identity and citizenship. The expansion and contraction of the included versus the excluded is not an accident of time but is a political manipulation of the population with significant consequences for how we understand citizenship.

Implications and Future Research

China's local citizenships continue to dramatically shape the relationship between individuals and the state with far-reaching consequences. The COVID-19 pandemic provides an unfortunate example of how unequal local citizenship membership dictates the rights and protections individuals enjoy from the state. Migrants working away from their hometowns during strict COVID lockdowns were often not entitled to food rations provided by the state, which created a "looming subsistence crisis for vast swathes of [megacities'] underclass" (Friedman 2022b). Locals enjoyed better access to government relief and support throughout shutdowns. Migrant workers without *hukou* were 2.7 times as likely to face food insecurity during the Shanghai COVID lockdown as Shanghai natives. Even migrants who

Conclusion: Beyond Hukou 185

transferred their *hukou* were 2 times as likely to face food insecurity as natives (Liu et al. 2023).

The continued impact local citizenship has on the lives of China's 376 million internal migrants highlights how rights and membership dictate the state-individual relationship in nondemocracies, just as in democratic countries. Citizenship institutions, or the rules on rights protected by the state, and membership, or who gets those rights, define citizenship regardless of regime type. The arguments presented in this book support a comparative approach to citizenship, one that values citizenship as a common concept across contexts and that can be used to understand the individual-state relationship.

Comparative authoritarian citizenship is a budding field of inquiry. Instead of being understood as a lesser form of democratic citizenship, it deserves theoretical explication in its own right. Authoritarian citizenship unites two related fields of inquiry, welfare redistribution in authoritarian states and the formal structures of inclusion and membership in citizenship research. Going beyond the understanding of authoritarian redistribution as a mere residual of what needs to be done for maintaining legitimacy, study of the diversified strategies autocrats use to strategically target and manipulate included and excluded groups provides a more nuanced understanding of how autocrats stay in power. Future research should build on the comparative framework included here to expand understanding of how autocrats delineate membership, especially in less institutionalized settings. China presents one possible mode: internal citizenship regimes based on geographic location. Autocrats could use any number of tools to divide and stratify the population that provide greater or lesser power to manipulate membership. As discussed earlier, for example, identity-based lines are more difficult—but certainly not impossible—to manipulate. Future research should build on this case study to understand the comparative forms of authoritarian citizenship and the consequences for manipulating membership below the national level.

These implications for authoritarian resilience are important not just for the state but also for the individuals who interact with that state. Too many theories gloss over the lived experiences of individuals, their agency, and their interaction with state institutions. The authoritarian citizenship framework allows these two intertwined levels of analysis to add perspective to understanding state-individual relations in authoritarian states. Existing research focuses on how individuals in authoritarian states claim citizenship by demanding rights provisions from their governments or practice localized forms of democratic rights. How do these actions by individuals interact with the structure of institutions? How do autocratic manipulations affect what and how individuals claim as part of citizenship?

An important implication of this book for all regime types is that citizenship varies below the national level. Building on Maas (2017), this book argues for examining citizenship below the national level. Understanding national-level membership and rights regimes provides only part of the picture for understanding how citizenship functions. The subnational nature of belonging and accessing citizenship requires a shift in our level of analysis. Access to and protection of citizenship rights often plays out at the local level because multiple, overlapping governments influence how individuals access rights. This greatly complicates the view of citizenship as Brubaker's (1992) internally inclusive membership category, regardless of regime type. How do local membership institutions vary across an array of citizenship types? How do local membership institutions affect the quality of democratic rights in electoral authoritarian and electoral democracy regimes? Examining these lower-level forms of belonging better aligns the concept of citizenship with the implementation and outcomes of citizenship and can help unite citizenship scholarship across a broad comparative spectrum.

Finally, this book has implications for the study of citizenship in general, not just in democratic contexts. By understanding how citizenship is manipulated, subdivided, and used for the authoritarian bargain, we can identify perversion of inclusive democratic citizenship. Just as the two categories of democratic and nondemocratic regime types can be decomposed into a spectrum of polyarchy, so too can citizenship be decomposed along a spectrum that begins with its ideal form and construction and includes its many varieties after disruption, curtailment, and manipulation.

APPENDIX A

Defining the *Hukou*: Key Terms

The *hukou* system is notoriously complicated, to insiders and outsiders alike. In the Health and *Hukou* Survey analyzed in chapter 5, 77 percent of respondents said they either did not really understand the *hukou* system or did not understand it at all. This appendix describes the modern *hukou* system, including the different forms of *hukou*s actively used today. In appendix B, I detail the data sources for measures of the population and migration.

Formal Hukou Types and Related Permits

Table A.1 identifies the different types of *hukou*s either previously or currently in use in China.

TABLE A.1.
Reform-era *hukou* registration types and related permits

Name		Description
Hukou classifications		
Individual *hukou*	个人户口 家庭户口	Standard household registration.
Collective *hukou*	集体户口	Household registration attached to a specific work unit.
Type of hukou		
Agricultural *hukou*	农业户口	Agricultural *hukou*, often called rural *hukou*, originally identified individuals living in rural counties and working in agriculturally assigned work units.

(continued)

187

188　*Appendix A*

TABLE A.1. (*continued*)

Name		Description
Nonagricultural *hukou*	非农户口	Nonagricultural *hukou*, often called urban *hukou*, originally identified individuals living in urban districts and those employed in urban state-owned work units. For example, a doctor or a teacher in a rural county might have had nonagricultural designation during the Mao period.
Resident *hukou*	居民户口	Local *hukou* status that does not distinguish between agricultural and nonagricultural.
New *hukou* labels after 2014 reform		
Urban *hukou*	城镇户口	After 2014, national reforms led some municipalities to relabel nonagricultural *hukou* as urban *hukou*. In some locations, this was a superficial name change, and urban *hukou* referred simply to nonagricultural. In other locations, urban *hukou* redefined urban by geographic designation of residence (urban districts, county-level cities, and urban neighborhoods in rural counties).
Rural *hukou*	农村户口	Rural *hukou* also saw changes after the 2014 national reform. In some locations, it is simply a name change for agricultural *hukou*. In other locations, it applies to individuals who live in rural jurisdictions (villages).
Reform subclasses		
Self-supplied grain *hukou*	自理口粮户口	Permit to live in cities without a grain ration certificate. Introduced nationally in 1984. No longer active.
Blue-print *hukou*	蓝印户口	China's green card–like system but in which investment provides status and holders are eligible to transfer to permanent *hukou* after three to five years. First introduced in the early 1990s and formalized nationally in 2000. Largely merged with naturalization processes for obtaining nonagricultural *hukou*, although some individuals still hold a blue-print *hukou* as a legacy of this transition system.
Residency permits		
Temporary resident permit	暂住证 暂居证 寄住证	Permit to live in cities; frequently requires annual reregistration and proof of formal work contract or legal housing. Introduced nationally in 1985. Currently used as a registration system for migrants. Does not replace original *hukou* status.
Long-term-resident permit	常住户口	Residence-based permit for staying in a place other than original *hukou* registration. Introduced nationally in 1996 as an extension of the temporary resident permit but does not require annual renewal. Migrants must hold a temporary resident permit before qualifying for long-term-resident permit. Long-term *hukou* and long-term population are two different measures.

NOTE: For more on collective *hukou*, or household registration related to work units, and its institutional evolution, see Li and Chan (2022).

Bureaus and offices at the local level collect data on the population and its composition. These organizations do not use standardized terms and measurements to define the population, primarily because of different sources of data. In the following I identify the commonly reported population measures and their bureaucratic sources. I use data from public security bureaus because they are directly tied to formal *hukou* status, unlike other measures of the population.

Hukou Population

The *hukou* population comprises any person with locally registered *hukou*, including agricultural, nonagricultural, and unified resident types of *hukou*s. Local public security bureaus maintain these data through the formal registration, cancellation, and transfer of *hukou*. Data used in this book come from the Hong Kong–based CEIC Database, which provides economic and investment data from local yearbooks reporting public security bureau statistics.

LONG-TERM RESIDENT POPULATION

People who have resided in a location for more than six months are long-term residents. This population includes individuals who are registered locally and nonlocal migrants. It excludes those who have a local *hukou* but have migrated out of the district and live elsewhere and those who returned to the district less than six months ago from living elsewhere. Simply put, the long-term resident population includes physical residents plus net migration. Long-term resident population numbers come from annual surveys rather than official registration data.

NONAGRICULTURAL POPULATION VERSUS URBAN POPULATION

The nonagricultural population as defined by official statistics refers to individuals with nonagricultural *hukou*. Because it is defined through the *hukou* system, the nonagricultural population is reported by local public security bureaus. I have also used the term *urban* to identify these groups, as is common convention.

There are official statistics that identify urban populations (城镇人口), especially after 2014. I surveyed all municipal-level statistical and annual yearbooks and many county-level yearbooks to compile a database

190   *Appendix A*

identifying which locations began reporting non-agricultural populations as urban populations. This survey resulted in three different categories of cities. Some cities never stopped reporting nonagricultural population. Some cities merely relabeled nonagricultural as urban without changing the underlying data definitions. Finally, some cities redefined urban to mean individuals whose *hukou* is registered in an urban locality, such as a city district, neighborhood, or town, which could have posed a significant problem for my study. Almost all mixing between these categories, however, arose after 2014, and for consistency, I use *nonagricultural population* to define urban population only when it is clearly distinguished from urban populations. This creates the end-scope condition for analysis using population data.

AGRICULTURAL POPULATION VERSUS RURAL POPULATION

Agricultural registration (农业户口) is a formal identifier distinct from current employment, as discussed in the book. Throughout, I use *rural* to identify these groups, as is the convention. As with the partial transition from *nonagricultural* to *urban*, official statistics have shown a transition from *agricultural* to *rural*. *Rural population* (乡村人口) is most often defined as those whose *hukou* is registered in rural units. With the same caveats as in the preceding, municipalities (or prefectures) and counties now vary in which data and which definition they report, primarily after 2014.

Defining and Measuring the Migrant Population

Internal migrant conjures an image of a mobile population traversing the countryside. For China, this image is, at times, appropriate, but at other times it misrepresents the population *treated* as migrants. Every country uses its own measures of internal migrants defined primarily along two dimensions. A time dimension provides a minimum threshold of settlement. This is largely used to exclude tourists or short-term, temporary travel. A distance dimension provides a minimum for how far an individual must travel to be considered a migrant. Usually, changes of address within a jurisdiction are excluded using the distance dimension, leaving the fundamental question of what defines the jurisdiction. In China, a third dimension, legal registration, marks formal bureaucratic integration with where people live.

TIME

The national standard for identifying the migrant population is six months (NBS 2019b). Individuals away from their *hukou* address for less than six months are not considered migrants in strict, statistical terms. Although this time limit isolates temporary, leisure travel from true migration, it also has the potential to miss circular migrants. These are the most temporary migrants, who routinely travel back and forth between home and work destination. At times, government reports contain statistics on the year-end workforce (年末（季末）外出务工劳动力口), which includes short-term migrants even if they have not reached the six-month mark. For this study, using six months for the time dimension is sufficient.

DISTANCE

Official statistics disaggregate the population along three geographic boundaries. The mobile population (人户分离) includes any individual whose de facto residence and de jure residence are in different townships, which are the lowest level of government administration. The mobile population is further subdivided into those who cross city districts (市辖区内) but stay within one city and all others (流动人口, or the floating population). The intracity mobile population is separated from the floating population because the municipal-level government governs urban districts directly, creating bureaucratic continuity. The total floating population is what most commonly constitutes the migrant population, excluding these intracity address changers.

Within the floating population, government reports regularly identify a subset of migrant workers (农民工). These migrant workers explicitly hold rural *hukou* but live and work in a township different from their registration.[1] Their having formal urban work also distinguishes these migrant workers from other migrants. A rural-to-rural migrant who engages in agricultural work would be included in the floating population but excluded from the migrant worker population, for example. This distinction stems from the legacy of urban work units during the Mao era.

LEGAL REGISTRATION

Some whom the *hukou* system treats as migrants have not actually moved, however. They are considered migrants because their employment status and geography do not align with their *hukou* type. Two related groups fall

192 *Appendix A*

into this category. First, the urbanized rural population comprises individuals whose *hukou* is formally registered in the countryside but whose land and village have been swallowed by urban development. These individuals live, and often work, in urban spaces, but retain rural registration. Although the urbanized rural population is de facto urban, the *hukou* system makes it a de jure rural population, and local offices and social service systems treat them as migrants.

Second, closely related to the urbanized rural population is the local migrant worker population. The annual survey of the migrant worker population also distinguishes between local migrant workers (本地农民工), who are rural *hukou* holders with urban jobs in the same township as their *hukou*, and nonlocal migrant workers (外出农民工), who are those who cross township borders.[2]

These two populations—the urbanized rural population and local migrant workers—blur the basic distance definition by including some migrants who do not actually move for their employment (local migrant workers). Yet they face barriers to accessing government services similar to the ones facing migrants who physically move between locations.

APPENDIX B

Methods, Data, and Sources

Semistructured Interviews

I completed 120 semistructured interviews with policy bureaucrats across central, provincial, municipal, and county levels of government; human resource officers; academics; policy research groups; and migrants themselves from five provinces in four regions of China. Interviews were completed between 2012 and 2019. Table B.1 lists the interviews cited in the book. General descriptions are used to ensure the confidentiality of respondents. I had multiple conversations with more than half the interviewees. Each line in table B.1 represents a unique interviewee. The month and year represent the first substantive conversation.

TABLE B.1.
Interviews

Code	Province	Date	Type	Institution
11140501	Beijing	May 2014	Academic	Professor, policy research consultant
11140502	Beijing	May 2014	Firm	Group interview, one human resource manager and three employees who changed *hukou* status through employment
11140502	Beijing	May 2014	Municipal	Government official
11140601	Beijing	Jun. 2014	Academic	Professor, policy research consultant
11140603	Beijing	Jun. 2014	Firm	Central-managed state-owned enterprise employee
11140701	Beijing	Jul. 2014	Firm	Employees involved in transferring *hukou*

(*continued*)

193

194 *Appendix B*

TABLE B.1. *(continued)*

Code	Province	Date	Type	Institution
11140802	Beijing	Aug. 2014	County	Policy research group
11140901	Beijing	Sep. 2014	Firm	Group interview, two human resource managers from private firms
11141001	Beijing	Oct. 2014	Central	National Development and Reform Commission affiliate
11141101	Beijing	Nov. 2014	Central	National Development and Reform Commission affiliate
11141102	Beijing	Nov. 2014	Central	National Development and Reform Commission affiliate
11141106	Beijing	Nov. 2014	Academic	Professor and policy researcher
11141108	Beijing	Nov. 2014	Individual	Migrant
11150103	Beijing	Jan. 2015	Individual	Migrant with experience changing *hukou*
11150301	Beijing	Mar. 2015	Firm	Private firm owner
11150306	Beijing	Mar. 2015	Firm	Small-factory owner
11150302	Beijing	Mar. 2015	Individual	Internal migrant
11160101	Beijing	Jan. 2016	Central	State-owned-enterprise employee
11171201	Beijing	Dec. 2017	Individual	Internal migrant, small-business owner
11171203	Beijing	Dec. 2017	Firm	Foreign financial firm founder
11171205	Beijing	Dec. 2017	Individual	Business consultant
31191205	Shanghai	Dec. 2019	Academic	Professor
32131101	Jiangsu	Nov. 2013	Academic	Professor
32131102	Jiangsu	Nov. 2013	County	*Hukou* police officer
32131103	Jiangsu	Nov. 2013	Municipal	Public security bureaucrat
32131104	Jiangsu	Nov. 2013	Municipal	Policy research group
34150301	Zhejiang	Mar. 2016	Provincial	Professor and human resources bureaucrat
34150305	Zhejiang	Mar. 2016	Municipal	Academic, policy working group
43150901	Hunan	Sep. 2015	County	*Hukou* police officer
43150902	Hunan	Sep. 2015	County	*Hukou* detective
44120801	Guangdong	Aug. 2012	Academic	Professor, policy research consultant
44120802	Guangdong	Aug. 2012	Law firm	Migrant rights lawyer
44120804	Guangdong	Aug. 2012	Municipal	Policy research group
44120806	Guangdong	Aug. 2012	Academic	Professor
44131201	Guangdong	Dec. 2013	Municipal	Public security bureaucrat
44131203	Guangdong	Dec. 2013	Firm	Group interview with six state-owned-enterprise human resource managers

Code	Province	Date	Type	Institution
44140501	Guangdong	May 2014	Firm	Migrant, private firm owner
44140502	Guangdong	May 2014	Municipal	Municipal government official
44140605	Guangdong	Jun. 2014	Firm	Province-managed state-owned-enterprise employee
44140607	Guangdong	Jun. 2014	Firm	Private firm manager
44140634	Guangdong	Jun. 2014	Individual	Internal migrant with Hong Kong residency
44140701	Guangdong	Jul. 2014	Municipal	Member of the military
44140702	Guangdong	Jul. 2014	Municipal	Publicity department bureaucrat
44140703	Guangdong	Jul. 2014	County	*Hukou* police officer
44141101	Guangdong	Nov. 2014	Academic	Professor
44141103	Guangdong	Nov. 2014	Academic	Professor, policy consultant
44141105	Guangdong	Nov. 2014	Firm	Factor headhunter (labor manager)
44141107	Guangdong	Nov. 2014	Central	State-owned-enterprise employee
44141111	Guangdong	Nov. 2014	Municipal	Public security bureau representative
44150701	Guangdong	Jul. 2015	County	*Hukou* detective
44150707	Guangdong	Jul. 2015	Firm	Private firm general manager
44150901	Guangdong	Sep. 2015	Individual	State-owned-enterprise employee
44150903	Guangdong	Sep. 2015	Municipal	Policy bureaucrat, city government
44150904	Guangdong	Sep. 2015	Academic	Professor
44150908	Guangdong	Sep. 2015	Individual	Internal migrant
44160201	Guangdong	Feb. 2016	Individual	Internal migrant, small-business owner
44160202	Guangdong	Feb. 2016	Individual	Internal migrant with Hong Kong residency
51131101	Sichuan	Nov. 2013	Municipal	Policy research group
51131102	Sichuan	Nov. 2013	Municipal	Ministry of Health bureaucrat
51131108	Sichuan	Nov. 2013	Individual	Migrant in service industry
51131105	Sichuan	Nov. 2013	County	Land management bureaucrat

Interviewees chose the location for interviews. Most occurred in public spaces such as coffee shops or restaurants, though a few also occurred in offices or homes. Interviewees were recruited through cold calling and through snowball techniques. Interviews were conducted without an interpreter and were one-on-one, unless otherwise noted that interviews were in a small group. To reduce the risk of disclosure of interviewee identity, I did not record conversations. Instead, with the permission of the interviewee,

196   *Appendix B*

I took notes during and after the conversation. All quotations in the manuscript are from my notes unless otherwise noted.

Subnational Policy

LEVEL OF ANALYSIS: THE MUNICIPALITY

China's subnational governments are nested hierarchies of bureaucracy and authority. Below the central government are local governments at the provincial, municipal, county, and township levels. Each level of government exerts control over policy and manipulates its implementation both directly and through the ministries and bureaus below it. For this study, the level of analysis is the municipality, also known as the prefecture-level city. The municipality both writes and implements *hukou* policies. Provincial governments exert varying degrees of pressure for policy on municipalities below them, but because implementation occurs at the municipal and county level, the municipality is the most important unit. Each *hukou* address is registered down to the county level—below the municipality. When interacting with the local government, a person must go to the local-township public security bureau (派出所) first. With this division of labor among government levels in a decentralized bureaucracy, variation within municipalities across counties and townships is inevitable, but it is particularistic rather than systematic, especially at the township level.

Variation across counties is a potential challenge for research because both policies and statistical records identify individuals who move across counties within the same municipality as migrants, and in some cities there can be restrictions across counties. For example, the education system in the municipality of Nanjing is unified, with no distinction among the counties of the city. *Hukou* holders living in the far reaches of the municipal area can technically access high schools in the central city districts if their scores are high enough. In Changsha, in contrast, the urban core and the rural outlying counties operate two separate education systems, and each system is homogenized within itself but not across the two.

Integration within municipal borders is a primary concern of the national reforms announced in 2014. Local governments announced dissolution of the urban-rural distinction in the system, but in actuality, they created systems either like Nanjing's, which has no internal boundaries between districts but still maintains urban-rural distinctions for individuals, or like

Changsha's, which maintains urban-rural distinction between counties but not across individuals. Additionally, there is no direct evidence that counties receive specific quotas for rural-to-urban transfers. Because the most likely reforms will integrate policies that vary below the municipal level, this is the most relevant level of analysis.

DATA SOURCES

Academics and policy makers often use analysis of media reports and small-scale case studies to understand policy innovations and historical evolution over time within the *hukou* system.[1] Although these studies provide essential understanding of individual policies, they cannot evaluate the system as a whole. Similarly, case studies provide valuable information on the evolution of policies over time, but the big cities are not representative of the rest of the country. I build on this literature by evaluating a nationwide database of local *hukou* policies at the municipal level. I rely on local policies below the provincial level because there is significant variation within provinces and because municipal governments exert significant control over the implementation of their *hukou* policies. I focus on formally stated policies from official municipal sources because media reports often diverge from real policies and actual policy implementation. For example, large reforms are often announced at the national or provincial level but are not carried out. Hubei, Hunan, Jiangsu, and Fujian Provinces all announced in 2003 that they were dissolving the urban-rural distinction in *hukou* registration. Fujian has made significant progress in integrating populations to dissolve the urban-rural distinction, but the other provinces have fallen well short of their goals.[2]

Three other studies build indexes of *hukou* policies on nonrandom samples. Zhang and Tao (2012) create a city-entry-barrier index that covers a nearly comprehensive set of entry tracks. They collect data on a nonrepresentative sample of 45 cities.[3] This limited sample includes only provincial capitals and large migrant-receiving cities. In reality, every city in the country receives migrants, either from across municipal lines or from the rural countryside. The *hukou* policies in these cities are often overlooked because they are supposedly the most liberal in the country. But little to no work has been done in these cities to see if *hukou* liberalization has actually occurred. Liu and Xu (2016) also create an index of barriers to *hukou* to estimate the openness of the *hukou* system. Their sample contains 63 cities, and they

198 *Appendix B*

include only five measures of policy openness, ignoring the many ways migrants can change their *hukou*. Finally, Zhang, Wang, and Lu (2019) collect formal government policies at multiple levels to quantify policy variation, focusing on investment, home purchase, high-skilled recruitment, and employment pathways to local citizenship for a sample of 120 cities.

This project builds on these three studies by taking a broad approach to measuring local naturalization regulations, examining policy implementation, and expanding the sample of cities. Actual policy implementation frequently deviates from formal policy regulations. To capture this difference, I collected data from the websites of local public security bureau, where the day-to-day management of local naturalization occurs. I also collected data on every pathway to local citizenship rather than only the most studied pathways of skilled labor recruitment and investment pathways. Finally, I gathered data from a census of cities, of which 317 of 333 had sufficient information publicly available for inclusion. This provides a better picture of variation across the country than more limited samples.

From my analysis of policy pathways and their restrictions, I develop an original index of naturalization openness for the four primary categories of local *hukou* naturalization: high skilled, low skilled, family, and investment. These categories mirror the four main pathways for immigration in the international context. Because disaggregating the types of targeted migrants is essential for this analysis, I treated each pathway to naturalization separately. Through numerous conversations with police officers involved in the day-to-day implementation of *hukou* enforcement, academics, and bureaucrats, I developed a standardized form for collecting information on all the ways to change *hukou* in each municipality and the standard barriers to accessing naturalization, such as age and time restrictions, necessary paperwork, and the formality of work requirements. Two research assistants and I filled out the data collection instrument for all 333 municipalities in China using instructions available on the local public security bureau websites. When the instructions were incomplete or information was not available, I randomly selected a local public security bureau office to call and asked the transfer requirement questions over the phone. This ultimately yielded 317 cities with sufficient information for analysis. Each index is measured as an openness index that ranges from 0 to 1. The higher the score on the index, the more open the naturalization policies are and the easier it is to meet the eligibility requirements.

In preparation for data collection, I began with a list of forms of citizenship acquisition identified in the comparative literature. I completed thirty-two semistructured interviews with academics, policy researchers, and bureaucrats including *hukou* police officers and detectives to identify the breadth of policies and the primary areas for variation in *hukou* policies. I conducted interviews in six different provinces to ensure the relevant policy details used to measure *hukou* openness were not region or province specific. Over the course of interviews, I identified which international citizenship acquisition pathways applied in China and which subsets of policies were specific to China.

Because the goal of the project was to create a dataset with national coverage, I created a protocol with forty questions identifying the types of *hukou* transfers present in each municipality and the specific regulations that make those policies more open (fewer barriers) or more closed (more barriers). This questionnaire provided a detailed description of each city's *hukou* policy landscape. Not every city provided the same level of detail in their policies, and not every city had the same set of policies.

Together with three research assistants, I attempted to collect *hukou* transfer policies for all 333 municipalities plus Beijing, Tianjin, Shanghai, and Chongqing, from May through June of 2016. The data collected represent policies at one point in time: a cross section of cities' policies in 2016. This timing was intentional. The central government announced a reform in fall of 2014. I collected data well after this reform to give sufficient time for local governments to formally adopt policies to reflect central reform. Because of China's five-year plans, these policies were expected to remain relatively stable until at least 2020.

When city public security bureau websites were insufficient, I used online bulletin boards (BBS) and local news sources.[4] If I used informal sources (nongovernmental), information was verified on at least three websites before it was included in the index. In the event of conflicting data, I had a research assistant call a random local public security bureau (at the street level) to clarify. To ensure intercoder reliability, two different research assistants coded a randomly selected 20 percent of the cities. Almost no differences were identified. Additionally, I randomly chose 10 percent of each research assistant's cities to verify all sources provided for the city's data. I entered all coding from the data collection sheets into the master database. The final sample yielded 317 cities with sufficient information for

200 *Appendix B*

TABLE B.2.
Main indicators of policy indexes

Naturalization type	Applies to	Requires
Family	Child registration: newborn, non-newborn	• Paperwork (amount) • Age limits
	Spouse	• Age or length limits
	Parent	• Age or length limits
High skilled	Employer selected	• Certification level minimum requirement • Education work requirements
	General pool: points-based, certified high-skilled work	• Program type (none, points-based, college, both; work only)
Residence	Rural integration: land-exchange, settlement	• Program type (land exchange, employment based, housing or settlement)
Investment	Capital investment: housing purchase, firm	• Minimum investment amount

inclusion in the study. Table B.2 summarizes the indicators used to construct the indexes.

POLICY INDEX

Family-Based Naturalization

Family-based policies had the most information available online. I disaggregated family-based *hukou* acquisition into four categories: newborn registration, non-newborn children naturalization, spousal naturalization, and parental naturalization. The administrative burdens related to family-based naturalizations derive from the paperwork necessary to apply and limitations on who is allowed to apply.

Newborn registration: The paperwork required to register a newborn can be difficult to obtain. All municipalities require a birth certificate issued by a hospital for registration.[5] Additionally, although only one parent must be local to register a child locally, most municipalities require both parents' identity documents, including national identity card (身份证) and *hukou*. Moreover, in most municipalities, parents must provide a marriage certificate to register children. Technically, all children born out of wedlock are considered out of plan according to family planning policies, and many municipalities use this as a pretext to deny or delay registration (Kennedy and Shi 2019).[6] Finally, similar to the marriage requirement, many municipalities require a certificate of family planning (准生证, 计划生育证) proving either that the child was born within the birth-planning regulations—either the one-child or two-child policy—or that the "social burden fee[s]" for children born "out of plan" were paid.[7] These regulations still hold even after the relaxation of birth-planning policies.

Some municipalities require additional paperwork or documentation, especially if one parent is not registered locally.[8] The most common additional paperwork needed is the "no-registration certificate" (未落户证明). Children born to parents from two different *hukou* locations or children following their father must also have a certificate verifying they are not registered anywhere else, such as policies in Jingdezhen, Jiangxi, require. Parents not registered locally (or mothers for children being registered in the father's location) must return to their *hukou* location to get a certificate attesting to no other registration. This can create a significant barrier to registration for children born to migrant parents and makes successful marriages and registration across *hukou* locations difficult. Although a child can now be registered at a father's location, some municipalities require DNA testing to prove paternity before children can be registered under their father.

Getting *hukou* is not automatic, and municipalities have differing time limits on registering newborns. The national regulation requires children be registered within one month of birth (State Council 1958). Just over half of municipalities require immediate registration, and the rest have more liberal policies, including no time limit on child registration. Informally, localities often allow newborn children registration as late as six years old, when compulsory education begins (Shi and Kennedy 2016).

Non-newborn children: The requirements for non-newborn children registration are similar to newborn registration requirements, but applications for non-newborn children are reviewed through a process more like adult naturalizations than newborn (Interview 44140703). Age limit is the primary determinant of how open registration for non-newborns is. The most restrictive policies, employed by just under half of all municipalities, require that children must be minors, or under age eighteen. Approximately 20 percent of municipalities have the most open policy: that children of any age can naturalize where their parents are registered. This is the only widely available right-of-return policy, which allows young adults to return to their previous *hukou* status if their parents are still living. In practice, however, this right of return is likely limited to urban settings, because rural returns are incredibly rare and likely to face informal restrictions.

Spouse: The two most common requirements beyond marriage length and minimum age are family planning certificates and proof of housing or livelihood.[9] A family planning certificate proves that the couple followed family planning regulations of the previous location of registration. Ten cities require proof of stable housing or proof of livelihood, again emphasizing the importance of stability in the destination location.

Parents: The standard policy through the 1980s allowed only retired parents to transfer to their children's *hukou* location and type, and the policy was not specifically loosened in the 1998 reform. Local policy relaxation rather than central edicts in the late 1990s and 2000s led to variation in the restrictions placed on parents. Approximately 40 percent of municipalities still require parents to be above retirement age—fifty-five for women and sixty for men—and provide proof of retirement (退休证, 无就业证) before they are eligible to transfer to their child's location. Approximately 35 percent of cities set an age limit below retirement age, most commonly fifty and fifty-five, for women and men, respectively. The more liberal cities removed age limits for parental transfers, requiring only that children be older than eighteen (成年) before they can transfer their parents. Sixteen municipalities, approximately 5 percent of the total sample, do not place any restrictions on parental transfers, representing the most liberal policy arrangement.

High-Skilled Naturalization

In most cases, to qualify for a government-distributed quota, workers must obtain a specified level of credential to qualify for the broadly classified high-skilled recruitment (引进人才入户 or 优秀人才落户). Variation across cities derives from the level of rank or certification a city uses to define eligibility.

High-skilled programs have various names. I classified high-skilled programs on the basis of requirements for advanced credentials, either education or rank and certification requirements, rather than looking at policies with specific names related to skilled labor. High-skilled programs go by names such as "outstanding talents," "Model Workers," and "Courageous and Advanced Individuals." Some policies even appeared, superficially, to target lower-skilled workers, such as ones targeting "peasant workers in the city," but in reality these policies still required education or technical training that many rural migrant workers do not have.

Formal high-skilled credentials take one of two forms: professional rank (职称) and certifications (资格). Each system has general and specialist categories, and specialists rank higher than generalists. Professional rank is a bureaucratic ranking of a formal job title and is divided into junior, intermediate, advanced intermediate, and advanced (初级, 中级, 副高, 高). Certifications are divided into junior, intermediate, advanced, master, and advanced master (初级, 中级, 高级, 技师, 高级技师). These certifications and their tiered rankings allow local governments to define what counts as high-skilled labor. Each ranking represents educational attainment and professional experience.[10] For example, a person with a high school education and ten years of work experience can apply for a formally recognized intermediate professional rank credential. Cities specify which level high-skilled workers must obtain before they are considered high-skilled and eligible to transfer their *hukou* through one of the high-skilled labor pathways. Those that require a higher level for eligibility are more restrictive because they take longer and more resources to achieve.

Larger cities and provincial capitals now use a points-based system to rank and select migrants for naturalization. These programs benefit the general pool of labor, distinct from employer-based naturalizations. See Zhang (2012) for a description of points-based systems.

To construct an index for high-skilled transfer programs, I divided these policies into two categories: employer selected and general pool. Employer-selected models are further subdivided into rank and certification versus education. These two tracks are parallel hierarchies, if you will. Because there is no obvious mapping of one onto the other, I divided each into four levels and used the sum of the two to measure a high-skilled employer-selected index.

General-pool models allow transfers without specific work requirements. Both points-based systems and education-based transfers with no work requirement fall under the general-pool model. To create an index of the general-pool policies, I rated each city on whether they had a points-based system, college-based transfers, both, or neither. College-based transfers are more open than points-based programs, because in most points-based programs, although education provides the most points, it rarely is sufficient for application. For example, in Shenzhen, having a college degree is worth eighty out of one hundred points. College graduates need additional qualifications or contributions to the city to be eligible for transfer.

To get an aggregate index, I sum these two subindexes. This strategy places a theoretically equal weight on the two programs. One could argue that general-pool policies are inherently more open because they do not require employer support. But more quotas may be set aside for employer-selected policies. Because these are multiple pathways, an additive index is appropriate. As a robustness check, I completed a principal component analysis (PCA) of the individual pieces of the program. On the basis of the loadings and a Kaiser-Meyer-Olkin test, PCA was inappropriate for this case. The results of the PCA suggested that the indicators do not move in tandem and, in fact, diverge. Because of this, to verify the results of the high-skilled index, I also run models on both employer-selected and general-pool indicators separately from each other, as discussed in chapter 3.

Residence-Based Naturalization

For the rest of the country without a college education, what I classify as permanent residence transfers are more feasible. These programs are considered suitable for low-skilled workers because they do not have a skill requirement and are open to all migrants. Cities have two low-skilled naturalization mechanisms: rural-to-urban transfers and the newer permanent-housing-based transfers. These low-skilled transfer systems target different populations and represent the most open policies because they have the lowest requirements.

One of the earliest transfer programs other than family-based transfers was the transfer of rural populations to urban status. This process accompanied the loosening of migration controls in the 1980s. Under this program, local rural migrants—those who moved from rural counties to the urban core for work within the same municipality—could petition to become urban residents after securing a labor contract. Meant as a way for low-skilled workers with jobs to transfer to the location of their jobs (Solinger 1999), the system morphed from marketization into a mechanism for local governments to accelerate urbanization, including through the reclassification of rural land to urban construction land (Meina Cai 2012). Local governments began using rural-to-urban transfer (农转非) to integrate rural populations living on the periphery of the city's urban core. When rural residents become urban, the state can claim their rural land for urban development, which is highly profitable for the local government. The central government condemned this because rural landholders were rarely compensated fairly, but some residual policies remain today. According to the 2002 China Household Income Project Survey, of urban residents who changed *hukou* status, 6 percent did so because the government confiscated their land (NBS, *China Household Income Project Survey* 2002).

Notably, these rural-to-urban transfer programs targeted local rural residents, especially those displaced by urbanization pressures. Nonlocal residents had "nothing to offer" local governments because their valuable asset, land, was in some other municipality (Interviews 44120802, 32131103). These early policies are the institutional origins of low-skilled policies promoting local over nonlocal naturalization.

Transitioning away from land-for-*hukou* exchanges, central-level reforms pushed for a more general rural-to-urban program beginning in 2003 and again in 2014. The resulting policies have four forms: land, family, work, and residence. Land-based rural-to-urban transfer is the residual land-for-*hukou* policy of *nongzhuanfei*, or local leaders encouraging rural land use rights holders to sign over their rights in order to get access to urban status. Initially, all rural-to-urban transfers required giving up land, but the central government banned this practice because of the negative consequences for rural residents' social security (State Council 2011a). At the time of data collection, nineteen municipalities still stipulated rural residents must give up their land. In practice, this number is much higher, because municipal governments do not want to formally publish this requirement (Interview 11141001).

Under family-based low-skilled programs, only holders of rural *hukou* with family in the urban center can change their registration status. When family is required, the local government wants to ensure those who transfer from rural to urban status have access to a minimum livelihood: rural migrants who have urban family members are more likely to be wealthier and economically established in the city. Under work-based low-skilled programs, individuals who establish permanent housing in an urban area and secure work are allowed to integrate into the urban *hukou* system. These policies vary by the type of proof of employment required for transfer. Relaxed policies require only a letter from a registered employer, whereas more closed programs require full contracts, which are much harder to get.

206 *Appendix B*

According to the urban sample of the China Household Income Project Survey of 2002, just 23 percent of rural and migrant workers had either long-term contracts or permanent positions, compared with 72 percent of local urban residents (NBS, *China Household Income Project Survey* 2002). Finally, residence programs require only secure residence to transfer *hukou* and are by far the most open of all the programs. In most cases, stable housing is defined as contracted rentals, but in a minority of cases, migrants must own their own home. Rural-to-urban transfers can be further limited by minimum stay requirements and by requiring migrants to pay into social insurance programs. Minimum stay requirements range from three months to seven years. Some cities also require family planning certificates.

Although formally not limited to local rural residents except when rural transfers are required to relinquish land use rights, these programs almost solely admit local rural residents. Nonlocal residents are generally not eligible (Interviews 44120802, 44120804).

Classifying low-skilled programs had several challenges, as did the high-skilled programs. Many rural-to-urban programs are not distinct from other programs. For example, nine cities require rural transfers to have family members in the city. This means that, in these cities, rural integration programs are simply family transfers without a distinct pathway unique to local rural residents. These cities are coded as not having low-skilled transfer programs. Similarly, two cities require rural residents to have high-skill certificates or education. These programs were coded as high-skilled rather than low-skilled programs because they require a certain skill level. A few cities require a migrant to purchase a house instead of renting a house. For these cities, as for the family requirement discussed earlier, the policy is classified as an investment policy rather than a rural integration policy.

A handful of cities formally allow *nongzhuanfei* but only in certain districts, primarily targeting smaller urban centers outside the main municipal districts. The index does not code these cities separately because urban status is the level of analysis and what is most important for welfare entitlements. Future research should look at the rise of satellite cities and their importance in urbanization in China.

The resultant low-skilled policies are, ranked from most difficult requirements to easiest, rural integration programs through land forfeiture, employment, housing, and general programs with no specific requirements. Programs that require land forfeiture are the strictest because they require relinquishing the most significant rural right. Contracted employment is the next-most difficult, especially because formally contracted employment can be difficult for migrants to secure. Securing stable housing is the third-most difficult. Finally, general programs specify no requirements.

Investment-Based Naturalization

I measure investment-based naturalizations by the minimum amount of investment required for transfer. Policies either state an explicit amount or state that a house of average price must be purchased. When policies state a minimum amount, this is the value I use. When housing purchase is the standard, I use average two-bedroom apartment purchase price in 2015, according to online sources.[11] To calculate the index, I normalized the inverse of the log of this housing value.

As discussed in chapter 3, investment can be housing, individual investment, or firm-based investment. The most common policy was purchase of a house. In most cities, the most open investment policies require migrants to purchase an average-priced home. I divided investment programs into two categories: those that required investment equal to the average housing price and those that required investment greater than the average home cost. I used a real estate firm's data on average housing cost in a city to estimate the breaking point between the two.

An alternative measure would include the actual value of the average house price instead of categories. This would better capture the actual value of capital investment needed, but it would be highly, and artificially, correlated with economic development of a city. To avoid this correlation, I included the above- and at-average ordinal variable instead.

Creating Indexes

I score cities on how easy it is to naturalize through a specific channel. When a naturalization pathway is not available in a municipality, the index is zero, meaning most restrictive. When multiple measures combine to make one index, such as the high-skilled index that considers both general-pool and employment-based pathways, I use PCA to combine the measures. These scores are then normalized to range between 0 and 1 to provide comparability across indexes. A PCA of all four indexes suggests that combining the scores into one master index is methodologically questionable, because the indicators diverge significantly from each other. For that reason,

208   Appendix B

I keep the indexes separate from each other, with unique pathways identified throughout.

CLUSTER ANALYSIS

Cluster analysis is routinely used for creating typologies that identify distinct groupings of observations that vary together across multiple indicators. This analysis is the first descriptive cut to identify variation in *hukou* policies across the country. I use hierarchical clustering, which sequentially divides observations into groups on the basis of dissimilarities between groups. I use the most applied measure of Euclidian distance. I use Ward's method of analysis of variance to identify the link function, or when two groups are far enough away from each other to be identified as a separate group (Ward 1963). Finally, I use the Duda-Hart classification rule to identify the ideal number of clusters. This measure captures the existence of each additional cluster and is known as a stopping rule, or the point to stop breaking the data down into subsequently smaller clusters (Milligan and Cooper 1985). According to the Duda-Hart rule, the ideal number of clusters is three.

NET NATURALIZATION ESTIMATES

Measuring the total *hukou* population and identifying migrants can be challenging because of the many different measures of a population outlined in appendix A.

I can estimate the approximate size of the naturalized population in each city in a given year using the growth of the population and a city's natural growth rate. Using data from statistical yearbooks, collected from the CEIC database on the *hukou*-registered population of each city, and on natural growth rates reported in the *Chinese Population Statistical Materials* (中华人民共和国分县市人口统计资料) from 2002 to 2013 (Ministry of Public Security, *Chinese Population Statistical Materials*, various years), I define the net total naturalized population as the growth in the *hukou* population not attributed to natural growth. The registered population grows because of births, and natural growth is calculated as registered births of local citizens minus death of local citizens plus net *hukou* transfers. Net total naturalization uses urban *hukou* as the base population; net nonlocal naturalization uses total *hukou* population as the base population; and local rural naturalization is total naturalization minus nonlocal naturalization. Population data are highly irregular in China and subject to political manipulation.[12] For this reason, results from analyses of these data should be taken as general trends rather than point estimates.[13]

The measure would ideally be identified as naturalization rate, in which the naturalized population is divided by the total number of migrants in a given city. Because of its sensitive nature, the total number of nonlocal residents is reported only in the census. Instead, I use nonlocal naturalization per estimated migrant stock and rural naturalization per *hukou* population to scale these estimates.

One of the larger concerns when using government-reported population data is falsifications. I screened the data for outlier values I suspected to be data entry errors or blatant data falsification. Although many cities did dramatically increase their nonagricultural populations in the study period, changes the next year indicate when dramatic increases may be false. In some cases, a sharp increase in the nonagricultural population was immediately followed by a dramatic decrease, such as in Wuhan in 2009 and 2010. The urban population increased by almost three million between 2008 and 2009 but decreased by nearly two million between 2009 and 2010. The back-to-back opposing fluctuations hint that the population recorded in 2009 was incorrect, as does the actual process of changing *hukou*. *Hukou* records are now stored digitally, but transfers are still paper based, and it is unlikely even the most efficient bureaucracy could process two million *hukou* transfers in one year.

Comparing dramatic changes in urban population between cities reveals further evidence of falsification in the Wuhan data. Shenzhen also expanded its urban population suddenly in 2004, but I am more confident about those official numbers reflecting reality because they are in line with subsequent years. Wuhan's fluctuations could be the result of political incentives to falsely state the urbanization rate, or they could be the result of a simple data entry error.

More than likely, this dramatic in-migration followed by immediate out-migration is politically motivated data manipulation. Hubei was one of four provinces that announced it would end the urban-rural distinctions in *hukou* by 2010. The 2009 data in Wuhan is, therefore, more likely a manipulation of statistics before the end of policy reform than a reflection of dramatic change. These falsified patterns are more likely in provinces and cities that have announced major reform.[14] These patterns will be discussed

210   Appendix B

in future work. Significant expansion (more than 25 percent of the total population) is followed by a significant decline of approximately the same size in eight occurrences. These are treated as missing for the purpose of this analysis.

Survey Methods

To assess migrants' demand for local urban status, I implemented a probability sample survey with experimental questions in Beijing and Changsha, Hunan, in 2015 and 2016. The survey was cosponsored by Peking University's China Center for Health Economic Research and hosted locally by Hunan University in Changsha.[15]

Hukou is not a typical market good with a price that estimates demand. Few opportunities exist to purchase it, and the government has monopoly power over price setting.[16] Contingent valuation, used widely in public policy and environmental studies,[17] provides an estimated willingness to pay (WTP) for nonmarket goods. Survey respondents are asked how much they are willing to pay for a given good, service, or policy, usually either by direct payment or through taxation. Although estimates of WTP can be biased because the technique relies on a hypothetical rather than observed behavior (Ehmke, Lusk, and List 2008), it is used widely in measuring the value of nonmarket goods and policies (Carson and Groves 2007; Cummings, Brookshire, and Schulze 1986; Arrow et al. 1993).

Respondents received a vignette about a proposed government program that would allow anyone to purchase local urban *hukou*. To ensure respondents had the same understanding of what *hukou* includes, they saw a show card listing all the welfare and assistance packages local urban *hukou* provided access to, including health insurance and housing assistance. Respondents were then asked if they would buy this *hukou* at a given bid price that randomly varied across seven prices, from RMB 1,000 to 600,000 (US\$145–US\$87,000). We set bid prices based on real-world parameters of a reasonable price and the black-market price. Respondents said yes or no to purchasing the *hukou* at the given price.[18] Respondents were then asked if they wanted to purchase the *hukou* for themselves, and a follow-up question asked if they would buy it for a family member. The analysis here defines the dependent variable as purchasing *hukou* for anyone in the family.

Methods, Data, and Sources 211

The second experiment involved a classic choice experiment. Respondents were asked if they would be interested in applying for a *hukou* through a special program that did not have additional requirements. These programs allowed only specific rights, however, and varied in provision of land, education, and pension rights. Land rights would allow migrants to retain existing family land use rights or require them to relinquish the rights. For education, the programs would provide free education or require respondents to pay a school selection fee for their children. For pension rights, respondents would automatically qualify for a local pension or would not qualify for a local pension. Respondents were asked to pick between two randomly paired programs or to retain their current status. All nonstrictly dominated pairings were included in the factorial design, and order was randomly assigned to each of the questions. Each respondent was presented with three pairs of policy choices.

APPENDIX C

Policy List and Results Tables

TABLE C.I.
Main central-government reform policies, 1977–2019

Organization	Policy title
MPS (1977)	Regulation regarding Dealing with *Hukou* Transfer
MPS, MF, MoP (1980)	Regulation regarding Resolving Issues of Grain Rationing for Rural Families of Cadre with Professional Skills Migrating to Urban Areas
SC (1982)	Measures for Internment and Deportation of Urban Vagrants and Beggars
SC (1984)	Regarding the Problem of Peasants Settling in Market Towns
MPS (1985)	Provisional Regulations for the Management of Temporary Residents in Cities and Towns
SC (1988)	Notification regarding Preventing Public Sales of Urban Hukou by Some Cities and Counties
SC (1989)	Notification regarding Strictly Controlling Overly Rapid Increase in "*Nongzhuanfei*"
MPS (1989)	Regulations for Management of Temporary Identification Permits
MPS (1992a)	Notification on Implementing Locally Effective Urban Residential *Hukou* Systems
MPS (1992b)	Urgent Notification regarding Resolving and Preventing the Flawed Method of Public Selling Nonagricultural *Hukou*
SC (1993)	Decision regarding Household Registration System Reform
MPS (1994)	Notification regarding the Use of New *Hukou* Relocation Certificates and *Hukou* Permits for Resettlement

(*continued*)

214   *Appendix C*

TABLE C.I. *(continued)*

Organization	Policy title
MPS, MoF, PBOC (1994)	Notification on Resolving and Preventing the Continued Sale of Nonagricultural *Hukou*
MPS, MoP, MLSS (1994)	Notification regarding Issues Relating to *Hukou* Transfer for Redeployed Cadres and Laborers
MPS (1995a)	Application Procedures for Temporary Residency Permits
MPS (1995b)	Notification regarding Introducing New Permanent Population Registration Forms and Resident *Hukou* Registers
MoC (1995)	Notification regarding Earnestly Carrying Out Small City and Town Household Registration Reform Work
SC (1997)	The Pilot Plan for Reform of the Household Registration Management System in Small Towns and the Notice on Improving the Rural Household Registration Management System
MPS (1997a)	Blueprint for Experiments in Small City and Town Household Registration Management Reform
MPS (1997b)	Opinion on Improving the Rural Household Registration Management system
MPS, SC (1998)	Recommendations on Resolving Several Issues with Current *Hukou* Management Work
CC (2000)	Recommendations on Accelerating the Healthy Development of Small Cities and Towns
MPS (2001)	Opinions on Accelerating Reform of the Small City and Town *Huji* [Household Registration] Management System
SC (2011a)	Notice of the General Office of the State Council on Actively and Steadily Promoting the Reform of the Household Registration System
SC (2014c)	Opinions of the State Council on Further Promotion of Reform of the Household Registration System
MPS (2014)	Notice on Earnestly Implementing the "Opinions of the State Council on Further Promoting the Reform of the Household Registration System"
SC (2015)	Opinions on Solving the Problems of Household Registration for People without Household Registration
SC (2016)	On Promoting the Settlement of 100 million nonregistered people in cities
MPS (2019)	Notice on Printing and Distributing the Guidelines for the Publicity of Basic-Level Government Affairs in Household Registration Management

NOTE: CC: Central Committee; MF: Ministry of Food; MLSS: Ministry of Labor and Social Security; MoC: Ministry of Construction; MoF: Ministry of Finance; MoP: Ministry of Personnel, National Bureau of Personnel; MPS: Ministry of Public Security; PBOC: People's Bank of China; SC: State Council.

Policy List and Results Tables   215

TABLE C.2.
Full results for chapter 4

Variable	High skilled	Low skilled	Family	Investment
Top tier	−0.0459	0.0287	−0.0938**	−0.0910
	(0.0592)	(0.0805)	(0.0451)	(0.0644)
Minority county	0.0116	−0.0108	−0.0542*	−0.0868*
	(0.0391)	(0.0503)	(0.0301)	(0.0521)
Foreign output (proportion)	0.233***	0.0174	0.0648	−0.0560
	(0.0707)	(0.0914)	(0.0644)	(0.0862)
FDI (per GDP)	−0.354	−1.018	0.249	−0.296
	(0.971)	(1.302)	(0.919)	(2.304)
Machinery (per sq. kilometer arable land)	0.000668	0.0635**	0.0548***	0.0293*
	(0.0132)	(0.0281)	(0.0115)	(0.0160)
Land price	1.20e-5*	−1.16e-5	−2.54e-5***	−1.18e-5
	(7.16e-6)	(1.36e-5)	(6.52e-6)	(1.11e-5)
Poverty county	0.00587	0.0545	0.0733***	0.0242
	(0.0354)	(0.0481)	(0.0278)	(0.0409)
Migrants per capita				
2nd quartile	0.101***	−0.0394	0.0477	0.0371
	(0.0365)	(0.0563)	(0.0319)	(0.0418)
3rd quartile	−0.00153	−0.0913	0.0717**	0.0170
	(0.0355)	(0.0577)	(0.0334)	(0.0499)
4th quartile	0.0172	−0.101	0.0825*	−0.0215
	(0.0500)	(0.0675)	(0.0427)	(0.0650)
GDP (log)	0.0162	0.00681	0.0197	0.0484
	(0.0237)	(0.0354)	(0.0194)	(0.0326)
Region				
Central	0.0775*	0.174***	−0.128***	0.0126
	(0.0398)	(0.0574)	(0.0326)	(0.0449)
West	0.0516	0.102*	−0.0117	0.0151
	(0.0415)	(0.0547)	(0.0327)	(0.0398)
Constant	0.144	0.244	0.456**	0.343
	(0.293)	(0.410)	(0.231)	(0.400)
Observations	264	264	264	264
R squared	0.090	0.135	0.175	0.069

NOTE: Robust standard errors are in parentheses. FDI: foreign direct investment; GDP: gross domestic product.
*** $p < .01$, ** $p < .05$, * $p < .1$

TABLE C.3.
Net naturalization rates

Variable	Total per capita	Total	Non-local per migrant	Non-local	Rural per cap	Rural
Lagged DV	−0.0543***	−0.0199	0.0325***	0.0528***	−0.121***	−0.148***
	(0.0116)	(0.0149)	(0.0126)	(0.00986)	(0.0163)	(0.0168)
FDI (per GDP)	0.0141**	34,473	−0.000812	−210.8	0.0155*	39,841
	(0.00621)	(31,691)	(0.0134)	(7,623)	(0.00834)	(42,382)
Foreign output (%)	−0.0226***	−102,348**	−0.0202	−8,360	−0.00920	−49,702
	(0.00784)	(40,006)	(0.0165)	(9,412)	(0.0106)	(53,945)
Machinery (kW)	2.14e−5***	107.8**	−4.84e−5***	−41.54***	1.33e−5	117.0**
	(8.24e−6)	(42.06)	(1.76e−5)	(10.03)	(1.11e−5)	(56.18)
Poverty county (%)	−0.0351***	−303,388***	−0.0433**	−845.3	−0.0271*	−280,942***
	(0.0122)	(62,524)	(0.0212)	(12,060)	(0.0165)	(83,640)
Migrant stock	−1.66e−8***	−0.0632**	−3.14e−8***	−0.0334***	4.49e−9	−0.109*
	(4.97e−9)	(0.0254)	(9.89e−9)	(0.00571)	(1.29e−8)	(0.0656)
Constant	0.0351***	178,040***	0.0403***	42,643***	0.0157	219,537***
	(0.00561)	(28,638)	(0.0113)	(6,489)	(0.0105)	(53,297)
Observations	2,657	2,657	2,775	2,776	2,633	2,644
Economic controls	Y	Y	Y	Y	Y	Y
Year FE	Y	Y	Y	Y	Y	Y
Municipal FE	Y	Y	Y	Y	Y	Y
R squared	0.068	0.065	0.139	0.151	0.063	0.076
Number of municipalities	281	281	279	279	278	279

NOTE: Standard errors are in parentheses. FDI: foreign direct investment; GDP: gross domestic product.

*** $p < .01$, ** $p < .05$, * $p < .1$

Notes

Introduction

1. The 2020 census estimates the internal migrant population, those who cross administrative boundaries and thus lack local citizenship, at 376 million people (NBS 2021a).

2. For example, out of thirty-seven chapters in *The Oxford Handbook of Citizenship*, three chapters—on mesolevel citizenship (Chung 2017), on citizenship in "transition" states (Shevel 2017), and on postcolonial citizenship (Sadiq 2017)—are dedicated to citizenship outside the Western, democratic context. None directly address the content of authoritarian citizenship. Other chapters engage partially with non-Western or nondemocratic contexts, including one on Gulf States as immigrant-receiving states (Joppke 2017) and another on performative citizenship in nondemocracies (Isin 2017).

3. On subjecthood and citizenship, see Lohr (2012).

4. According to the Varieties of Democracy project, 54 percent of the world's population lives under autocratic rule (Lührmann et al. 2020).

5. For example, participatory institutions, such as local elections and small-scale deliberative democracy, allow individuals to create democratic influence on governance outcomes through grassroots activities (He 2018; O'Brien 2001; O'Brien and Li 2000; Xia and Guan 2017).

6. Individuals perform citizenship under authoritarian rule by making claims on the state (Brown 2021; Distelhorst and Fu 2019; Isin 2017). Even in authoritarian settings, individuals carve out space to perform acts of citizenship (Ong 1999; Saeidi 2010). Individuals contest and claim citizenship, whether that means democratic norms of citizenship or broader socioeconomic rights of belonging (Goldman 2007; Solinger 1999).

217

218   *Notes to Introduction*

7. Existing literature in this area is relatively limited. Autocrats shape national-level citizenship to balance redistribution among local populations and immigration needs of economic development processes (Shin 2017). Autocrats also use citizenship education to shape identity (Jones 2018; Nasir and Turner 2013). Much less is known about citizenship variation inside autocratic states.

8. On citizenship boundaries and membership, see Lohr (2012).

9. See, for example, Feinberg (2006) on how preservation of traditional gendered family norms undermined democratic citizenship for women.

10. For example, Skocpol (1995) demonstrates how veterans and women organized after the Civil War to establish early social benefits such as pensions in the United States, known as a relatively weak welfare state. But as the Civil War generation declined, so too did these welfare benefits, and the US welfare system reverted to its less generous form.

11. The idea of internal citizenship can be similar to what Maas (2017) calls multilevel citizenship in democracies when defined geographically. Individuals hold both a national citizenship and a local citizenship, which more directly defines the individual-state relationship because of local rights provisions.

12. On formal, industrial employment bestowing access to citizenship rights under the António de Oliveira Salazar (Portugal) and Francisco Franco (Spain) dictatorships, see Pinto (2012).

13. Apartheid South Africa and the Bantustan system is a quintessential case of race-based citizenship. Black South Africans were stripped of citizenship rights and geographically isolated from white full citizens (Claassens 2014).

14. Religious minorities are regularly stripped of citizenship rights, including in Turkey (Yılmaz and Turner 2019), China's northwest (Byler 2021), and Myanmar (Boyraz 2019).

15. Nonlocal populations also face discriminatory practices in access to education, loans, jobs in the state sector, and medical insurance, such as higher fees, restricted access, and outright denial of services (Huang 2014; Zhang 2012). For example, one white-collar worker without local *hukou* in southern China was reimbursed for only 25 percent of a hospital bill for surgery because the worker's health insurance was in a different province (Interview 44150707).

16. Before 1999, *hukou* status was inherited only matrilineally.

17. Rubins (1998) identifies two types of internal migration systems: permit based and notification based. Notification based systems simply require individuals to notify the state of internal movements, whereas permit-based systems require individuals to gain formal permission from the state to relocate.

18. Chinese economic and social institutions, based on the Soviet system, divide society into urban and rural systems managed separately (Chan and Wei

2019). The *hukou* is a key institution dividing the population into these two management systems.

19. China has four levels of subnational government: provincial, municipal (sometimes called prefectural), county, and township. This analysis uses *municipality* to refer to China's 333 prefectural-level cities (地级市), which include an urban core, rural counties, and in some cases, satellite county-level cities. I use *municipality* instead of *prefecture* because it aligns better with comparative cases.

20. See, for example, Wang (2005), which argues that the *hukou* allows the Chinese Communist Party to organize the economy by excluding individuals from redistribution, thus protecting state resources.

21. As Pan (2020) argues, government redistribution can be used to repress groups that threaten the regime.

22. Chengdu is larger than Xi'an (21 million versus 12 million people in 2020), has a higher proportion of migrants (41 percent of the total population compared with 34 percent), and it is more ethnically diverse (1.86 percent compared with 1.04 percent minority populations), all of which are traditional security concerns in China (NBS 2021a, c).

23. *Rights consciousness* refers to popular movements that target fundamental, ideological rights that individuals should have from the state and directly challenge the regime's order. *Rules consciousness* refers to accepting institutional rules as they are with mass movements focused on the application of those rules. See Li (2010) for a discussion of rights versus rules consciousness.

24. On market reform and *hukou* change in the cities of Beijing, Shenzhen, and Chongqing, see Young (2013).

25. Even modern democratic welfare states in Europe began as a means of preventing regime change (Esping-Andersen 1990). On welfare and the selectorate theory, see Bueno de Mesquita et al. (2003) and Haber (2006). On welfare as a tool to buy off challengers, see Haggard and Kaufman (2009); Knutsen and Rasmussen (2017); and Gandhi (2008).

26. On welfare and coercion, see Albertus, Fenner, and Slater (2018). On repression, see Pan (2020).

27. On who benefits from welfare, see Desai and Rudra (2019); Rudra (2008); Rudra and Tobin (2017); Huang (2020); and Yang (2021).

28. See, for example, Ansell (2008) and Wintrobe (1998).

29. This builds on work addressing mesolevel citizenship (Chung 2017) and multilevel citizenship (Maas 2017).

30. See, for example, Chan and Zhang (1999) and Chan, Liu, and Yang (1999). For a discussion of migration and more recent *hukou* policies, see Mu et al. (2021).

220   *Notes to Introduction and Chapter 1*

31. See, for example, Cheng and Selden (1994) and Cheng (1991).

32. See, for example, Chan (2009); Chan and Buckingham (2008); and Zhang (2008).

33. For discussion of social identity and *hukou*, see, for example, Afridi, Li, and Ren (2015).

34. The literature on wage and employment inequality is vast. For a selection of approaches, see Song (2014, 2015); Wu and Treiman (2007); Guo and Iredale (2004); and Liu (2005).

35. Many studies show the difference in access to welfare based on *hukou* registration, often using *hukou* as a control variable in service acquisition. For discussions that center *hukou* in the discussion of welfare, see Cai (2011); Yang (2021); Huang (2020); and Solinger (1999).

36. See, for example, Wallace (2014) and Wang (2004, 2005).

37. A related study by Young (2013) argues that *hukou* reform stems from marketization. Although marketization plays a role in development, this angle ignores the ways in which the central and local states use labor management long after dismantling the command economy.

38. See, for example, Young (2013).

39. For a discussion of interview protocols, locations, and coverage, see appendix B.

40. The county level is another possible alternative to the municipal level, because county governments have a history of manipulating local naturalization (Zweig 1992), but the county level misses the larger urban-rural balance most important at the municipal level.

Chapter 1

1. Political rights are not the only rights attached to democratic citizenship. T. H. Marshall's evolutionary theory posits that citizenship rights evolved from civil to political to social rights (Marshall 1950).

2. See, for example, the edited volumes on political citizenship in China by Goldman and Perry (2002a) and social citizenship in the Middle East by Meijer and Butenschøn (2017a).

3. The study of autocratic performance on legitimacy is largely overlooked in the literature. See Przeworski (2022).

4. Direct elections occur for village committees, neighborhood committees, and local People's Congresses in counties and townships (Goldman and Perry 2002b; Manion 2015; O'Brien and Li 2000).

5. Sometimes this is also known as nested citizenships (Faist 2001).

6. Federal systems are likely to develop weak local citizenship: in federal systems, individuals have both a local citizenship and a national citizenship (Miller

1995), and the relative importance of these two identities dictates the strength and importance of local citizenship (Keating 2009). Free movement of people and nationalized welfare states reduce the importance of local citizenship (Maas 2013), but as these distinctions increase, so too does the impact of local citizenship on social equality and cohesion.

7. The overview here draws from Cheng (1991), Wang (2005), and Zhang and Wang (2010).

8. For a review of studies of the *juntian* system, see Zhang (2015).

9. Some scholars also argue that the household register in the Tang dynasty was the first use of democratic institutions because individuals in the register elected bureaucratic leadership and because weak property rights developed. See, for example, Dutton (1992).

10. Land redistribution and household registration coevolved rather than *hukou* immediately bestowing lifetime land use rights. Some scholars argue that the *juntian* system was meant explicitly as a means of fully registering populations, whereas land distribution led to registration rather than the reverse. See, for example, Han (1990) and Zhao (2006).

11. The system implemented during the Republican Era is still the basis for the household registration system in Taiwan, which requires that individuals register with their local police station, but they can register in a new location after a short wait period. The system was never meant as a means of migration control (Chan 2010).

12. The Second Sino-Japanese War, from 1937 to 1945, devastated the central coast. The Chinese Civil War lasted from 1927 until 1949, after the formation of the new PRC in 1949, and resulted in six million casualties (Lynch 2010).

13. For an overview of the Soviet command economy, see Gregory (1990). Gregory argues that labor was allocated by the will of the people, whereby individuals chose their work and work location and population control was used only for protecting valuable assets, such as access to urban areas. But this ignores the role of the *propiska* in managing labor throughout the Soviet command economy era. Chan and Wei (2019) highlight how Soviet leaders explicitly extracted resources and value from the agricultural sector to support industrialization, and population controls through the *propiska* were a core tool for extraction.

14. On the use of the *hukou* system as a labor management system under the command economy, see Cheng and Selden (1994). For a detailed discussion of the Soviet system, which China emulated, see Chan and Wei (2019).

15. Large, state-owned farms also had *propiska*, but the bulk of rural residents were expressly left out of the Soviet internal citizenship system (Buckley 1995; Matthews 1993).

16. This echoes the contradictions found in the lead-up to Stalinist command economy policies and the implementation of the Soviet *propiska*. See Cheng and

222 *Notes to Chapter 1*

Selden (1994) for a discussion of the policies implementing the *hukou* system in the 1950s.

17. As Walder (1986) argues, the individual depended on the enterprise for life-sustaining resources in all contexts, but especially so in a communist regime. Because the work unit *was* the state in the Mao era in China, employment in this formal unit provided the individual's legitimacy as a citizen (16). This system developed into "iron rice bowl" welfare, funded by the state through state-owned enterprises, which provided for individuals' needs from cradle to grave (Fung 2001; Leung 1994; Walder 1986).

18. This labor market dualism institutionalized inequality in terms of getting a job and in welfare and redistribution (Gallagher 2015).

19. On the Great Leap Forward and failures of policy, see Yang (1996).

20. This distinction is even more evident when looking at other citizenship rights such as education. Unlike health care, social assistance, old-age care, and social insurance, which are explicitly granted to workers, education is a universal right granted to all citizens (1954 constitution, Article 94). On the development of urban citizenship, see, for example, Chan, Liu, and Yang (1999); Fan (2002); Guo (2014); He et al. (2010); Janoski (2014); Li, Li, and Chen (2010); Peng (2011); Sun and Fan (2011); Li Zhang (2012); and Zhang and Wang (2010).

21. For a detailed discussion of the Mao-era *hukou* system contrasted with imperial structures, see Han (1999).

22. Reform and Opening Up was Deng Xiaoping's major policy effort to move the Chinese economy away from the stagnated command economy of the Mao era and open up China to the global market to advance development.

23. Temporary residence permits were trialed in Wuhan in the early 1980s before becoming national policy (Solinger 1985).

24. The State Council discussed reforming the entire *hukou* system to one of permanent, temporary, and visitor *hukou* in 1993 (State Council 1993). Ultimately rejected because of cost, this reform would have eventually expanded access to local-government services for all migrants who settled in urban areas (Zhang 2003).

25. People with local-urban *hukou* could also be considered migrants by those looking at the experience of physically moving, as most studies of internal migration do. But in the Chinese context, a person who has moved and become a local-urban resident is usually no longer considered a migrant because that person has been integrated or settled into the *hukou* system. In my analysis, with its focus on internal exclusion, these populations are not considered migrants. For a detailed discussion of formal *hukou* institutional labels and how they overlap with the concept of migration, see appendix A.

Notes to Chapter 1 223

26. Changing *hukou* between rural locations during the Mao period was relatively easier, especially within a county. Often, in practice, this form of *hukou* naturalization needed approval from only the migrant's original agricultural commune and the commune the migrant was moving to, without higher-level approval (Interview 11150103).

27. In addition to the interview, this is based on a series of internal memos from the National Development and Reform Commission.

28. On policy experimentation as a form of institutional change, see Heilmann (2008a).

29. The system could be particularly abusive because many urban work units, both historically and today, hold their employees' formal paperwork. Many migrant workers cannot access their *hukou* because their identity documents are held by the factory where they work. Still to this day, *hukou* paperwork and passports are often centrally managed by employers in larger and state-owned firms (Interview 44150901). Migrant workers stopped on the street and asked for paperwork, through no fault of their own, cannot always produce it, resulting in excessive detention. For a report on human rights abuses in the Custody and Repatriation System, see Becquelin (2003).

30. On how the reform to the social service provision led to state retrenchment in health care, see Duckett (2011).

31. On the transition from state employment to informal employment, see Kuruvilla, Lee, and Gallagher (2011); Hughes (1998); and Leung (1994).

32. Solinger (2014) argues that a shift from plan-based management of resources allocated by the center to a scarcity mindset of how to redistribute finite resources caused rising inequalities in local-government redistribution, not identity-based discrimination against outsiders.

33. On direct elections at the local level, see Goldman and Perry (2002b); Manion (2015); and O'Brien and Li (2000).

34. On subnational welfare states in China, see Ratigan (2017). On variation in health care generosity, see Huang (2015).

35. On the 2001 reform and institutional change, see Chan and Buckingham (2008).

36. These provinces and the year of their announcement are Fujian (2001), Hunan (2002), Jiangsu (2005), Sichuan (2004), Hubei (2004), Henan (2006), Yunnan (2005, 2007), Shandong (2005), Liaoning (2005), Shaanxi (2005), and Jiangxi (2005) (various sources including *People's Daily* 2001, 2002, 2004a, 2004b, 2006, 2007; Xinhua News Agency 2002; *Sina News* 2005).

37. The decentralization of control over many *hukou* policies coincided with municipal governments having more direct control over urban districts and

224   *Notes to Chapter 1*

more coordinating power over counties. During the Mao era, urban district governments—prefectures (地区)—had relatively little power, largely acting as provincial outposts. During the 1980s and 1990s, however, the urbanization movement upgraded these governments from weak prefectural governments with little influence over rural areas to prefecture-level cities (市) with administrative power over the entire municipality, including coordinating power over counties (Chung and Lam 2004).

38. These cities and the year of implementation are Zhuhai (2003), Shantou (2003), Foshan (2003), Shenzhen (2004), Wuhai (2004), Karamay (2006), Fangchenggang (2010), and Jiayuguan (2011) (Ministry of Public Security 1999–2013).

39. This includes a homestead plot for housing and often agricultural land.

40. The role of land in *hukou* reform is discussed in more detail in chapter 2.

41. The 2014 reform also implemented a new city-size categorization. Towns (镇) are officially designated urban spaces within counties and city districts that do not constitute cities and should completely remove naturalization restrictions for migrants. Small cities, either county-level cities (县级市) or municipal-level cities (地级市), with a population of less than half a million should similarly remove naturalization restrictions. Medium-sized cities, between half a million and one million, should gradually phase out restrictions for *hukou* naturalization, targeting individuals who pay into social insurance for naturalization. Large cities are divided into two subgroups. Type I cities, with a population of one to three million, should set minimum lengths for naturalizations, and Type II cities, three to five million, should require permanent employment and maintain strict quotas for local naturalizations. Extralarge cities of five million or more should implement institutionalized naturalization policies that strictly limit naturalizations. Chapter 4 discusses these forms of naturalization in more detail.

42. The central government pushed small areas to naturalize rural populations with stable employment as early as the 1980s (Zweig 1992), and the 2014 reform reflects a continuation of this policy. See, for example, State Council (2011a); Central Committee of the Communist Party of China and State Council (2000); State Council (1984); State Council (1997); Ministry of Public Security (2001).

43. On the evolution of the *propiska*, especially its earlier stages of implementation, see Buckley (1995) and Hatcher and Thieme (2015).

44. On household registration in Central Asia, see Hatcher and Thieme (2015); Hojaqizi (2008); and Tukmadiyeva (2016).

45. Residence permits also require citizenship responsibilities previously required only of *hukou* holders. Those with a residence permit "shall fulfill their civil obligations prescribed by the State and local regions including military service and participation in militia organizations" (State Council 2014c, paragraph 10, official translation).

Notes to Chapters 1 and 2 225

46. The phrase "new-type urbanization" appears as early as 2007 in an article in the CCP's *People's Daily*. Condemning the pollution, crowding, and unequal development of urban spaces, the article reports the then dean of Jiangsu Academy of Social Sciences, Song Linfei, calling for a new type of urbanization that stresses moderate accumulation, sustainable development, and universal guarantees (Bao and Xu 2007).

47. The 2014 reform continued *hukou* as an information gathering mechanism. *Hukou* reform should be used to collect information on "labor employment, education, income, social security, housing, credit, public health, family planning, taxation, marriage, nationality, etc.," through national information systems to support "population development strategies and policies, and to provide support for population service and management" (State Council 2014c, paragraph 11).

48. The other dramatic peaks in health insurance enrollment show the introduction of residence-based insurance programs and the nationwide push for universal access to health insurance by 2009.

49. Because urban populations have a low natural growth rate, many localities have declining school age populations. An increase in school enrollment is due either to growth in the population, which has been slow, or to allowing migrant children to attend schools in urban centers.

50. On multilevel citizenship, see Maas (2017), who distinguishes state citizenship from local citizenship: state citizenship is defined by birthright citizenship, and municipal, or local, citizenship is defined by residency (661). He does so to distinguish hierarchies: state citizenship is more definitive and closer to the general conceptions of citizenship. But in China, local citizenship is also a birthright, giving this form of citizenship more importance in implementation of citizenship.

Chapter 2

1. Municipalities are also known as prefectures.

2. This is not to say that democracies do not also use citizenship institutions for unequal redistribution. All regime types can use citizenship institutions to manipulate redistribution. This inequality is particularly prevalent in nondemocracies.

3. This manipulation of welfare generosity across different groups within a polity is the focus of the authoritarian welfare state literature. See, for example, Albertus, Fenner, and Slater (2018); Huang (2020); Pan (2020); and Yang (2021). The distinction here is the manipulation, not of redistribution itself, but of eligibility through membership.

4. This aligns with the first rule in the "dictator's handbook" of minimizing the people whose support you depend on (Bueno de Mesquita and Smith 2011), but here I expand beyond the top elite and apply this logic to the broader society. On restricting resources as a means of organizing society, see Wang (2005).

226 Notes to Chapter 2

5. Broadly speaking, this is the logic behind the selectorate theory, in which autocrats must maintain a privileged winning coalition, who receive greater benefits from the autocrat for their support (Bueno de Mesquita et al. 2003). On redistribution to elite classes in general as a necessity of authoritarian longevity, see Huang (2020).

6. In many cases, the neglect of the countryside became active extraction and exploitation, with resources flowing from the countryside to the urban centers to support the centrally planned economy (Chan and Wei 2019).

7. In other words, authoritarian redistribution can be interpreted as including access to privileged spaces, such as urban centers. Autocrats restrict access to urban spaces because the concentration of people and resources can more easily facilitate regime-threatening movements (Wallace 2014).

8. For a discussion of the targeted populations, see Wang (2005) and Pan (2020). Using the *hukou* to exclude targeted populations is the reverse logic of Pan (2020), who describes redistribution through poverty alleviation programs that target troublemakers. This incongruency stems from different base populations. Pan's study focuses on recipients of the minimum livelihood subsidies, who are already in the local *hukou* system. My analysis looks at who can *become* local and gain access from the outside.

9. Xiao Han's parents were intellectuals, a class of people accused during the Cultural Revolution (1966–1976) of being antirevolutionary. During this time, many urban and eastern elites moved out of cities to avoid violence against them and their families.

10. Most recently, the central government has detained and arrested millions of minority citizens, primarily Muslim Uyghurs, to "reeducate" them, essentially stripping them of their citizenship rights. The government calls Islam an extremist-driven sickness to justify restricting them from citizenship rights (Zenz 2019).

11. Nominally democratic institutions are regularly used by autocrats to co-opt opposition parties (Gandhi 2008). Albertus, Fenner, and Slater (2018) call this "coercive distribution" because would-be challengers are coerced into supporting the regime through redistributive mechanisms.

12. As Pan (2020) argues, the mechanisms of authoritarian redistribution increase the state's reach into the lives of its recipients, allowing greater information gathering and surveillance, creating a means of repression.

13. According to Göbel (2021), approximately 42 percent of 74,425 protests reported in social media between 2013 and 2016 were labor protests, and migrant workers were one of the largest groups of participants.

14. On urban concentration of migrant workers and protest formation, see Becker (2014) and Chan and Ngai (2009).

Notes to Chapter 2 227

15. See Lee (2007) on variation in protest movement goals and their relation to the state.

16. Rentier states, which gain financial resources and power through natural resources and means not specific to development, are excluded from the scope of this argument.

17. This logic is similar to the idea of developmental citizenship, which ties the rights and responsibility of citizenship to engagement in economic life. See Kyung-Sup (2020) for more on developmental citizenship. However, the arguments presented here are broader than those outlined for developmental citizenship because of the focus on membership institutions rather than rights and the engagement with the state apparatus.

18. The developmental state engages with industries the state deems strategically important, aligning industrial policies with government-directed development goals. On the developmental state, see Johnson (1982) and Öniş (1991).

19. The 1954 constitution outlines social security, health, education, and old-age care for working populations. For more discussion of rights related to labor, see chapter 1.

20. For more on central planning and labor allocation, see Cheng and Selden (1994) and Zhang and Wang (2010).

21. Keeping family members out of the city was a key motivation behind the creation of weeklong holidays that would allow factory workers to visit family in the countryside (State Council 1957).

22. For an overview of early decentralization and the rise of local-government authority relative to the central government, see Wei (2001).

23. Local economic development policy depends on a wide variety of factors. On the proliferation of economic policies, see Ma and Cui (2002). Local state corporatism occurs when the local state treats industries as part of the local whole, creating a corporation organization locally, representing the blend of market and state forces present for much of China's economic reform period (Oi 1995). Local-leader backgrounds influence the types of development policies they pursue (Donaldson 2009). The famous Wenzhou model uses existing market towns to encourage private entrepreneurship (Liu 1992).

24. For a review of China's fiscal decentralization, see Wang and Ma (2014).

25. On urban size and social stability concerns, see Wallace (2014).

26. The CDR became a commission under the Central Committee in 2018, but at the time of *hukou* reform it was a leading small group.

27. On the strategic value of flexibility and ambiguity in policy making, see Ang (2016).

28. On black *hukou*, see Vortherms (2019).

228 Notes to Chapter 2

29. Zhang Gaoli is now infamous for an alleged affair with and assault of the tennis star Peng Huai.

30. Before joining the central-level government, he was a member of the Standing Committee for Guangdong Province (1993–1997), governor and eventually party secretary of Shandong Province (2001–2007), and party secretary of Tianjin Province (2007–2012).

31. The Ministries of Personnel and Labor and Social Security were merged in 2008.

32. Two provinces, Beijing and Tibet, took an additional year to publish *hukou* policies in response to the 2014 reforms and published theirs in 2016. By 2020, all provinces had announced some form of provincial policy.

33. The decentralization of control over many *hukou* policies coincided with the rise of municipal governments' direct control over urban districts and coordinating power over counties. During the Mao era, urban district governments—prefectures (地区)—had relatively little power, largely acting as provincial outposts. During the 1980s and 1990s, however, the urbanization movement upgraded these weak prefectural governments with little influence over rural areas to prefecture-level cities (市) with administrative power over the entire municipality, including coordinating power over counties (Chung and Lam 2004).

34. It is also interesting to note that the provincial policy states a higher population in Harbin than any other source: 4.8 million in the urban center. Every statistical yearbook puts that population at around 4.7 million.

35. See, for example, Zhejiang Provincial Government (2015).

36. Local officials are evaluated annually using the Target Responsibility System, which provides quantified targets across a range of economic and social indicators. The evaluations are written one bureaucratic level above—municipal officials' evaluations are written by the provincial-level Organization Department (组织部) and provincial officials' evaluations are written by the Central Organization Department. This nested level of accountability ensures centralization of political authority and is the mechanism for central-level priorities influencing local-level policies. On the system and the *nomenklatura* system more generally, see Burns (1987); Landry (2008); Manion (1985); and Zuo (2015).

37. I collected municipal government policies via Peking University's law database and from the municipal government websites themselves.

38. For more discussion on this, see chapter 4.

39. Municipal governments manage the county-level governments below them, which are primarily responsible for day-to-day welfare distribution such as health and education programs. Municipalities must hold in reserve a fund to cover the costs of social welfare to cover any county-level shortcomings (Liu, Vortherms, and Hong 2017).

Notes to Chapters 2 and 3 229

40. In the Target Responsibility System, protests add significant negative points, becoming a veto, on a local leader's evaluation. See, for example, Zuo (2015).

41. In many cities, a local *hukou* is required to purchase a home. Additionally, having multiple *hukou*s allows individuals to hide and move assets (Kao 2013).

42. On health insurance reform, for example, see Liu, Vortherms, and Hong (2017) and Huang (2020). On education, see Friedman (2022a).

43. In Beijing, for example, the Human Resources and Social Security Administration instructed city-district governments to allocate *hukou* transfer quotas to firms on the basis of sector, economic prospects, tax contribution, and employment contribution to support key sectors (Beijing Human Resources and Social Security Administration 2018).

44. On *hukou* as a form of job benefit, see Vortherms and Liu (2022).

45. Each pathway is enumerated in detail in chapter 3.

46. Globalization decreases local wage competition by creating an external market for labor. More outwardly oriented economies benefit from investment in human capital because there are higher returns to human capital investment (Ansell 2008).

Chapter 3

1. See, for example, the comparison between *hukou* and Canadian permanent residency in Ho (2011).

2. I use *administrative burdens* in a manner similar to burdens related to "compliance costs," as defined by Herd and Moynihan (2018), who argue that administrative burdens can reduce access to citizenship rights, such as voting in their study of the United States, and have significant distributional consequences.

3. Caste systems are usually defined as hereditary systems of social stratification characterized by social hierarchies of group identities often related to occupation and supported by endogamy. The *hukou* is hereditary, inherently hierarchical, and historically related to family occupation—agricultural versus nonagricultural. It lacks the practice of endogamy.

4. Comparable numbers are not available for rural residents, because of how the China Household Income Project Survey (CHIPS) questions are worded. Because there are essentially no transfers to rural *hukou*, it is likely that this 80 percent figure underestimates the number of people who have their birth-registered *hukou*, because all rural residents would also fall into this category (NBS, *China Household Income Survey Project* 2002).

5. See chapter 1 for a discussion of this process.

6. The data were collected in 2016 to allow time for local governments to publish their regulations regarding *hukou* policies after the 2014 national reform. Autonomous municipalities are underrepresented in the sample because of missing data. See appendix B for a more detailed discussion.

230 *Notes to Chapter 3*

7. Zhang, Wang, and Lu (2019), for example, investigate high-end employment, other employment, housing purchase, and investment pathways, leaving out residence- and family-based transfers.

8. In Zhang, Wang, and Lu's (2019) thorough analysis, the sample is limited to 120 cities. Liu and Xu (2016) include 63 cities in their analysis. Zhang and Tao (2012), although compiling a more comprehensive list of naturalization pathways, include only 45 cities in a nonrepresentative sample.

9. One limitation of this design, however, is the time-limited element. By focusing on formal government policies rather than implementation of those policies, Zhang, Wang, and Lu (2019) are able to build a dynamic measure that captures policy changes over time.

10. See, for example, Beine et al. (2015) for a discussion of international naturalization regimes measured by entry tracks.

11. A quota for total immigrant visas may create a wait, but this is separate from country-specific quotas.

12. Children needing care implies adult children with disabilities or children being adopted (Interview 44150701). There are other, less standard, ways of transferring family members. In most municipalities, adult children requiring care can transfer to a relative's location. Family members present a certificate from a community welfare office saying the person needs care, and that entitles the adult child to a transfer. Generally, the legal regulation of these transfers has little variation. Some municipalities, including Shanghai, allow grandparents to transfer their grandchildren, similar to parents transferring their children, creating greater right of return for older Shanghai families.

13. For example, in 2016, Beijing required spouses to be over forty-five to transfer. These age limits reduce the potential demand on local-government resources. Women are more likely to move to their husbands' *hukou* location than vice versa, and women are eligible for pensions after the age of fifty-five. Beijing's spousal *hukou* regulation, written in the late 1990s, required individuals seeking a local pension to have paid into the local pension system for at least ten years locally, and benefits—and qualifying work years—were not transferable. A woman who became a Beijing *hukou* holder at forty-five and who was unable to find formal employment before transferring *hukou* was significantly less likely to be eligible for a locally provided pension. Similarly, local governments do not want to add additional children to their school system. A woman transferring her registration at the age of forty-five is less likely to have school age children transferring with her.

14. An analogous system is the four tiers of nursing in the United States: certified nursing assistants, licensed practical nurses, registered nurses, and advanced-practice registered nurses. Each level denotes a higher skill, education, and experience level, and all are regulated through formal credentialing practices.

Notes to Chapter 3   231

15. This framework of understanding skilled-labor migration is based on Papademetriou and Sumption (2011).

16. Most programs specify applicants must be within two years of graduation if they include college education. In Suizhou, Hubei, for example, employment-based transfers are available only to employees who have been employed for two years or less.

17. For a systematic comparison of the early points models, see Zhang and Wang (2010).

18. In Shenzhen, applicants summoned to the police station to prove their innocence lose eighty points per incident.

19. Guangdong highlights the importance of focusing on active policies. Points systems began in Guangdong and, eventually, every city announced a program. By 2015, however, some cities, such as Shanwei, canceled their programs within years of their implementation. Descriptions of the points systems can be found on older versions of the municipal security bureau websites but have since been taken down.

20. For a discussion of investment-based immigration around the world, see Xu, El-Ashram, and Gold (2015).

21. US Citizenship and Immigration Service, "EB-5 Immigrant Investor Program," March 1, 2023, https://www.uscis.gov/eb-5.

22. The pilot Venture Capital program requires a Can$2 billion investment in a high-risk Immigrant Investor Venture Capital fund (https://www.canada.ca/en/immigration-refugees-citizenship/services/immigrate-canada/immigrant-investor-venture-capital/eligibility.html). Initially, under the short-lived Immigrant Investor program in Canada, individuals were required to invest Can$800,000 to be used by province and territorial governments (www.canada.ca/en/immigration-refugees-citizenship/services/immigrate-canada//investors.html).

23. See, for example, Shanghai Municipal Government (1993). Rural *hukou*s were traditionally stamped in black ink and urban *hukou*s were stamped in red or green ink up until 2000, when the usefulness of color disaggregation was mediated by digital records (Wang 2005).

24. Since 2016, however, this rural advantage no longer exists because of the national unconditional two-child policy.

25. In my conversations with officials, quotas were regularly mentioned as upper bounds on the number of transfers allowed but not as an explicit requirement, so they should be seen as ceilings rather than floors.

26. Reports conflict on the actual number of transfers in Shenzhen. According to official sources, all applicants with more than one hundred points received transfers, which would put the figure above 200,000, based on lists of transfer applicants posted on the internet. But this statement masks later reviews of

232 *Notes to Chapters 3 and 4*

applicants governed by unwritten rules that reduce actual transfers, such as people with disabilities being rejected. Statistics provided by the Guangdong Provincial Statistics Bureau suggest approximately 160,000 migrants transferred their *hukou* to Shenzhen in 2014 (Guangdong Provincial Government 2016).

27. At best, cities announce their quotas or targets for one specific pathway to citizenship, such as Guangzhou's six thousand points for transfers or Beijing's Education Bureau quotas for college graduates. These posted quotas are neither widely available across cities nor comprehensive within one location. Some cities in Guangdong do publish their transfers, such as Guangzhou, which reports local rural transfers to urban *hukou*.

28. The household income survey is a nationally representative sample, which provides a random sample of the total population. Although its results are illustrative of *hukou* transfer types, it should not be considered nationally representative of *hukou* changers because the sample was not specifically designed to identify people who had changed their *hukou*.

29. A detailed methodology is available in appendix B.

30. A principal component analysis also suggests a master index combining all the measures is inappropriate, because the primary principal explains only 25 percent of the overall variation. See appendix B.

31. This is based on a chi-square distribution test; chi-square: 20.9721, Pr = 0.000.

Chapter 4

1. As discussed in chapter 3, many provinces simply stopped reporting the number of nonagricultural *hukou* in 2014, preventing me from extending this analysis in a nationally representative way after 2014.

2. On the securitization of migration, see Huysmans (2000).

3. Chinese cities are unofficially classified into tiers based on administrative rank, population, and economic development. See Sun (2017) for a 2017 ranking of cities by tier.

4. Not all cities maintain this hard line. One notable exception is Chengdu. It commissioned a three-year study of the costs of urban-rural integration, which concluded the government would be able to integrate services (Chengdu Party Committee of Urban and Rural Work 2012).

5. See the edited volume by Chung (1999) for a discussion on how variation in development is driven by these sets of actors; Heilmann (2008b) on experimentation in policy making; and Rithmire (2015), Shen and Tsai (2016), and Yang (1997) on subnational development strategies. For a comparative discussion, see Sinha (2005).

Notes to Chapter 4 233

6. For a discussion on the central-local power balance and how economic policies decentralize even with centralized political power, see Yang (2006) and Cai and Treisman (2011).

7. For a broad discussion on foreign investment and reforms, see Malesky (2009). For a discussion of FDI and its impact on capital and labor policies, see Chen (2018) and Gallagher (2011).

8. *Foreignness* is defined here in the international context. Within one state, however, this openness can also be domestic, from one region to another. The same logic holds, that investment from a developed region to an underdeveloped region can create incentives for human capital development. Openness to capital from other municipalities would work similarly to the two mechanisms linking foreign capital and labor incentives, but the effect would be smaller. For example, a firm from Shanghai opening a branch in internal Henan would provide "foreign" technology from the technologically more advanced Shanghai. That foreignness is difficult to measure is an area for future research.

9. Because there is no free market for land, local governments had monopoly power on converting rural land to urban and construction land. By converting rural land to construction land, the local government captured significant financial gains from construction companies building on the land while compensating rural farmers very little for their taken land. For a discussion of the rise of rural land markets, see Cai (2012) and Cai et al. (2021).

10. The law was subsequently revised in 1988 and 1998.

11. On the evolution of land markets, see Ho and Lin (2003) and Rithmire (2015).

12. See, for example, Rithmire (2013a, 2015).

13. See, for example, Guo (2001); Lin et al. (2018); and Sargeson (2013).

14. For more discussion of the land-for-*hukou* process, see chapter 5.

15. Variation in agricultural mechanization is a result of both government policy and appropriateness of specific crop production for mechanized cultivation. For a regional analysis on mechanization by agricultural zone, see Feng, Liu, and Qu (2019).

16. Fiscal transfers can be capacity-balancing transfers, which provide budgetary support for central-level policies that increase expenditures, such as wage increases for civil servants (Huang and Chen 2012).

17. For a discussion of the evolution of poverty alleviation in China, see Guo, Zhou, and Liu (2019).

18. Local governments have long used the complicated system of measuring population to spin local statistics in their favor. Localities that wish to emphasize economic growth per capita, for example, may use only their *hukou* population in per capita estimates, leaving out hundreds of thousands of migrant workers whose

234   Notes to Chapters 4 and 5

de facto residence is in the city (Chan and Wang 2008g). Excluding a key portion of the population from estimation makes per capita figures more impressive.

19. Because of a significant missing data, rural machinery use is measured in 2012, because this is the last year that most provinces reported the data. After 2013, the indicator is not available for municipalities in eight provinces.

20. Additionally, a principal component analysis suggested that combining the indexes into a master index was inappropriate because of high variation across indicators.

21. All models also control for FDI per GDP, land price, migrant stock (quartiles), GDP, and regional indicators.

22. Growth in city-center construction land is also correlated with more open residence-based naturalization policies. As land taking increases, more construction land becomes available because the local government must convert agricultural land to construction land to develop it. When more construction land becomes available, naturalization rules loosen, lowering barriers to naturalization. This correlation loses statistical significance, however, when economic controls are included in the model.

23. Based on two sample t-tests with unequal variance, the low-skilled index is 10 percent more open ($p < .001$), the family index is 3 percent more open ($p < .1$), and the investment index is 7 percent more open ($p < .001$). See appendix B for t-test means and results.

24. See chapter 3 for a description of the strengths and weaknesses of these estimates. These data do not include urban upgrading, in which changed administrative boundaries shift the population from rural to urban, creating an expected upward bias in overall estimates.

25. See appendix C for full results.

Chapter 5

1. According to the 2014 reform, municipalities and county governments write policies in line with their economic and social conditions, to be approved by provincial governments.

2. Six provinces, Tianjin, Zhejiang, Hubei, Hunan, Guangdong, and Chongqing, state that individuals should be free to choose where they live but do not mention voluntarism in *hukou* naturalization. Five provinces, Beijing, Heilongjiang, Shanghai, Sichuan, and Gansu, make no mention of respecting the will of the masses.

3. In particular, the National Health Commission ran an annual China Migrant Dynamics Survey from 2009 to 2018 (National Health Commission 2021).

4. On assimilation and the naturalization decision, see also DeVoretz and Pivnenko (2005); Diehl and Blohm (2003); Dronkers and Vink (2012); Logan,

Oh, and Darrah (2012); Nam and Kim (2012); Peters, Vink, and Schmeets (2015); Portes and Curtis (1987); Portes and Mozo (1985); and Zimmermann et al. (2009).

5. Most state-owned enterprises have quotas for local employees, and many smaller businesses hire only local *hukou* holders because of perceived stability compared with unreliable, unstable migrant workers who might leave at any time (Interviews 11160101, 11150306).

6. These results align with related survey experiments measuring the impact of *hukou* on wages in different cities. See Vortherms and Liu (2022).

7. On the impact of these rights in the international setting, see Bevelander and DeVoretz (2008); FitzGerald and Cuesta-Leiva (1997); Jasso and Rosenzweig (1986); Kahanec and Tosun (2009); and Nam and Kim (2012).

8. Shanghai allows grade school children to attend public schools, regardless of *hukou* status, for example. The 2014 "Opinion on Further Promotion of *Hukou* Reform" explicitly mentions education as a right all migrant children should have. As of 2022 there is no clear evidence if and where this reform has been implemented.

9. See, for example, college quotas by major and province, available on universities' websites.

10. On the gap between urban and rural education systems, see work by Rozelle (2020).

11. Hyperlocal naturalization, in which location does not change but *hukou* type changes from rural to urban or from rural to resident *hukou*, was the only type of local naturalization that did not require relinquishing land (Interview 44120802). Any *hukou* naturalization that crossed municipal or even at times county boundaries required relinquishing land use rights because the new location's municipal government "had no power over other places to protect land use rights" (Interview 44131201).

12. This came up in every interview on the subject with every bureaucrat and policy maker.

13. The 2014 reform stresses that migrants should not be stripped of their land use rights. Close readings of provincial policies indicate that migrants should not have to give up contracted land before the contract runs out. These protections might not hold for land redistributions, which occur regularly.

14. This effect holds regardless of how pensions are measured—as any pension, employment-based pension, or residence pension.

15. After analyzing 874 advertisements at the Shanghai marriage market, *The Paper* (www.thepaper.cn) reported 53 percent of ads included information on *hukou*. A minority of ads required *hukou*, and nonlocal women sought local men more than the reverse (*The Paper* 2018).

16. For more discussion on policies to explicitly restrict access to urban places, see chapter 1.

236 *Notes to Chapter 5, Conclusion, Appendix A, and Appendix B*

17. To evaluate the potential role of language and identity, I limited the Changsha sample to migrants from within Hunan. Within Hunan, there are six major dialects (Chen and Bao 2007). Of Hunan migrants in Changsha, those who come from counties that primarily speak the same dialect as Changsha are no more or less likely to apply for a new *hukou*.

18. This is a benefit of the contingent valuation survey over alternative valuations such as using the value of government services to identify the value of *hukou*.

19. The new economic theory of migration posits that out-migration is a household diversification strategy. Remittances sent home buffer agricultural families from crop failures (Massey et al. 1993).

20. Having a younger sibling is not correlated with buying for oneself but is with buying for family (marginal effect: 0.12, $p < .01$). Having an older sibling reduces the desire to buy for oneself (marginal effect: –0.09, $p < .01$) or for family (marginal effect: –0.08, $p < .10$).

Conclusion

1. *People's Daily* (2018a).

2. Xinhua News Agency (2018b).

3. The categories were based on registered and de facto residence: permanent resident, resident of the same province but different district, long-term temporary resident, and short-term temporary resident.

4. Circular 6-TT/BNV(C13) (1997), https://thukyluat.vn/vb/thong-tu-6-tt -bnv-c13-nam-1997-thuc-hien-nghi-dinh-51-cp-1997-ve-viec-dang-ky-va-quan-ly -ho-khau-do-bo-noi-vu-ban-hanh-9f26.html.

5. See, for example, Light (2012) and Matthews (1993).

6. On whether the *propiska* affected urbanization, see Buckley (1995) and Gang and Stuart (1999).

7. For an account of the forced removal of people from white-controlled areas to Bantustans, see Desmond (1971).

Appendix A

1. See NBS, *Migrant Monitoring Report* (various years).

2. See NBS, *Migrant Monitoring Report* (various years).

Appendix B

1. Policy innovations include the implementation of the temporary resident card in Wuhan, as described in Solinger (1985), or the points-based systems in Shanghai and Guangdong, as described in Zhang (2012).

2. I base my assertion on population data from each province's statistics bureau.

3. The authors state that the sample is representative because it covers all provinces of mainland China, except Tibet, but the sample is not randomly chosen.

4. In some cases, *hukou* policy varied below the municipal level, and the urban core and rural peripheral counties had different policies. When these variations occurred, I coded the policies for the urban core. This standard arose from the concept of measuring what it takes to get full urban status rather than a potentially less valuable status in a smaller periphery location.

5. Children not born in a hospital and therefore lacking a birth certificate must take additional legal measures to secure a *hukou*.

6. In Yibin, Sichuan, for example, children born out of wedlock must have three witnesses attesting to paternity before an unmarried father can register a newborn.

7. Families must present the family planning certificate (生育证) to the Family Planning Bureau before starting a *hukou* transfer. A standard birth certificate (准生证) is obtained before the birth to prove it meets family planning limits. Almost all *hukou* transfer policies require the family planning certificate, an additional step in the transfer process. Fewer than five municipalities stated that, when transferring children, the child's standard birth certificate was needed, which requires one fewer step than for children born within the limitations of the one-child policy. Although that policy has changed to a three-child policy, past violators have not been absolved, and having more than three children is still considered out of plan. Additionally, second children born too soon after the first one are also considered out of plan and could be denied a *hukou* (Vortherms 2019).

8. An example is proof of payment for hospital charges related to birth, such as required in Changchun, Jilin.

9. Proof of housing often includes property deeds (房产证); if there are no deeds to the property, individuals must provide the house purchase contract and the formal tax receipts (购房合同, 发票原件). If the house was purchased with a loan, individuals must also include the bank contract for the loan with the bank's formal stamp.

10. For example, a person with a college degree and one year of work experience would have the bureaucratic rank of junior. After ten years, the person achieves the advanced rank.

11. The primary source for this was a website called China Rental Data (租房大数据). The website moved to City Real Estate Web (城市房产网) (http://www.cityhouse.cn/city.html).

12. This measurement has two key weaknesses. First, population data in China is notoriously of poor quality. I use data from CEIC that reports *hukou* population. Local governments have been known to misrepresent their real population numbers, and some provinces report registered long-term residents instead of

238   *Notes to Appendix B*

hukou population in other publications. Guangdong, for example, reports long-term resident population in all versions of Chinese Population Statistical Materials. Because no documentation verifies the use of either *hukou* population or other population measure, I randomly checked approximately 5 percent of the city-year observations with the city yearbook data, which reports *hukou* population more frequently than city statistical yearbooks. Second, determining net natural growth rate using the reported natural growth rate only estimates the total number of people added to the population by natural growth, which can introduce error. The calculation for the natural growth rate used by the central Statistics Bureau is based on "average population," although the Statistics Bureau does not state how average population is calculated. This introduces a small amount of measurement error in the estimation.

13. Additionally, I remove outlier observations when the reported population change varies by more than two standard deviations from the year's average across all municipalities. The results remain the same.

14. Fujian, for example, had nearly province-wide fluctuations consistent with overestimation of urban-rural population integration, although the negative correction the year after was not as dramatic as in Wuhan.

15. A detailed discussion of survey methodology is on my website under "Health and *Hukou* Survey," http://www.samanthavortherms.com/data-1.

16. There have been limited opportunities to purchase *hukou* since the late 1980s. But not all cities allow the sale of *hukou*, there is no transparency of prices where it does exist, and because of the monopoly power of the state, prices do not necessarily reflect demand from consumers (*Inside China Mainland* 1992).

17. See, for example, Bishop and Heberlein (1979) and Diener, O'Brien, and Gafni (1998) for reviews.

18. The dichotomous-choice contingent-value survey presents the most accurate and unbiased WTP estimation. To reduce bias from the hypothetical nature of the question, the design followed the recommendations of Arrow et al. (1993).

Works Cited

Acemoglu, Daron. 2003. "Patterns of Skill Premia." *Review of Economic Studies* 70 (2): 199–230.

Acemoglu, Daron, and James A. Robinson. 2006. *Economic Origins of Dictatorship and Democracy*. New York: Cambridge University Press.

Afridi, Farzana, Sherry Xin Li, and Yufei Ren. 2015. "Social Identity and Inequality: The Impact of China's Hukou System." *Journal of Public Economics* 123: 17–29.

Aiyede, Emmanuel Remi. 2009. "The Political Economy of Fiscal Federalism and the Dilemma of Constructing a Developmental State in Nigeria." *International Political Science Review* 30 (3): 249–269.

Albertus, Michael, Sofia Fenner, and Dan Slater. 2018. *Coercive Distribution*. Cambridge: Cambridge University Press.

Andreas, Joel, and Shaohua Zhan. 2016. "Hukou and Land: Market Reform and Rural Displacement in China." *Journal of Peasant Studies* 43 (4): 798–827.

Ang, Yuen Yuen. 2016. *How China Escaped the Poverty Trap*. Ithaca, NY: Cornell University Press.

Ansell, Ben W. 2008. "Traders, Teachers, and Tyrants: Democracy, Globalization, and Public Investment in Education." *International Organization* 62 (2): 289–322.

Arrow, Kenneth, Robert Solow, Paul R. Portney, Edward E. Leamer, Roy Radner, and Howard Schuman. 1993. "Report of the NOAA Panel on Contingent Valuation." *Federal Register* 58: 4601–4614.

Azimov, U., and T. Azimov. 2009. "Discrimination against Internal Migrants in the Kyrgyz Republic: Analysis and Recommendations." Bishkek, Kyrgyzstan: Social Research Center (American University of Central Asia).

240 Works Cited

Banister, Judith. 1987. *China's Changing Population*. Stanford, CA: Stanford University Press.

Bao, Hongjun, and Zhifeng Xu. 2007. "New-Type Urbanization: Far from 'Metropolitan Disease.'" *People's Daily*, March 10.

Becker, Jeffrey. 2014. *Social Ties, Resources, and Migrant Labor Contention in Contemporary China: From Peasants to Protesters*. Lanham, MD: Lexington Books.

Becquelin, Nicolas. 2003. "Enforcing the Rural-Urban Divide: Use of Custody and Repatriation Detention Triples in 10 Years." *Human Rights in China*. Accessed March 2018. https://www.hrichina.org/en/content/4682.

Beijing Human Resources and Social Security Administration. 2018. "Beijing shi renli ziyuan he shehui baozhang ju guanyu yinfa 'Beijingshi yinjin fei beijing sheng yuan biyesheng gongzuo libanfa' de tongzhi" 北京市人力资源和社会保障局关于印发《北京市引进非北京生源毕业生工作管理办法》的通知 [Notice from the Beijing Municipal Human Resources and Social Security Bureau on the issuance of the "Beijing Management Measures for the Introduction of Graduates from Non-Beijing Sources"]. Beijing.

Beine, Michel, Anna Boucher, Brian Burgoon, Mary Crock, Justin Gest, Michael Hiscox, Patrick McGovern, Hillel Rapoport, Joep Schaper, and Eiko Thielemann. 2015. "Comparing Immigration Policies: An Overview from the IMPALA Database." *International Migration Review* 50 (4): 827–863.

Berman, Eli, and Stephen Machin. 2000. "Skill Biased Technology Transfer around the World." *Oxford Review of Economic Policy* 16 (3): 12–22.

Bevelander, Pieter, and Don J. DeVoretz. 2008. "The Economics of Citizenship: A Synthesis." In *The Economics of Citizenship*, edited by Pieter Bevelander and Don J. DeVoretz, 155–168. Sweden: Malmö University.

Bishop, Richard C., and Thomas A. Heberlein. 1979. "Measuring Values of Extra market Goods: Are Indirect Measures Biased?" *American Journal of Agricultural Economics* 61 (5): 926–930.

Blaydes, Lisa. 2011. *Elections and Distributive Politics in Mubarak's Egypt*. New York: Cambridge University Press.

Blitz, Brad K. 2007. "Decentralisation, Citizenship and Mobility: Residency Restrictions and Skilled Migration in Moscow." *Citizenship Studies* 11 (4): 383–404.

Boix, Carles. 2003. *Democracy and Redistribution*. Cambridge: Cambridge University Press.

Boyraz, Cemil. 2019. "The Alevi Question and the Limits of Citizenship in Turkey." *British Journal of Middle Eastern Studies* 46 (5): 767–780.

Brown, Junius F. 2021. "Development and Citizenship in the Chinese 'Mayor's Mailbox' System." *Asian Survey* 61 (3): 443–472.

Brubaker, Rogers. 1992. *Citizenship and Nationhood in France and Germany*. Cambridge, MA: Harvard University Press.

Buckley, Cynthia. 1995. "The Myth of Managed Migration: Migration Control and Market in the Soviet Period." *Slavic Review* 54 (4): 896–916.

Bueno de Mesquita, Bruce, and Alastair Smith. 2011. *The Dictator's Handbook: Why Bad Behavior Is Almost Always Good Politics*. New York: Public Affairs.

Bueno de Mesquita, Bruce, Alastair Smith, Randolph M. Siverson, and James D. Morrow. 2003. *The Logic of Political Survival*. Cambridge, MA: MIT Press.

Burns, John P. 1987. "China's Nomenklatura System." *Problems of Communism* 36 (5): 36–51.

Byler, Darren. 2021. *Terror Capitalism: Uyghur Dispossession and Masculinity in a Chinese City*. Durham, NC: Duke University Press.

Cai, Fang. 2011. "Hukou System Reform and Unification of Rural-Urban Social Welfare." *China and World Economy* 19 (3): 33–48.

Cai, Hongbin, and Daniel Treisman. 2011. "Did Government Decentralization Cause China's Economic Miracle?" *World Politics* 58 (4): 505–535.

Cai, Meina. 2012. "Land-Locked Development: The Local Political Economy of Institutional Change in China." PhD diss., Political Science, University of Wisconsin, Madison.

———. 2016. "Land for Welfare in China." *Land Use Policy* 55: 1–12.

Cai, Meina, Jianyong Fan, Chunhui Ye, and Qi Zhang. 2021. "Government Debt, Land Financing and Distributive Justice in China." *Urban Studies* 58 (11): 2329–2347.

Carson, Richard T., and Theodore Groves. 2007. "Incentive and Informational Properties of Preference Questions." *Environmental and Resource Economics* 37 (1): 181–210.

Central Committee. 1980. "Zhonggong zhongyang guanyu kongzhi woguo renkou zeng chang wenti zhi quanti gongchandang yuan gongqingtuan yuan de gongkaixin" 中共中央关于控制我国人口增长问题致全体共产党员共青团员的公开信 [An open letter from the Central Committee of the Communist Party of China to all members of the Communist Party of China and the Communist Youth League on the issue of controlling population growth in China]. Beijing.

———. 2000. "Zhonggong zhongyang guanyu zhiding guomin jingji he shehui fazhan di shi ge wu nian jihua de jianyi" 中共中央关于制定国民经济和社会发展第十个五年计划的建议 [Proposals for the Tenth Five-Year Plan]. Beijing.

———. 2005. "Zhonggong zhongyang guanyu zhiding guomin jingji he shehui fazhan di shiyi ge wu nian jihua de jianyi" 中共中央关于制定国民经济和社会发展第十一个五年计划的建议 [Proposals for the Eleventh Five-Year Plan]. Beijing.

Central Committee and State Council. 2000. "Guanyu cujin xiao chengzhen jiankang fazhan de ruogan yijian" 关于促进小城镇健康发展的若干意见 [Recommendations on accelerating the healthy development of small cities and towns]. Beijing.

Chan, Chris King-Chi, and Pun Ngai. 2009. "The Making of a New Working Class? A Study of Collective Actions of Migrant Workers in South China." *China Quarterly* 198: 287–303.

Chan, Kam Wing. 2004. "Zhongguo huji zhidu gaige he chengxiang renkou qianyi" 中国户籍制度改革和城乡人口迁移 [Reform to China's household registration system and rural to urban population migration]. *Zhongguo laodong jingjixue* 中国劳动经济学 [China Labor Economics], 108–123.

———. 2007. "Misconceptions and Complexities in the Study of China's Cities: Definitions, Statistics, and Implications." *Eurasian Geography and Economics* 48 (4): 383–412.

———. 2009. "The Chinese Hukou System at 50." *Eurasian Geography and Economics* 50 (2): 197–221.

———. 2010. "The Household Registration System and Migrant Labor in China: Notes on a Debate." *Population and Development Review* 36 (2): 357–364.

———. 2014. "Achieving Comprehensive Hukou Reform in China." Paulson Institute Memorandum. Paulson Institute.

———. 2021. "What the 2020 Chinese Census Tells Us about Progress in Hukou Reform." *China Brief* 21 (15): 11–17.

Chan, Kam Wing, and Will Buckingham. 2008. "Is China Abolishing the Hukou System?" *China Quarterly* 195: 582–606.

Chan, Kam Wing, Ta Liu, and Yunyan Yang. 1999. "Hukou and Non-hukou Migrations in China: Comparisons and Contrasts." *International Journal of Population Geography* 5: 425–448.

Chan, Kam Wing, and Man Wang. 2008. "Remapping China's Regional Inequalities, 1990–2006: A New Assessment of de Facto and De Jure Population Data." *Eurasian Geography and Economics* 49 (1): 21–55.

Chan, Kam Wing, and Yanning Wei. 2019. "Two Systems in One Country: The Origin, Functions, and Mechanisms of the Rural-Urban Dual System in China." *Eurasian Geography and Economics* 60 (4): 422–454.

Chan, Kam Wing, and Li Zhang. 1999. "The Hukou System and Rural-Urban Migration in China: Processes and Changes." *China Quarterly* (160): 818–855.

Changsha City Government. 2017. "Zhangsha shi qingnian rencai zhu meng gongcheng shishi xize" 长沙市青年人才筑梦工程实施细则 [Detailed rules for the implementation of the dream building project for young talents in Changsha]. Changsha.

Chen, Chih-Jou Jay. 2020. "Peasant Protests over Land Seizures in Rural China." *Journal of Peasant Studies* 47 (6): 1327–1347.

Chen, Chuanbo, and Cindy C. Fan. 2016. "China's Hukou Puzzle: Why Don't Rural Migrants Want Urban Hukou?" *China Review* 16 (3): 9–39.

Chen, Hui, and Houxing Bao. 2007. "Hunan sheng de hanyu fangyan" 湖南省的汉语方言 [Chinese dialects in Hunan Province]. *Fangyan* 方言 [Dialects] (3): 250–259.

Chen, Juan. 2011. "Internal Migration and Health: Re-examining the Healthy Migrant Phenomenon in China." *Social Science and Medicine* 72 (8): 1294–1301.

Chen, Ling. 2018. *Manipulating Globalization: The Influence of Bureaucrats on Business in China*. Stanford, CA: Stanford University Press.

Chen, Yuqi, Xiubin Li, Yujun Tian, and Minghong Tan. 2009. "Structural Change of Agricultural Land Use Intensity and Its Regional Disparity in China." *Journal of Geographical Sciences* 19: 545–556.

Chen, Zhao, Ming Lu, and Yiqing Xu. 2015. "The Voice of Migrants: How Does Hukou Affect the Public Consciousness and Participation in China?" *Chinese Journal of Sociology* 1 (3): 447–468.

Cheng, Tiejun. 1991. "Dialectics of Control: The Household Registration (Hukou) System in Contemporary China." PhD diss., Sociology, State University of New York at Binghampton.

Cheng, Tiejun, and Mark Selden. 1994. "The Origins and Social Consequences of China's Hukou System." *China Quarterly* (139): 644–668.

———. 1997. *The Construction of Social Hierarchies: China's Hukou and Danwei Systems*. Armonk, NY: M. E. Sharpe.

Cheng, Zhiming, Fei Guo, Graeme Hugo, and Xin Yuan. 2013. "Employment and Wage Discrimination in the Chinese Cities: A Comparative Study of Migrants and Locals." *Habitat International* 39: 246–255.

Chengdu Party Committee of Urban and Rural Work and Tsinghua University School of Public Administration Innovation and Social Responsibility Research Center. 2012. *Chengxiang yitihua gongzuo dianzhang* 城乡一体化工作典章 [Urban-rural integration work]. Beijing: Tsinghua University Press.

Chung, Erin Aeran. 2017. "Citizenship in Non-Western Contexts." In *The Oxford Handbook of Citizenship*, edited by Ayelet Shacher, Rainer Bauböck, Irene Bloemraad, and Maarten Vink, 431–452. Oxford: Oxford University Press.

Chung, Jae Ho, ed. 1999. *Cities in China: Recipes for Economic Development in the Reform Era*. New York: Routledge.

———. 2005. "Preferential Policies, Municipal Leadership, and Development Strategies: A Comparative Analysis of Qingdao and Dalian." In *Cities in Post-Mao China*, edited by Jae Ho Chung, 117–152. London: Routledge.

244 *Works Cited*

———. 2013. *Central Control and Local Discretion in China: Leadership and Implementation during Post-Mao.* Oxford: Oxford University Press.

Chung, Jae Ho, and Tao-chiu Lam. 2004. "China's "City System" in Flux: Explaining Post-Mao Administrative Changes." *China Quarterly* (180): 945–964.

Citrin, Jack, Donald P. Green, Christopher Muste, and Cara Wong. 1997. "Public Opinion towards Immigration Reform: The Role of Economic Motivations." *Journal of Politics* 59 (3): 858–881.

Claassens, Aninka. 2014. "Denying Ownership and Equal Citizenship: Continuities in the State's Use of Law and 'Custom', 1913–2013." *Journal of Southern African Studies* 40 (4): 761–779.

Clarke, Michael. 2007. "China's Internal Security Dilemma and the "Great Western Development": The Dynamics of Integration, Ethnic Nationalism and Terrorism in Xinjiang." *Asian Studies Review* 31 (3): 323–342.

Croll, Elisabeth J. 1999. "Social Welfare Reform: Trends and Tensions." *China Quarterly* 159: 684–699.

Cummings, Ronald G. 1986. *Valuing Environmental Goods: An Assessment of the Contingent Valuation Method.* Totowa, NJ: Rowman & Allanheld.

Dahl, Robert A. 2005. "What Political Institutions Does Large-Scale Democracy Require?" *Political Science Quarterly* 120 (2): 187–197.

Desai, Raj M., and Nita Rudra. 2019. "Trade, Poverty, and Social Protection in Developing Countries." *European Journal of Political Economy* 60: 101744.

Desmond, Cosmas. 1971. *The Discarded People: An Account of African Resettlement in South Africa.* London: Penguin.

DeVoretz, Don J., and Sergiy Pivnenko. 2005. "The Economic Causes and Consequences of Canadian Citizenship." *Journal of International Migration and Integration* 6 (3/4): 435–468.

Dickson, Bruce J. 2003. *Red Capitalists in China.* New York: Cambridge University Press.

Diehl, Claudia, and Michael Blohm. 2003. "Rights or Identity Naturalization Processes among 'Labor Migrants' in Germany." *International Migration Review* 37 (1): 133–162.

Diener, Alan, Bernie O'Brien, and Amiran Gafni. 1998. "Health Care Contingent Valuation Studies: A Review and Classification of the Literature." *Health Economics* 7 (4): 313–326.

Distelhorst, Greg, and Diana Fu. 2019. "Performing Authoritarian Citizenship: Public Transcripts in China." *Perspectives on Politics* 17 (1): 106–121.

Donaldson, John A. 2009. "Why Do Similar Areas Adopt Different Developmental Strategies? A Study of Two Puzzling Chinese Provinces." *Journal of Contemporary China* 18 (60): 421–444.

Dronkers, Jaap, and Maarten P. Vink. 2012. "Explaining Access to Citizenship in Europe: How Citizenship Policies Affect Naturalization Rates." *European Union Politics* 13 (3): 390–412.

Duckett, Jane. 2011. *The Chinese State's Retreat from Health: Policy and the Politics of Retrenchment*. New York: Routledge.

Dutton, Michael R. 1992. *Politics and Punishment in China: From Patriarchy to "the People."* Cambridge: Cambridge University Press.

Edin, Maria. 2003. "State Capacity and Local Agent Control in China: CCP Cadre Management from a Township Perspective." *China Quarterly* 173: 35–52.

Egerö, Bertil. 1991. *South Africa's Bantustans: From Dumping Grounds to Battlefronts*. Sterling, VA: Stylus.

Ehmke, Mariah D., Jason L. Lusk, and John A. List. 2008. "Is Hypothestical Bias a Universal Phenomenon? A Mlutinational Investigation." *Land Economics* 84 (3): 489–500.

Epenshade, Thomas J., and Charles A. Calhoun. 1993. "An Analysis of Public Opinion toward Undocumented Immigration." *Population Research and Policy Review* 12: 189–224.

Ergenc, Ceren. 2014. "Political Efficacy through Deliberative Participation in Urban China." *Journal of Chinese Political Science* 19 (2): 191–213.

Escobar, Cristina. 2002. "Clientelism and Citizenship: The Limits of Democratic Reform in Sucre, Colombia." *Latin American Perspectives* 29 (5): 20–47.

Esping-Andersen, Gøsta. 1990. *The Three Worlds of Welfare Capitalism*. Princeton, NJ: Princeton University Press.

Faist, Thomas. 2001. "Social Citizenship in the European Union: Nested Membership." *Journal of Common Market Studies* 39 (1): 37–58.

Fan, C. Cindy. 1995a. "Development from Above, Below and Outside: Spatial Impacts of China's Economic Reforms in Jiangsu and Guangdong Provinces." *Chinese Environment and Development* 6 (1/2): 85–116.

———. 1995b. "Of Belts and Ladders: State Policy and Uneven Regional Development in Post-Mao China." *Annals of the Association of American Geographers* 85 (3): 421–449.

———. 2002. "The Elite, the Natives, and the Outsiders: Migration and Labor Market Segmentation in Urban China." *Annals of the Association of American Geographers* 92 (1): 103–124.

Feenstra, Robert C., and Gordon H. Hanson. 1997. "Foreign Direct Investment and Relative Wages: Evidence from Mexico's Maquiladoras." *Journal of International Economics* 42 (3): 371–393.

Feinberg, Melissa. 2006. *Elusive Equality: Gender, Citizenship, and the Limits of Democracy in Czechoslovakia, 1918–1950*. Pittsburgh, PA: University of Pittsburgh Press.

Works Cited

Feng, Esther. 2013. "Official's 41 Properties Prompt Detentions." *Wall Street Journal*. February 1.

Feng, Wang, Yong Cai, and Baochang Gu. 2012. "Population, Policy and Politics: How Will History Judge China's One-Child Policy?" *Population and Development Review* 38 (S): 115–129.

Feng, Weilun, Yansui Liu, and Lulu Qu. 2019. "Effect of Land-Centered Urbanization on Rural Development: A Regional Analysis in China." *Land Use Policy* 87: 104072.

FitzGerald, Valpy, and J. A. Cuesta-Leiva. 1997. The Economic Value of a Passport: A Model of Citizenship and the Social Dividend in a Global Economy. QEH Working Paper Series. QEHWPS04.

Freeman, Gary P., and Alan K. Kessler. 2008. "Political Economy and Migration Policy." *Journal of Ethnic and Migration Studies* 34 (4): 655–678.

Friedman, Eli. 2022a. *The Urbanization of People: The Politics of Development, Labor Markets, and Schooling in the Chinese City*. New York: Columbia University Press.

———. 2022b. "Escape from the Closed Loop." *Boston Review*. November 28. https://www.bostonreview.net/articles/escape-from-the-closed-loop/.

Fu, Danni. 2018. "Officer Sentenced to 10 Years for 'Hukou' Profiteering." *Sixth Tone*. July 16. https://www.sixthtone.com/news/1002624.

Fu, Xiaolan, Carlo Pietrobelli, and Luc Soete. 2011. "The Role of Foreign Technology and Indigenous Innovation in the Emerging Economies: Technological Change and Catching Up." *World Development* 39 (7): 1204–1212.

Fung, Ho-lup. 2001. "The Making and Melting of the 'Iron Rice Bowl' in China, 1949 to 1995." *Social Policy and Administration* 35 (3): 258–273.

Gagnon, Jason, Theodora Xenogiani, and Chunbing Xing. 2014. "Are Migrants Discriminated against in Chinese Urban Labour Markets?" *IZA Journal of Labor and Development* 3 (17).

Gallagher, Mary E. 2011. *Contagious Capitalism: Globalization and the Politics of Labor in China*. Princeton, NJ: Princeton University Press.

———. 2015. "Transformation without Transition: China's Maoist Legacies in Comparative Perspective." In *Working through the Past: Labor and Authoritarian Legacies in Comparative Perspective*, edited by Teri Caraway, Stephen Crowley, and Maria Cook, 207–226. Ithaca, NY: Cornell University Press.

Gallagher, Mary E., and Jonathan K. Hanson. 2015. "Power Tool or Dull Blade? Selectorate Theory for Autocracies." *Annual Review of Political Science* 18 (1): 367–385.

Gandhi, Jennifer. 2008. *Political Institutions under Dictatorship*. Cambridge: Cambridge University Press.

Gandhi, Jennifer, and Ellen Lust-Okar. 2009. "Elections under Authoritarianism." *Annual Review of Political Science* 12: 403–422.

Gang, Ira N., and Robert C. Stuart. 1999. "Mobility Where Mobility Is Illegal: Internal Migration and City Growth in the Soviet Union." *Journal of Population Economics* 12: 117–134.

Gilley, Bruce. 2007. "Legitimacy and Institutional Change: The Case of China." *Comparative Political Studies* 41 (3): 259–284.

Göbel, Christian. 2021. "The Political Logic of Protest Repression in China." *Journal of Contemporary China* 30 (128): 169–185.

Goldman, Merle. 2007. *From Comrade to Citizen: The Struggle for Political Rights in China.* Cambridge, MA: Harvard University Press.

Goldman, Merle, and Elizabeth J. Perry, eds. 2002a. *Changing Meanings of Citizenship in Modern China.* Cambridge, MA: Harvard University Press.

———. 2002b. "Political Citizenship in Modern China." In *Changing Meanings of Citizenship in Modern China*, edited by Merle Goldman and Elizabeth J. Perry, 1–22. Cambridge, MA: Harvard University Press.

Gravemeyer, Stefan, Thomas Gries, and Jinjun Xue. 2010. "Income Determination and Income Discrimination in Shenzhen." *Urban Studies* 48 (7): 1457–1475.

Greenhalgh, Susan. 2005. "Missile Science, Population Science: The Origins of China's One-Child Policy." *China Quarterly* 182: 253–276.

Gregory, Paul R. 1990. "The Stalinist Command Economy." *Annals of the American Academy of Political and Social Science* 507 (1): 18–25.

Grünberg, Nis, and Vincent Brussee. 2022. "The Central Commission for Deepening Reform as Policy Accelerator." In *CPC Futures: The New Era of Socialism with Chinese Characteristics*, edited by Frank N. Pieke and Bert Hofman, 71–77. Singapore: National University of Singapore Press.

Gu, Hengyu, Yingkai Ling, Tiyan Shen, and Lindong Yang. 2020. "How Does Rural Homestead Influence the Hukou Transfer Intention of Rural-Urban Migrants in China?" *Habitat International* 105: 102267.

Gu, Hengyu, Ziliang Liu, and Tiyan Shen. 2020. "Spatial Pattern and Determinants of Migrant Workers' Interprovincial Hukou Transfer Intention in China: Evidence from a National Migrant Population Dynamic Monitoring Survey in 2016." *Population, Space and Place* 26 (2): e2250.

Guangdong Provincial Government. 1994. "Chengli zhujiang sanjiaozhou jingji qu guihua xietiao lingdao xiaozu" 成立珠江三角洲经济区规划协调领导小组 [The establishment of the Pearl River Delta Economic Region Planning and Coordinating Leading Small Group]. Guangzhou. Retrieved December 2023. https://www.gd.gov.cn/zwgk/gongbao/1994/21/content/post_3357340.html.

———. 2016. *2015 Guangdong Statistical Yearbook.* Beijing: China Statistics Press.

248   Works Cited

Guo, Fei, and Robyn R. Iredale. 2004. "The Impact of Hukou Status on Migrants' Employment: Findings from the 1997 Beijing Migrant Census." *International Migration Review* 38 (2): 709–731.

Guo, Taihui. 2014. "Rights in Action: The Impact of Chinese Migrant Workers' Resistances on Citizenship Rights." *Journal of Chinese Political Science* 19 (4): 421–434.

Guo, Xiaolin. 2001. "Land Expropriation and Rural Conflicts in China." *China Quarterly* 166: 422–439.

———. 2010. "'Jumin zheng' li hukou you duoyuan? jiyu guangdong diqu de fenxi jianyu shanghai bijiao" "居住证" 离户籍有多远? -- 基于广东地区的分析兼与上海比较 [How far away is the resident permit from the hukou status in China: A comparison between Guangdong and Shanghai]. *Nanfang Renkou* [South China Population] 25 (3): 28–34.

Guo, Yuanzhi, Yang Zhou, and Yansui Liu. 2022. "Targeted Poverty Alleviation and Its Practices in Rural China: A Case Study of Fuping County, Hebei Province." *Journal of Rural Studies* 93: 430–440

Haber, Stephen. 2006. "Authoritarian Government." In *Oxford Handbook of Political Economy*, edited by Barry R. Weingast and Donald A. Wittman, 693–707. New York: Oxford University Press.

Haggard, Stephan, and Robert R. Kaufman. 2009. *Development, Democracy, and Welfare States: Latin America, East Asia, and Eastern Europe.* Princeton, NJ: Princeton University Press.

Hainan Provincial Government. 2018. *Bai wan rencai jin hainan xingdong jihua* 百万人才进海南行动计划 [Action plan for millions of talents to enter Hainan]. Haikou.

Han, Dongping. 1999. "The Hukou System and China's Rural Development." *Journal of Developing Areas* 33 (3): 355–378.

Han, Guopan. 1990. *Nanbei Chao Jingji Shi lv* 南北朝经济史略 [A brief economic history of the southern and northern dynasties]. Xiamen: Xiamen University Press.

Handan Municipal Government. 2015. "Handan shi renmin zhengfu guanyu tuijin huji zhidu gaige de shishi yijian" 邯郸市人民政府关于推进户籍制度改革的实施意见 [Implementation opinions of the Handan Municipal People's Government on promoting the reform of the household registration system]. Handan, Hebei.

Hanson, Gordon H., Kenneth F. Scheve, and Matthew J. Slaughter. 2007. "Public Finance and Individual Preferences over Globalization Strategies." *Economics and Politics* 19 (1): 1–33.

Hardee-Cleveland, Karen, and Judith Banister. 1988. "Fertility Policy and Implementation in China, 1986–88." *Population and Development Review* 14 (2): 245–286.

Works Cited

Hardy, Andrew. 2001. "Rules and Resources: Negotiating the Household Registration System in Vietnam under Reform." *Sojourn: Journal of Social Issues in Southeast Asia* 16 (2): 187–212.

Hatcher, Craig, and Susan Thieme. 2015. "Institutional Transition: Internal Migration, the Propiska, and Post-socialist Urban Change in Bishkek, Kyrgyzstan." *Urban Studies* 53 (10): 2175–2191.

He, Baogang. 2018. "Deliberative Citizenship and Deliberative Governance: A Case Study of One Deliberative Experimental in China." *Citizenship Studies* 22 (3): 294–311.

He, Shenjing, Yuting Liu, Fulong Wu, and Chris Webster. 2010. "Social Groups and Housing Differentiation in China's Urban Villages: An Institutional Interpretation." *Housing Studies* 25 (5): 671–691.

Heilmann, Sebastian. 2008a. "From Local Experiments to National Policy: The Origins of China's Distinctive Policy Process." *China Journal* 59: 1–30.

———. 2008b. "Policy Experimentation in China's Economic Rise." *Studies in Comparative International Development* 43 (1): 1–26.

Heilmann, Sebastian, Lea Shih, and Andreas Hofem. 2013. "National Planning and Local Technology Zones: Experimental Governance in China's Torch Programme." *China Quarterly* 216: 896–919.

Heilongjiang Ministry of Public Security. 2017. *Heilongjiang City and County Yearbook.* Heilongjiang.

Heilongjiang Provincial Government. 2014. "Heilongjiang xing renmin zhengfu guanyu jinyibu tuijin huji zhidu gaige gongzuo de tongzhi [shixiao]" 黑龙江省人民政府关于进一步推进户籍制度改革工作的通知[失效] [Heilongjiang provincial government notice on further promoting the reform of the household registration system (rescinded)]. Heilongjiang.

Heinemann, Torsten, and Thomas Lemke. 2012. "Suspect Families: DNA Kinship Testing in German Immigration Policy." *Sociology* 47 (4): 810–826.

Heisler, Martin O. 2005. "Introduction: Changing Citizenship Theory and Practice: Comparative Perspective in a Democratic Framework." *PS: Political Science and Politics* 38 (4): 667–670.

Helbling, Marc. 2013. "Local Citizenship Politics in Switzerland: Between National Justice and Municipal Particularities." In *Multilevel Citizenship*, edited by Willem Maas, 149–167. Philadelphia: University of Pennsylvania Press.

Henry, Laura A. 2009. "Redefining Citizenship in Russia." *Problems of Post-Communism* 56 (6): 51–65

Herd, Pamela, and Donald P. Moynihan. 2018. *Administrative Burden.* New York: Russell Sage Foundation.

Highton, Benjamin. 2004. "Voter Registration and Turnout in the United States." *Perspectives on Politics* 2 (3): 507–515.

Ho, Elaine Lynn-Ee. 2011. "Caught Between Two Worlds: Mainland Chinese Return Migration, Hukou Considerations and the Citizenship Dilemma." *Citizenship Studies* 15 (6–7): 643–658.

Ho, Samuel P. S., and George C. S. Lin. 2003. "Emerging Land Markets in Rural and Urban China: Policies and Practices." *China Quarterly* 175: 681–707.

Hojaqizi, Guliatir. 2008. "Citizenship and Ethnicity: Old Propiska and New Citizenship in Post-Soviet Uzbekistan." *Inner Asia* 10 (2): 305–322.

Holliday, Ian. 2000. "Productivist Welfare Capitalism: Social Policy in East Asia." *Political Studies* 48 (4): 706–723.

Hong, Ren-Jie, Yu-Chi Tseng, and Thung-Hong Lin. 2022. "Guarding a New Great Wall: The Politics of Household Registration Reforms and Public Provision in China." *China Quarterly* 251: 776–797.

Hu, Angang, and Lianhe Hu. 2011a. "Dierdai Minzu Zhengce: Cuijin Minzu Jiaorong Yiti He Fanrong" 第二代民族政策：崔进民族较容易体和繁荣 [Second generation minzu policies: Promoting organic ethnic blending and prosperity] *Journal of Xinjiang Shifan University* (Philosophy and Sociology Edition) 32 (5): 1–13.

Hu, Biliang, and Tony Saich. 2012. "Developing Social Citizenship? A Case Study of Education and Health Services in Yantian Village of Guangdong Province." *China and World Economy* 20 (3): 69–87.

Hu, Chen-chong, Yu Zhu, Li-yue Lin, and Wan-ling Wang. 2011. "Liudong renkou de huji qianyi yiyuan ji qi yingxiang yinsu fenxi————jiyu yi xiang zai fujian sheng de wenjuan diaocha" 流动人口的户籍迁移意愿及其影响因素分析————基于一项在福建省的问卷调查 [Analysis on floating population's Hukou transfer intention and its influencing factors: Insights from a survey in Fujian Province]. *Population and Development* 17 (3): 1–10.

Hu, Lianhe, and Angang Hu. 2011b. "'Minzu da ronglu' he 'minzu da pinpan': guowai minzu zhengce de liangda moshi" "民族大熔炉"和"民族大拼盘": 国外民族政策的两大模式 [The "melting pot" and the "hors d'oeuvre platter": Two grand models of overseas ethnic policies]." *Chinese Social Sciences Today* 231: 7.

Huang, Bihong, and Kang Chen. 2012. "Are Intergovernmental Transfers in China Equalizing?" *China Economic Review* 23 (3): 534–551.

Huang, Xian. 2014. "Expansion of Chinese Social Health Insurance: Who Gets What, When and How?" *Journal of Contemporary China* 23 (89): 923–951.

————. 2015. "Four Worlds of Welfare: Understanding Subnational Variation in Chinese Social Health Insurance." *China Quarterly* 222: 449–474.

————. 2020. *Social Protection under Authoritarianism: Health Politics and Policy in China*. Oxford: Oxford University Press.

Huang, Xiyi. 1999. "Ground-Level Bureaucrats as a Source of Intensification of Rural Poverty in China." *Journal of International Development* 11: 637–648.

Huang, Xu, Ye Liu, Desheng Xue, Zhigang Li, and Zhilei Shi. 2018. "The Effects of Social Ties on Rural-Urban Migrants' Intention to Settle in Cities in China." *Cities* 83: 203–212.

Hughes, Neil C. 1998. "Smashing the Iron Rice Bowl." *Foreign Affairs* 77 (4): 67–77.

Huysmans, Jef. 2000. "The European Union and the Securitization of Migration." *Journal of Common Market Studies* 38 (5): 751–777.

Inside China Mainland. 1992. "Cities, Wake Up to the Migration Afoot." *Inside China Mainland* 14 (12): 75–81.

Isin, Engin. 2017. "Performative Citizenship." In *The Oxford Handbook of Citizenship*, edited by Ayelet Shachar, Rainer Baubock, Irene Bloemraad, and Maarten Vink. Oxford: Oxford University Press.

Janoski, Thomas. 2014. "Citizenship in China: A Comparison of Rights with the East and West." *Journal of Chinese Political Science* 19 (4): 365–385.

Jaros, Kyle. 2019. *China's Urban Champions: The Politics of Spatial Development*. Princeton, NJ: Princeton University Press.

Jasso, Guillermina, and Mark R. Rosenzweig. 1986. "Family Reunification and the Immigration Multiplier: U.S. Immigration Law, Origin-Country Conditions, and the Reproduction of Immigrants." *Demography* 23 (3): 291–311.

Johnson, Chalmers. 1982. *MITI and the Japanese Miracle: The Growth of Industrial Policy, 1925–1975*. Palo Alto, CA: Stanford University Press.

Jones, Calvert W. 2018. "New Approaches to Citizen-Building: Shifting Needs, Goals, and Outcomes." *Comparative Political Studies* 51 (2): 165–196.

Joppke, Christian. 2017. "Citizenship in Immigration States." In *The Oxford Handbook of Citizenship*, edited by Ayelet Shachar, Rainer Baubock, Irene Bloemraad, and Maarten Vink, 385–406. Oxford: Oxford University Press.

Kahanec, Martin, and Mehmet Serkan Tosun. 2009. "Political Economy of Immigration in Germany: Attitudes and Citizenship Aspirations." *International Migration Review* 43 (2): 263–291.

Kan, Karita. 2020. "The Social Politics of Dispossession: Informal Institutions and Land Expropriation in China." *Urban Studies* 57 (16): 3331–3346.

Kao, Ernest. 2013. "Multiple Identities: A Recurring Theme in Chinese Corruption." *South China Morning Post*, February 4.

Keane, Michael. 2001. "Redefining Chinese Citizenship." *Economy and Society* 30 (1): 1–17.

Keating, Michael. 2009. "Social Citizenship, Solidarity and Welfare in Regionalized and Plurinational States." *Citizenship Studies* 13 (5): 501–513.

Kennedy, John James, and Yaojiang Shi. 2019. *Lost and Found: The "Missing Girls" in Rural China*. New York: Oxford University Press.

Kennedy, Scott. 2005. *The Business of Lobbying in China*. Cambridge, MA: Harvard University Press.

Keyssar, Alexander. 2009. *The Right to Vote: The Contested History of Democracy in the United States*. New York: Basic Books.

Knight, John, and Lina Song. 1999. "Employment Constraints and Suboptimality in Chinese Enterprises." *Oxford Economic Papers* 51: 284–299.

Knutsen, Carl Henrik, and Magnus Rasmussen. 2017. "The Autocratic Welfare State: Old-Age Pensions, Credible Commitments, and Regime Survival." *Comparative Political Studies* 51 (5): 659–695.

Kovacheva, Vesela, Dita Vogel, Xiaonan Zhang, and Bill Jordon. 2012. "Comparing the Development of Free Movement and Social Citizenship for Internal Migrants in the European Union and China—Converging Trends?" *Citizenship Studies* 16 (3–4): 545–561.

Kratou, Hajer, and Mohamed Goaied. 2016. "How Can Globalization Affect Income Distribution? Evidence from Developing Countries." *International Trade Journal* 30 (2): 132–158.

Kuruvilla, Sarosh, Ching Kwan Lee, and Mary E. Gallagher, eds. 2011. *From Iron Rice Bowl to Informalization: Markets, Workers, and the State in a Changing China*. Ithaca, NY: Cornell University Press.

Kyung-Sup, Chang. 2020. "Why Developmental Citizenship, Why China? An Analytic Introduction." *Citizenship Studies* 24 (7): 847–855.

Landry, Pierre. 2008. *Decentralized Authoritarianism in China: The Communist Party's Control of Local Elites in the Post-Mao Era*. Cambridge: Cambridge University Press.

Landry, Pierre F., Xiaobo Lü, and Haiyan Duan. 2017. "Does Performance Matter? Evaluating Political Selection Along the Chinese Administrative Ladder." *Comparative Political Studies* 51 (8): 1074–1105.

Lao, Xin, and Hengyu Gu. 2020. "Unveiling Various Spatial Patterns of Determinants of Hukou Transfer Intentions in China: A Multi-scale Geographically Weighted Regression Approach." *Growth and Change* 51 (4): 1860–1876.

Lee, Ching Kwan. 2007. *Against the Law: Labor Protests in China's Rustbelt and Sunbelt*. Oakland: University of California Press.

Lee, Leng. 2012. "Decomposing Wage Differentials between Migrant Workers and Urban Workers in Urban China's Labor Markets." *China Economic Review* 23 (2): 461–470.

Leng, Ning, and Cai Zuo. 2021. "Tournament Style Bargaining within Boundaries: Setting Targets in China's Cadre Evaluation System." *Journal of Contemporary China*, 1–20.

Leung, Joe C. B. 1994. "Dismantling the 'Iron Rice Bowl': Welfare Reforms in the People's Republic of China." *Journal of Social Policy* 23 (3): 341–361.

Li, Jiayuan, Xing Ni, and Rui Wang. 2021. "Blame Avoidance in China's Cadre Responsibility System." *China Quarterly* 247: 681–702.

Li, Jing. 2012. "Naming of Guo Shengkun as Security Minister Divides Opinion." *South China Morning Post.* December 29. https://www.scmp.com/ news/china/article/1114732/naming-guo-shengkun-security-minister-divides -opinion.

Li, Lianjiang. 2010. "Rights Consciousness and Rules Consciousness in Contemporary China." *China Journal* (64): 47–68.

Li, Limei, Si-ming Li, and Yingfang Chen. 2010. "Better City, Better Life, but for Whom? The Hukou and Resident Card System and the Consequential Citizenship Stratification in Shanghai." *City, Culture and Society* 1 (3): 145–154.

Li, Keqiang. 2014. "Li Keqiang: Tuijin yi renwei hexin de xinxing chengzhen hua" 李克强：推进以人为核心的新型城镇化 [Li Keqiang: Promote new urbanization with people at the core]. State Council. Retrieved August 2018. http://www .gov .cn/ guowuyuan/ 2014 -03/ 05/ content 2629422 .htm.

Li, Meng, and Kam Wing Chan. 2022. "The Collective Hukou in Urban China." *Eurasian Geography and Economics* 63 (2): 259–270.

Liang, Zai, and Zhongdong Ma. 2004. "China's Floating Population: New Evidence from the 2000 Census." *Population and Development Review* 30 (3): 467–488.

Liaoning Provincial Government. 2015. "Liaoning xing renmin zhengfu guanyu jinyibu tuijin huji zhidu gaige de yijian" 辽宁省人民政府关于进一步推进户籍制度改革的意见 [Opinions of the People's Government of Liaoning Province on further promoting the reform of the household registration system]. Shenyang.

Light, Matthew A. 2012. "What Does It Mean to Control Migration? Soviet Mobility Policies in Comparative Perspective." *Law and Social Inquiry* 37 (2): 395–429.

Lin, Qiaowen, Shukui Tan, Lu Zhang, Siliang Wang, Chao Wei, and Yanan Li. 2018. "Conflicts of Land Expropriation in China during 2006–2016: An Overview and Its Spatio-temporal Characteristics." *Land Use Policy* 76: 246–251.

Liu, Alan P. L. 1992. "The "Wenzhou Model" of Development and China's Modernization." *Asian Survey* 32 (8): 696–711.

Liu, Gordon G., Samantha A. Vortherms, and Xuezhi Hong. 2017. "China's Health Reform Update." *Annual Review of Public Health* 38: 431–448.

Liu, Jinwei, and Le Xu. 2016. "Woguo chengshi huku kaifang chengdu jiqi yinxiang yinsu fenxi—jiyu quanguo 63 yangben chengshi de pinggu" 我国

城市户籍开放程度及其影响因素分析—基于全国63个样本城市的评估 [Analysis of the degree of openness of urban household registration in China and its influencing factors—based on an assessment of 63 sample cities across the country] In *Zhongguo shehui tizhi gaige baogao* 中国社会体制改革报告 [Report on social institutional reform in China] no. 4: 40–55. Beijing: Shehuikexue wenxuan chubanshe [Sociology Literature Press].

Liu, Tao, and Qiujie Shi. 2020. "Acquiring a Beijing Hukou: Who Is Eligible and Who Is Successful?" *China Quarterly* 243: 855–868.

Liu, Yuming, Gen Li, Xiang Qi, Bei Qu, Carl A. Latkin, Weiming Tang, and Brian J. Hall. 2023. "Prevalence and Determinants of Food Insecurity during the 2022 COVID-19 Related Lockdown in Shanghai." *Global Public Health* 18 (1).

Liu, Zhiqiang. 2005. "Institution and Inequality: The Hukou System in China." *Journal of Comparative Economics* 33 (1): 133–157.

Lo, Kevin, Longyi Xue, and Mark Wang. 2016. "Spatial Restructuring through Poverty Alleviation Resettlement in Rural China." *Journal of Rural Studies* 47: 496–505.

Logan, John R., Sookhee Oh, and Jennifer Darrah. 2012. "The Political and Community Context of Immigrant Naturalization in the United States." *Journal of Ethnic and Migration Studies* 38 (4): 535–554.

Lohr, Eric. 2012. *Russian Citizenship: From Empire to Soviet Union*. Cambridge, MA: Harvard University Press.

Lührmann, Anna, Seraphine F. Maerz, Sandra Grahn, Nazifa Alizada, Lisa Gastaldi, Sebastian Hellmeier, Garry Hindle, and Staffan I. Lindberg. 2020. Democracy Report 2020: Autocratization Surges – Resistance Grows. Gothenburg, Sweden: V-Dem Institute.

Lynch, Michael. 2010. *The Chinese Civil War, 1945–1949*. Oxford, UK: Osprey Press.

Ma, Laurence J. C., and Gonghao Cui. 2002. "Economic Transition at the Local Level: Diverse Forms of Town Development in China." *Post-Soviet Geography and Economics* 43 (2): 79–103.

Maas, Willem. 2013. "Equality and the Free Movement of People: Citizenship and Internal Migration." In *Democratic Citizenship and the Free Movement of People*, edited by Willem Maas, 9–30. Leiden, Netherlands: Martinus Nijhoff.

———. 2017. "Multilevel Citizenship." In *The Oxford Handbook of Citizenship*, edited by Ayelet Shachar, Rainer Bauböck, Irene Bloemraad, and Maarten P. Vink, 644–668. Oxford: Oxford University Press.

Magaloni, Beatriz. 2006. *Voting for Autocracy: Hegemonic Party Survival and Its Demise in Mexico*. Cambridge: Cambridge University Press.

Malchow-Møller, Nikolaj, Jakob Roland Munch, Sanne Schroll, and Jan Rose Skaksen. 2008. "Attitudes towards Immigration: Perceived Consequences and Economic Self-Interest." *Economic Letters* 100 (2): 254–257.

Malesky, Edmund J. 2009. "Foreign Direct Investors as Agents of Economic Transition: An Instrumental Variables Analysis." *Quarterly Journal of Political Science* 4 (1): 59–85.

Manion, Melanie. 1985. "The Cadre Management System, Post-Mao: The Appointment Promotion, Transfer and Removal of Party and State Leaders." *China Quarterly* 102: 203–233.

———. 2015. *Information for Autocrats: Representation in Chinese Local Congresses.* New York: Cambridge University Press.

Mann, Michael. 1987. "Ruling Class Strategies and Citizenship." *Sociology* 21 (3): 339–354.

Marshall, T. H. 1950. *Citizenship and Social Class and Other Essays.* Cambridge: Cambridge University Press.

Massey, Douglas S., Joaquin Arango, Graeme Hugo, Ali Kouaouci, Adela Pellegrino, and J. Edward Taylor. 1993. "Theories of International Migration: A Review and Appraisal." *Population and Development Review* 19 (3): 431–466.

Matthews, Mervyn. 1993. *The Passport Society: Controlling Movement in Russia and the USSR.* Boulder, CO: Westview.

Meijer, Roel, and Nils Butenschøn, eds. 2017a. *The Crisis of Citizenship in the Arab World.* Boston: Brill.

———. 2017b. "The Crisis of Citizenship in the Arab World." In *The Crisis of Citizenship in the Arab World,* edited by Roel Meijer and Nils Butenschøn, 1–38. Boston: Brill.

Merkle, Rita. 2003. "Ningxia's Third Road to Rural Development: Resettlement Schemes as a Last Means to Poverty Reduction?" *Journal of Peasant Studies* 30 (3–4): 160–191.

Miller, Gary T. 1995. "Citizenship and European Union: A Federalist Approach." In *Federal-Type Solutions and European Integration,* edited by C. Lloyd Brown-John. Lanham, MD: University Press of America.

Milligan, G., and M. C. Cooper. 1985. "An Examination of Procedures for Determining the Number of Clusters in a Dataset." *Psychometrika* 50: 159–179.

Ministry of Construction. 1995. "Guanyu renzhen peihe hao xiao chengzhen huji gaige gongzuo de tongzhi" 关于认真配合好小城镇户籍改革工作的通知 [Notification regarding earnestly carrying out small city and town household registration reform work]. Beijing.

Ministry of Land. 2016. *China Land and Resources Statistical Yearbook.* Beijing: Geological Press.

256 Works Cited

Ministry of Education. 2014. "2014 Niandu Approval form for demand plan for introducing overseas students." **2014** 年度引进留学人才需求计划核准 [Approval form for demand plan for introducing overseas students]. China Service Center for Scholarly Exchange. Retrieved July 2015. http://www.cscse .edu.cn/publish/portal0/tab89/info1644.htm.

Ministry of Public Security. 1977. "Guanyu chuli hukou qianyi de guiding" 关于处理户口迁移的规定 [Regulation regarding dealing with hukou transfer]. Beijing.

———. 1985. "Guanyu chengzhen zan zhu renkou guanli de zhan hang guiding" 关于城镇暂住人口管理的暂行规定 [Provisional regulations for the management of temporary residents in cities and towns]. Beijing.

———. 1989. "Linshi shenfen zheng guanli zhan hang guiding" 临时身份证管理暂行规定 [Regulations for management of temporary identification permits]. Beijing.

———. 1992a. "Guanyu shi hang dang di youxiao chengzhen jumin hukou zhidu de tongzhi" 关于实行当地有效城镇居民户口制度的通知 [Notification on implementing locally effective urban residential hukou systems]. Beijing.

———. 1992b. "Guanyu jianjue zhizhi gongkai mai fei nongye hukou cuowu zuofa de jinji tongzhi" 关于坚决制止公开卖非农业户口错误做法的紧急通知 [Urgent notification regarding resolving and preventing the flawed method of public selling non-agricultural hukou]. Beijing.

———. 1994. "Guanyu qiyong xin de hukou qianyi zheng, hukou zhun qian zheng de tongzhi" 关于启用新的户口迁移证、户口准迁证的通知 [Notification regarding the use of new hukou relocation certificates and hukou permits for resettlement). Beijing.

———.1995a. "Zanzhu zheng shenling banfa" 暂住证申领办法 (Application Procedures for Temporary Residency Permits). Beijing.

———.1995b. "Guanyu qiyong xin de changzhu renkou dengji biao he jumin hukou bu youguan shixiang de tongzhi" 关于启用新的常住人口登记表和居民户口簿有关事项的通知 (Notification regarding Introducing New Permanent Population Registration Forms and Resident *Hukou* Registers). Beijing.

———. 1997a. "Xiao chengzhen huji guanli zhidu gaige shidian fang'an" 小城镇户籍管理制度改革试点方案[Blueprint for experiments in small city and town household registration management reform]. Beijing.

———. 1997b. "Guanyu wanshan nongcun huji guanli zhidu de yijian" 关于完善农村户籍管理制度的意见[Opinion on improving the rural household registration management system]. Beijing.

———. 2001. "Guanyu tuijin xiao chengzhen huji guanli zhidu gaige de yijian" 关于推进小城镇户籍管理制度改革的意见 [Opinions on accelerating reform of the small city and town household registration management system]. Beijing.

———. 2014. "Guanyu renzhen guanche luoshi 'Guowuyuan guanyu jin yi bu tuijin huji zhidu gaige de yijian' de tongzhi" 关于认真贯彻落实《国务院关于进一步推进户籍制度改革的意见》的通知 [Notice on Earnestly Implementing the "Opinions of the State Council on Further Promoting the Reform of the Household Registration System"]. Beijing.

———. 2019. "Guanyu yinfa huji guanli lingyu jiceng zhengwu gongkai biaozhun zhiyin de tongzhi" 关于印发户籍管理领域基层政务公开标准指引的通知 [Notice on Printing and Distributing the Guidelines for the Publicity of Basic-Level Government Affairs in Household Registration Management]. Beijing.

———. Various Years. *Zhonghua renmin gongheguo quanguo fen xian shi renkou tongji ziliao* 中华人民共和国全国分县市人口统计资料 [Chinese Population Statistical Materials]. Zhongguo ditu chuban she 中国地图出版社 [China Map Press]. Beijing.

Ministry of Public Security, Ministry of Finance, and People's Bank of China. 1994. "Guanyu jianjue zhizhi jixu chumai fei nongye hukou de tongzhi" 关于坚决制止继续出卖非农业户口的通知 [Notification on resolving and preventing the continued sale of non-agricultural hukou]. Beijing.

Ministry of Public Security, Ministry of Food, and National Bureau of Personnel. 1980. "Guanyu jiejue bufen zhuanye jishu bu de nongcun jiashu qianwang chengzhen you guojia gongying liangshi wenti de guiding" 关于解决部分专业技术部的农村家属前往城镇由国家供应粮食问题的规定 [Regulation regarding resolving issues of grain rationing for rural families of cadre with professional skills migrating to urban areas]. Beijing.

Ministry of Public Security, Ministry of Personnel, and Ministry of Labour. 1994. "Guanyu ganbu, gongren diaodong banli hukou qianyi shouxu youguan wenti de tongzhi" 关于干部、工人调动办理户口迁移手续有关问题的通知 [Notification regarding issues relating to hukou transfer for redeployed cadres and laborers]. Beijing.

Ministry of Public Security, State Council. 1998. "Guanyu jiejue dangqian hukou guanli gongzuo zhong jige tuchu wenti yijian de tongzhi" 关于解决当前户口管理工作中几个突出问题意见的通知. [Recommendations on Resolving Several Issues with Current *Hukou* Management Work]. Beijing.

Ministry of the Interior and Ministry of Labor. 1954. "Guanyu jixu guance (quangzhi nongmin mangliu ru chengshi) de zhibiao" 关于继续观测（观致

农民盲流如城市）的指标 [Joint directive to control the blind influx of peasants into cities]. Beijing.

Money, Jeannette. 1999. *Fences and Neighbors: The Geography of Immigration Control*. Ithaca, NY: Cornell University Press.

Montinola, Gabriella, Yingyi Qian, and Barry R. Weingast. 1995. "Federalism, Chinese Style: The Political Basis for Economic Success in China." *World Politics* 48 (1): 50–81.

Mu, Xiaoyan, Anthony Gar-On Yeh, Xiaohu Zhang, Jiejing Wang, and Jian Lin. 2021. "Moving Down the Urban Hierarchy: Turning Point of China's Internal Migration Caused by Age Structure and Hukou System." *Urban Studies* 59 (7): 1389–1405.

Müller, Armin. 2017. *China's New Public Health Insurance: Challenges to Health Reforms and the New Rural Co-operative Medical System*. New York: Routledge.

Murphy, Rachel, and Vanessa L. Fong. 2006. "Introduction: Chinese Experiences of Citizenship at the Margins." In *Chinese Citizenship: Views from the Margins*, edited by Rachel Murphy and Vanessa L. Fong, 1–8. New York: Routledge.

Muste, Christopher. 2013. "The Dynamics of Immigration Opinion in the United States, 1992–2012." *Public Opinion Quarterly* 77 (1): 398–416.

Nam, Yunju, and Wooksoo Kim. 2012. "Welfare Reform and Elderly Immigrants' Naturalization: Access to Public Benefits as an Incentive for Naturalization in the United States." *International Migration Review* 46 (3): 656–679.

Nasir, Kamaludeen Mohamed, and Bryan S. Turner. 2013. "Governing as Gardening: Reflections on Soft Authoritarianism in Singapore." *Citizenship Studies* 17 (3–4): 339–352.

Nasritdinov, Emil 2008. "Discrimination of Internal Migrants in Bishkek." Retrieved December 2021. https://www.auca.kg/uploads/Migration _Database/Discrimination%20of%20internal%20migrants%20in %20Bishkek.pdf.

National Bureau of Statistics (NBS). 2002. *China Household Income Project Survey*. Beijing: China Statistics Press.

———. 2011. *2010 Zhonghua Renmin Gonghe Guo di Liu Ci Quanguo Renkou Pucha* 中华人民共和国第六次全国人口普查 [2010 Sixth National Population Census of the People's Republic of China]. Beijing: China Statistics Press.

———.2013. *China Household Income Project Survey*. Beijing: China Statistics Press.

———. 2019. "Renkou" 人口 [Population]. Retrieved February 6, 2023. http://www.stats.gov.cn/tjsj/zbjs/201912/t20191202_1713059.html.

———. 2021a. "Main Data of the Seventh National Population Census News Release." National Bureau of Statistics. Beijing. Retrieved August 2021. http://www.stats.gov.cn/english/PressRelease/202105/t20210510_1817185.html.

———. 2021b. "2020 *Zhonghua Renmin Gonghe Guo di Qi Ci Quanguo Renkou Pucha* 中华人民共和国第七次全国人口普查 [2020 Seventh National Population Census of the People's Republic of China]. Beijing: China Statistics Press.

———.Various Years. *China City Statistical Yearbook*. Beijing: China Statistics Press.

———. Various Years. *China Statistical Yearbook*. Beijing: China Statistics Press.

———. Various Years. *Migrant Workers Monitoring and Investigation Report*. Beijing.

———. Various Years. *Regional Economic Yearbook*. Beijing: China Statistics Press.

National Health Commission. 2019. *China Health Statistical Yearbook*. Beijing: China Health Yearbook Press.

———. 2021. "China Migrants Dynamic Survey." Beijing: Migrant Population Service Center. Retrieved October 4, 2021. https://chinaldrk.org.cn/wjw/#/home.

National People's Congress. 1988. "Zhonghua renmingongheguo tudi guanlifa" 中华人民共和国土地管理法 [Land administration law]. National People's Congress. Beijing.

———. 2013. Law of the People's Republic of China on Protection of the Rights and Interests of the Elderly. National People's Congress. Beijing.

O'Brien, Kevin J. 2001. "Villagers, Elections, and Citizenship in Contemporary China." *Modern China* 27 (4): 407–435.

O'Brien, Kevin J., and Lianjiang Li. 2000. "Accommodating "Democracy" in a One-Party State: Introducing Village Elections in China." *China Quarterly* 162: 465–489.

Oi, Jean C. 1995. "The Role of the Local State in China's Transitional Economy." *China Quarterly* 144: 1132–1149.

Ong, Aihwa. 1999. "Muslim Feminism: Citizenship in the Shelter of Corporatist Islam." *Citizenship Studies* 3 (3): 355–371.

Öniş, Ziya. 1991. "'The Logic of the Developmental State.' Review of Asia's Next Giant: South Korea and Late Industrialization, Alice H. Amsden; The Political Economy of the New Asian Industrialism, Frederic C. Deyo; MITI and the Japanese Miracle, Chalmers Johnson; Governing the Market: Economic Theory and the Role of Government in East Asian Industrialization, Robert Wade." *Comparative Politics* 24 (1): 109–126.

260 *Works Cited*

Pan, Jennifer. 2020. *Welfare for Autocrats: How Social Assistance in China Cares for Its Rulers*. New York: Oxford University Press.

Papademetriou, Demetrios G., Will Somerville, and Hiroyuki Tanaka. 2008. "Hybrid Immigrant-Selection Systems: The Next Generation of Economic Migration Schemes." Washington, DC: Migration Policy Institute.

Papademetriou, Demetrios G., and Madeleine Sumption. 2011. "Rethinking Points Systems and Employer-Selected Immigration." In *Improving US and EU Immigration Systems*. European University Institute, Migration Policy Institute.

Peng, Thomas. 2011. "The Impact of Citizenship on Labour Process: State, Capital and Labour Control in South China." *Work, Employment, and Society* 25 (4): 726–741.

People's Daily. 2001. "Fujian huji guanli: Quxiao nongye hukou zhun ru tiaojian daiti jin cheng zhibiao" 福建户籍管理: 取消农业户口 准入条件代替进城指标 [Fujian household registration management: Cancel agricultural household registration and replace urban entry quota with conditional transfer]. *People's Daily*. December 24.

———. 2002. "Hunan shishi huji guanli xin guiding lizheng jinnian di quxiao nongye renkou, fei nongye renkou hukou 'er yuan zhi' guanli moshi, bensheng huji renkou an shiji juzhu di dengji hukou, tongcheng 'hunan jumin hukou'" 湖南实施户籍管理新规定 力争今年底取消农业人口、非农业人口户口"二元制"管理模式, 本省户籍人口按实际居住地登记户口, 统称"湖南居民户口" [Hunan has implemented new regulations on household registration management and strives to abolish the "dual system" management model of agricultural and non-agricultural population household registration by the end of this year. The province's household registration population will be registered according to their actual place of residence, collectively referred to as "Hunan resident household registration"]. *People's Daily*. January 4.

———. 2004a. "Sichuan goujian chengxiang tongyi hukou dengji zhidu 300 yu wan nongmin luohu chengzhen" 四川构建城乡统一户口登记制度300余万农民落户城镇 [Sichuan has established a unified urban and rural household registration system and more than 3 million farmers have settled in cities and towns]. *People's Daily*. July 23

———. 2004b. "Hubei zhengshi qidong huji gaige chengxiang tongyi dengji wei jumin hukou" 湖北正式启动户籍改革 城乡统一登记为居民户口 [Hubei officially launches household registration reform, unified urban and rural registration as resident household registration]. *People's Daily*. August 14.

———. 2006. "Henan quan sheng tongyi chengxiang hukou guanli jiang an juzhu di dengji huji" 河南全省统一城乡户口管理将按居住地登记户籍

[Unified urban and rural household registration management in Henan Province will register household registration according to place of residence]. *People's Daily*. January 16.

———. 2007. "Yunnan jiang quxiao nongye hukou" 云南将取消农业户口 [Yunnan will cancel agricultural household registration]. *People's Daily*. October 25

———. 2014. "Xijinping zhuchi shen gaizu huiyi ding huji gaige yaoqiu" 习近平主持深改组会议 定户籍改革要求 [Xi Jinping presides over the comprehensively deepening reform meeting to set requirements for household registration reform]. *People's Daily*. June 7.

———. 2018a. "Xijinping yan li de 'di yi ziyuan' weihe ruci zhongyao" 习近平眼里的"第一资源"为何如此重要 [Why is the "first resource" in Xi Jinping's eyes so important?]. *People's Daily*, July 18.

———. 2018b. "San da chengshi de 'yin cai dajuan' (jujiao yin cai yong cai)" 三大城市的"引才答卷"（聚焦引才用才） ["Answers for introducing talents" in the three major cities (focusing on introducing talents)]. *People's Daily*. March 18.

Perry, Elizabeth J. 2002. *Challenging the Mandate of Heaven: Social Protest and State Power in China*. Armonk, NY: M. E. Sharpe.

———. 2008. "Chinese Conceptions of "Rights": From Mencius to Mao- and Now." *Perspectives on Politics* 6 (1): 37–50.

Peters, Floris, Maarten Vink, and Hans Schmeets. 2015. "The Ecology of Immigrant Naturalisation: A Life Course Approach in the Context of Institutional Conditions." *Journal of Ethnic and Migration Studies* 42 (3): 359–381.

Pinto, Pedro Ramos. 2012. "'Everyday Citizenship' under Authoritarianism: The Cases of Spain and Portugal." In *Civil Society Activism under Authoritarian Rule: A Comparative Perspective*, edited by Francesco Cavatorta, 13–33. London: Routledge.

Pipko, Simona, and Albert J. Pucciarelli. 1985. "The Soviet Internal Passport System." *International Lawyer* 19 (3): 915–919.

Pizzi, Elise, and Yue Hu. 2022. "Does Governmental Policy Shape Migration Decisions?" *Modern China* 48 (5): 1050–1079.

Po, Lanchih. 2012. "Asymmetrical Integration: Public Finance Deprivation in China's Urbanized Villages." *Environment and Planning A* 44 (12): 2834–2851.

Portes, Alejandro, and John W. Curtis. 1987. "Changing Flags: Naturalization and Its Determinants among Mexican Immigrants." *International Migration Review* 21 (2): 352–371.

Portes, Alejandro, and Rafael Mozo. 1985. "The Political Adaptation Process of Cubans and Other Ethnic Minorities in the United States: A Preliminary Analysis." *International Migration Review* 19 (1): 35–63.

262 Works Cited

Przeworski, Adam. 2022. "Formal Models of Authoritarian Regimes: A Critique." *Perspectives on Politics*, 1–10.

Ran, Ran. 2017. "Understanding Blame Politics in China's Decentralized System of Environmental Governance: Actors, Strategies and Context." *China Quarterly* 231: 634–661.

Ratigan, Kerry. 2017. "Disaggregating the Developing Welfare State: Provincial Social Policy Regimes in China." *World Development* 98: 467–484.

Reuters. 2017. "Beijing ziliao: Zhonggong zhongyang shen gai xiaozu lici huiyi ji tongguo de gaige fang'an shuli" 背景资料：中共中央深改小组历次会议及通过的改革方案梳理[Background information: A summary of previous meetings of the Deep Reform Group of the CPC Central Committee and the reform plans adopted.] Retrieved October 2023. https://www.reuters.com/article/factboxreform-1012-thursday-idCNKBS1CH0D9.

Rithmire, Meg. 2013a. "Land Politics and Local State Capacities: The Political Economy of Urban Change in China." *China Quarterly* 216: 872–895.

———. 2013b. "China's "New Regionalism": Subnational Analysis in Chinese Political Economy." *World Politics* 66 (1): 165–194.

———. 2015. *Land Bargains and Chinese Capitalism: The Politics of Property Rights under Reform*. Cambridge: Cambridge University Press.

Rogers, Sarah. 2014. "Betting on the Strong: Local Government Resource Allocation in China's Poverty Counties." *Journal of Rural Studies* 36: 197–206.

Rothstein, Richard. 2017. *The Color of Law: A Forgotten History of How Our Government Segregated America*. New York: Liveright.

Rozelle, Scott, and Natalie Hell. 2020. *Invisible China: How the Urban-Rural Divide threatens China's Rise*. Chicago: University of Chicago Press.

Rubins, Noah. 1998. "Recent Development: The Demise and Resurrection of the Propiska: Freedom of Movement in the Russian Federation." *Harvard International Law Journal* 39: 545–566.

Rudra, Nita. 2008. *Who Really Gets Hurt? Globalization and the Race to the Bottom in Developing Countries*. Cambridge: Cambridge University Press.

Rudra, Nita, and Jennifer Tobin. 2017. "When Does Globalization Help the Poor?" *Annual Review of Political Science* 20 (1): 287–307.

Sadiq, Kamal. 2017. "Postcolonial Citizenship." In *The Oxford Handbook of Citizenship*, edited by Ayelet Shachar, Rainer Baubock, Irene Bloemraad, and Maarten Vink, 178–199. Oxford: Oxford University Press.

Saeidi, Shirin. 2010. "Creating the Islamic Republic of Iran: Wives and Daughters of Martyrs, and Acts of Citizenship." *Citizenship Studies* 14 (2): 113–126.

Sargeson, Sally. 2013. "Violence as Development: Land Expropriation and China's Urbanization." *Journal of Peasant Studies* 40 (6): 1063–1085.

Schachar, Ayelet, Rainer Baubock, Irene Bloemraad, and Maarten Vink, eds. *The Oxford Handbook of Citizenship*. Oxford: Oxford University Press.

Schedler, Andreas. 2002. "Elections without Democracy: The Menu of Manipulation." *Journal of Democracy* 13 (2): 36–50.

Shaanxi Statistics Bureau. 2011. *Xi'an Statistical Yearbook 2011*. Beijing: China Statistical Press.

Shanghai Municipal Government. 1993. *Shanghai lanyin hukou guanli zanxing guiding* 上海蓝印户口管理暂行规定 [Temporary regulations of Shanghai blue-print *hukou*]. Shanghai.

Shaw, Jo. 2017. "Citizenship and the Franchise." In *The Oxford Handbook of Citizenship*, edited by Ayelet Schachar, Rainer Baubóck, Irene Bloemraad, and Maarten P. Vink, 290–313. Oxford: Oxford University Press.

Shen, Xiaoxiao, and Kellee S. Tsai. 2016. "Institutional Adaptability in China: Local Developmental Models under Changing Economic Conditions." *World Development* 87: 107–127.

Shepherd, Christian, and Natalie Thomas. 2017. "Beijing Evictions Leave Migrant Workers in Limbo as Winter Deepens." Reuters, December 15. https://www.reuters.com/article/us-china-migrants/beijing-evictions-leave-migrant-workers-in-limbo-as-winter-deepens-idUSKBN1E90F4/

Shevel, Oxana. 2017. "Citizenship and State Transition." In *The Oxford Handbook of Citizenship*, edited by Ayelet Schachar, Rainer Baubock, Irene Bloemraad, and Maarten Vink, 407–430. Oxford: Oxford University Press.

Shi, Tianjian, and Jie Lu. 2010. "The Meanings of Democracy: The Shadow of Confucianism." *Journal of Democracy* 21 (4): 123–130.

Shi, Yaojiang, and John James Kennedy. 2016. "Delayed Registration and Identifying the "Missing Girls" in China." *China Quarterly* 228: 1018–1038.

Shin, Adrian J. 2017. "Tyrants and Migrants: Authoritarian Immigration Policy." *Comparative Political Studies* 50 (1): 14–40.

Shue, Vivienne. 1994. "State Power and Social Organization in China." In *State Power and Social Forces: Domination and Transformation in the Third World*, edited by Joel S. Migdal, Atul Kohli, and Vivienne Shue, 63–88. New York: Cambridge University Press.

Sichuan Statistics Bureau. 2011. *Sichuan Statistical Yearbook 2011*. Beijing: China Statistics Press.

———. 2020. *Sichuan Statistical Yearbook 2020*. Beijing: China Statistics Press.

Sina News. 2005. "Zhongguo 11 sheng shi kaishi tongyi chengxiang hukou beijing zan wei lie ru qizhong" 中国11省市开始统一城乡户口 北京暂未列入其中 [11 Chinese provinces begin unified hukou; Beijing temporarily excluded]. *Sina News*, October 27. Retrieved May 2014. https://news.sina.com.cn/o/2005-10-27/17377286184s.shtml.

———. 2016. "Jiangsu kaosheng jiazhang fandui ming'e waidiao guanfang: Zheng yu gaoxiao goutong" 江苏考生家长反对名额外调 官方：正与高校沟通 [Parents of Jiangsu students oppose the extra transfer of enrollment quota]. *Sina News*. May 14. http://news.sina.com.cn/c/2016-05-14/doc-ifxsehvu8926759.shtml.

Sinha, Aseema. 2005. *The Regional Roots of Developmental Politics in India: A Divided Leviathan*. Bloomington: Indiana University Press.

Skocpol, Theda. 1995. *Protecting Soldiers and Mothers: The Political Origins of Social Policy in the United States*. Cambridge, MA: Belknap Press.

Smart, Alan, and George C. S. Lin. 2007. "Local Capitalisms, Local Citizenship and Translocality: Rescaling from below in the Pearl River Delta Region, China." *International Journal of Urban and Regional Research* 31 (2): 280–302.

Smart, Alan, and Josephine Smart. 2001. "Local Citizenship: Welfare Reform Urban/Rural Status, and Exclusion in China." *Environment and Planning A* 33: 1853–1869.

Solinger, Dorothy J. 1985. "'Temporary Residence Certificate' Regulations in Wuhan, May 1983." *China Quarterly* 101: 98–103.

———. 1999. *Contesting Citizenship in Urban China: Peasant Migrants, the State, and the Logic of the Market*. Oakland: University of California Press.

———. 2014. "The Modalities of Geographical Mobility in China and Their Impacts, 1980–2010." In *China-India: Pathways of Economic and Social Development*, edited by Delia Davin and Barbara Harriss-White, 139–156. London: British Academy.

Song, Yang. 2014. "What Should Economists Know about the Current Chinese Hukou System?" *China Economic Review* 29: 200–212.

———. 2015. "Hukou-Based Labour Market Discrimination and Ownership Structure in Urban China." *Urban Studies* 53 (8): 1657–1673.

Soysal, Yasemin Nuhoğlu. 1994. *Limits of Citizenship*. Chicago: University of Chicago Press.

Starr, Sered. Susan. 2021. "Diminished Citizenship in the Era of Mass Incarceration." *Punishment and Society* 23 (2): 218–240.

State Council. 1953. "Guanyu shixing liangshi de jihua shougou he jihua gongying de mingling" 关于实行粮食的计划收购和计划供应的命令 [The order on the planned purchase and planned supply of food]. Beijing.

———. 1957. "Guanyu gongren, zhiyuan huijia shentan qin de jiaqi he gongzuo daiou de zanxing guiding" 关于工人、职员回家探亲的假期和工资待遇的暂行规定 [Provisional regulations on home leave and wages of workers and employees]. Beijing.

———. 1958. "Zhonghua renmin gonghe guo hukou dengji jitiao lie" 中华人民共和国户口登记条例 [Household registration ordinance]. Beijing.

———. 1982. "Chengshi liuliang qitiao renyuan shourong qiansong banfa" 城市流浪乞讨人员收容遣送办法 [Measures for internment and deportation of urban vagrants and beggars]. Beijing.

———. 1984. "Guanyu nongmin jinru jizhen luohu wenti de tongzhi" 关于农民进入集镇落户问题的通知 [Regarding the problem of peasants settling in market towns]. Beijing.

———. 1988. "Guanyu zhizhi yixie shi, xian gongkai chumai chengzhen hukou de kongzhi" 关于制止一些市、县公开出卖城镇户口的控制 [Notification regarding preventing public sales of urban hukou by some cities and counties]. Beijing.

———. 1989. "Guanyu yange kongzhi 'nong zhuan fei' guo kuai zengzhang de tongzhi" 关于严格控制""过快增长的通知 [Notification regarding strictly controlling overly rapid increase in "nongzhuanfei"]. Beijing.

———. 1993. "Guanyu hujizhidu gaige de jueding" 关于户籍制度改革的决定 [Decision regarding household registration system reform]. Beijing.

———. 1997. "Guowuyuan pi zhuan gong'an bu xiao chengzhen huji guanli zhidu gaige shidian fang'an he guanyu wanshan nongcun huji guanli zhidu yijian de tongzhi" 国务院批转公安部小城镇户籍管理制度改革试点方案和关于完善农村户籍管理制度意见的通知 [The pilot plan for reform of the household registration management system in small towns and the notice on improving the rural household registration management system]. Beijing.

———. 1998. "Guanyu jiejue dangqian hukou guanli gongzuo zhong ji ge tuchu wenti de yijian" 关于解决当前户口管理工作中几个突出问题的意见 [Notice on resolving several acute problems facing current hukou management work]. Beijing.

———. 2001. "Guowuyuan guanyu yinfa zhongguo nongcun fupin kaifa gang-yao (2001–2010 nian) de tongzhi" 国务院关于印发中国农村扶贫开发纲要 (2001–2010年) 的通知 [Outline for poverty reduction and development of China's rural areas (2001–2010)]. Beijing.

———. 2011a. "Guowuyuan bangongting guanju jiji wentuo tuijin huji guanli zhidu gaige de tongzhi" 国务院办公厅关于积极稳妥推进户籍管理制度改革的通知 [Notice of the General Office of the State Council on actively and steadily promoting the reform of the household registration system]. Beijing.

———. 2011b. "Guowuyuan guanyu yinfa zhongguo nongcun fupin kaifa gang-yao (2011–2020 nian) de tongzhi" 国务院关于印发中国农村扶贫开发纲要 (2011–2020年) 的通知 [Outline for development-oriented poverty reduction for China's rural areas (2011–2020)]. Beijing.

———. 2014a. "Guanyu tongyi jianli tuijin xinxing chengzhen hua gongzuo bu ji lianxi huiyi zhidu de pifu" 关于同意建立推进新型城镇化工作部际联席会

议制度的批复 [State Council approval of the establishment of an interministerial joint meeting system for promoting new urbanization work]. Beijing.

———. 2014b. "Zhang gaoli: Zunxun chengzhen hua fazhan guillv zhashi tuijin huji zhidu gaige" 张高丽:遵循城镇化发展规律 扎实推进户籍制度改革 [Zhang Gaoli: Follow the laws of urbanization development and solidly promote the reform of the household registration system]. Retrieved October 2023. https://www.gov.cn/guowuyuan/2014-11/17/content_2779832.htm.

———. 2014c. "Guowuyuan guanyu jinyibu tuijin huji zhidu gaige de yijian" 国务院关于进一步推进户籍制度改革的意见 [Opinions of the State Council on further promotion of reform of the household registration system]. Beijing.

———. 2015. "Guanyu jiejue wu hukou renkou yuan dengji hukou wenti de yijian" 关于解决无户口人员登记户口问题的意见 [Opinions on Solving the Problems of Household Registration for People without Household Registration]. Beijing.

———. 2016. "Guanyu yin fa tuidong 1 yi fei huji renkou zai chengshi luohu fang'an de tongzhi" 关于印发推动1亿非户籍人口在城市落户方案的通知 [On promoting the settlement of 100 million nonregistered people in cities]. Beijing.

———. 2017. "Makai zhuchi guowuyuan nongmin gong gongzuo lingdao xiaozu quanti huiyi" 马凯主持国务院农民工工作领导小组全体会议 [Ma Kai presided over the plenary meeting of the State Council's leading small group on migrant workers' work]. Beijing. Retrieved October 2023. https://www.gov.cn/guowuyuan/2017-01/20/content_5161639.htm.

Street, Alex. 2014. "My Child Will Be a Citizen: Intergenerational Motives for Naturalization." *World Politics* 66 (2): 264–292.

Sun, Bin. 2019. "Outcomes of Chinese Rural Protest: Analysis of the Wukan Protest." *Asian Survey* 59 (3): 429–450.

Sun, Mingjie, and C. Cindy Fan. 2011. "China's Permanent and Temporary Migrants: Differentials and Changes, 1990–2000." *Professional Geographer* 63 (1): 92–112.

Sun, Qi. 2017. "2017 'Xin yixian' chengshi paihang bang fabu chengdu, hangzhou, wuhan chanlian sanjia zhengzhou, dongguan xin jin ru bang" "2017新一线"城市排行榜发布成都、杭州、武汉蝉联三甲郑州、东莞新晋入榜" [2017 "new first-tier" city ranking list released Chengdu, Hangzhou, and Wuhan remain in the top three, Zhengzhou, Dongguan newly entered the list]. *Yicai News.* May 31. Retrieved July 2018. https://www.yicai.com/news/5293378.html.

Surak, Kristin. 2016. "Global Citizenship 2.0: The Growth of Citizenship by Investment Programs." Investment Migration Working Paper, no. 3. Geneva, Switzerland: Investment Migration Council.

Tang, Jianjun, Yue Xu, and Huanguang Qiu. 2021. "Integration of Migrants in Poverty Alleviation Resettlement to Urban China." *Cities*, 103501.

Tang, Yongfeng, and Isabelle Côte. 2021. "How Large-Scale Land Protests Succeed in China: The Role of Domestic Media." *Journal of Chinese Political Science* 26 (2): 333–352.

Tao, Ran, Chen Shi, Hui Wang, and Guzhong Zhuang. 2011. "'Liuyisi zhuanzhedian bei lun' yu zhongguo huji—tudi—caishui zhidu liandong gaige" "刘易斯转折点悖论"与中国户籍—土地—财税制度联动改革 [Paradox of "Lewis Turning Point" and coordinated reforms of China's hukou-land-fiscal system]. *International Economic Review* (3): 120–147.

The Paper. 2018. "Women qule xiangqin jiao 6 ci, shoujile zhe 874 fen zhenghun qishi" 我们去了相亲角6次，收集了这874份征婚启事 [We went to the marriage market 6 times, and collected 874 advertisements]. *The Paper*. Retrieved December 2019. https://www.thepaper.cn/newsDetail_forward_2351635.

Tilly, Charles. 1995. "Citizenship, Identity and Social History." *International Review of Social History* 40 (S3): 1–17.

Toops, Stanley W. 2004. "The Demography of Xinjiang." In *Xinjiang: China's Muslim Borderland: China's Muslim Borderland*, edited by S. Frederick Starr, 241–263. New York: Routledge.

Tukmadiyeva, Malika 2016. "Propiska as a Tool of Discrimination in Central Asia." Central Asia Fellowship Papers, no. 2, January. Washington, DC: Central Asia Program.

Turaeva-Hoehne, Rano. 2011. "Propiska Regime in Post-Soviet Space: Regulating Mobility and Residence." CASI Working Paper. Bishkek, Kyrgyzstan: Central Asian Studies Institute.

Turner, Bryan S. 1990. "Outline of a Theory of Citizenship." *Sociology* 24 (2): 189–217.

———. 1993. *Contemporary Problems in the Theory of Citizenship and Social Theory*. London: Sage.

UNICEF, National Bureau of Statistics of China, and UNFPA. 2017. 2015 *nian zhongguo ertong renkou qingkuang: shishi yu shuju* 2015年中国儿童人口情况：事实与数据 [Population status of children in China in 2015: Facts and figures]. New York: UNICEF.

Vortherms, Samantha A. 2015. "Localized Citizenships: Household Registration as an Internal Citizenship Institution." In *Theorizing Chinese Citizenship*, edited by Zhonghua Guo and Sujian Guo, 85–108. Lanham, MD: Rowman and Littlefield.

———. 2019. "China's Missing Children: Political Barriers to Citizenship through the Household Registration System." *China Quarterly* 238: 309–330.

———. 2021. "Hukou as a Case of Multi-level Citizenship." In *The Routledge Handbook of Chinese Citizenship*, edited by Zhonghua Guo, 132–142.

Works Cited

Vortherms, Samantha A., and Gordon G. Liu. 2022. "Hukou as Benefits: Demand for Hukou and Wages in China." *Urban Studies* 59 (15): 3167–3183.

Walder, Andrew G. 1986. *Communist Neo-Traditionalism: Work and Authority in Chinese Industry*. Oakland: University of California Press.

Wallace, Jeremy. 2014. *Cities and Stability: Urbanization, Redistribution, and Regime Survival in China*. Oxford: Oxford University Press.

Wallner, Jennifer 2009. "Beyond National Standards: Reconciling Tension between Federalism and the Welfare State." *Publius: The Journal of Federalism* 40 (4): 646–671.

Wang, Fei-ling. 2004. "Reformed Migration Control and New List of the Targeted People: China's Hukou System in the 2000s." *China Quarterly* 177: 115–132.

———. 2005. *Organizing through Division and Exclusion: China's Hukou System*. Stanford, CA: Stanford University Press.

———. 2010. "Conflict, Resistance and the Transformation of the Hukou System." In *Chinese Society: Change, Conflict and Resistance*, edited by Elizabeth J. Perry and Mark Selden, 80–100. London: Taylor and Francis.

Wang, Feng. 1997. "The Breakdown of a Great Wall: Recent Changes in Household Registration System in China." In *Floating Population and Migration in China: The Impact of Economic Reforms*, edited by Thomas Sharping, 149–165. Hamburg, Germany: Institute of Asian Studies.

Wang, Feng, and Xuejin Zuo. 1999. "Inside China's Cities: Institutional Barriers and Opportunities for Urban Migrants." *American Economic Review* 88 (2): 276–280.

Wang, Li. 2012. "Social Exclusion and Education Inequality: Towards an Integrated Analytical Framework for the Urban-Rural Divide in China." *British Journal of Sociology of Education* 33 (3): 409–430.

Wang, Lianzhang. 2017. "Shenzhen Closes Door on Blind Migrants." *Sixth Tone*. January 12. http://www.sixthtone.com/news/1810/shenzhen-closes-door-on-blind-migrants.

Wang, Xiaobing, Futoshi Yamauchi, and Jikun Huang. 2016. "Rising Wages, Mechanization, and the Substitution between Capital and Labor: Evidence from Small Scale Farm System in China." *Agricultural Economics* 47 (3): 309–317.

Wang, Xiaobing, Futoshi Yamauchi, Keijiro Otsuka, and Jikun Huang. 2016. "Wage Growth, Landholding, and Mechanization in Chinese Agriculture." *World Development* 86: 30–45.

Wang, Yu. 2017. "Intermarriage, Social Mobility, and Inequality in China." PhD diss., Sociology, University of Wisconsin, Madison.

Wang, Zhiguo, and Liang Ma. 2014. "Fiscal Decentralization in China: A Literature Review." *Annals of Economics and Finance* 15 (2): 305–324.

Ward, Joe H. 1963. "Hierarchical Grouping to Optimize an Objective Function." *Journal of the American Statistical Association* 58 (301): 236–244.

Weaver, R. Kent. 1986. "The Politics of Blame Avoidance." *Journal of Public Policy* 6 (4): 371–398.

Wei, Yehua Dennis. 2001. "Decentralization, Marketization, and Globalization: The Triple Processes Underlying Regional Development in China" *Asian Geographer* 20 (1–2): 7–23.

Whiting, Susan. 2011. "Values in Land: Fiscal Pressures, Land Disputes and Justice Claims in Rural and Peri-urban China." *Urban Studies* 48 (3): 569–587.

Whyte, Martin. 2010. *Myth of the Social Volcano: Perceptions of Inequality and Distributive Injustice in Contemporary China.* Palo Alto, CA: Stanford University Press.

———. 2016. "China's Dormant and Active Social Volcanoes." *China Journal* 75: 9–37.

Wincott, Daniel 2006. "Social Policy and Social Citizenship: Britain's Welfare States." *Publius: The Journal of Federalism* 36 (1): 169–188.

Wintrobe, Ronald. 1998. *The Political Economy of Dictatorship.* Cambridge: Cambridge University Press.

World Bank. 2020. "Vietnam – Household Registration Study 2015." World Bank Dataset. Last updated May 21, 2020. https://wbwaterdata.org/dataset/vietnam-household-registration-study-2015.

World Bank and Vietnam Academy of Social Sciences. 2016. *Vietnam's Household Registration System.* Ha Noi: Hong Duc Publishing: World Bank Group, Vietnam Academy of Social Sciences.

Wu, Xiaogang, and Donald J. Treiman. 2007. "Inequality and Equality under Chinese Socialism: The Hukou System and Intergenerational Occupational Mobility." *American Journal of Sociology* 113 (2): 415–445.

Xia, Ying, and Bing Guan. 2017. "Practicing Democratic Citizenship in an Authoritarian State: Grassroots Self-Governance in Urban China." *Citizenship Studies* 21 (7): 809–823.

Xinhua News Agency. 2002. "Jiangsu quxiao nongye hukou: Tongcheng jumin hukou shishi qianyi zhun ru zhi" 江苏取消农业户口:统称居民户口 实施迁移准入制 [Jiangsu cancels agricultural household registration: Collectively referred to as resident household registration, and implements a migration system]. Xinhua News Agency. December 16.

———. 2013. "Xijinping ren zhongyang quanmian shenhua gaige lingdao xiaozu zu zhang" 习近平任中央全面深化改革领导小组组长 [Xi Jinping appointed leader of the Comprehensively Deepening Reforms Leading Small Group]. Xinhua News Agency. December 30.

———. 2017. "Chinese Police Solve 430 Fake ID Cases." Xinhua News Agency. April 27.

———. 2018a. "San da chengshi de 'yin cai dajuan'" 三大城市的"引才答卷" [The talent attraction sheet for three big cities). Xinhua News Agency. April 18.

———. 2018b. "Xijinping: Fazhan shi di yi yaowu, rencai shi di yi ziyuan, chuangxin shi di yi dongli" 习近平：发展是第一要务，人才是第一资源，创新是第一动力 [Xi Jinping: Development is the number one priority, talents are the number one resource, and innovation is the number one driving force]. Xinhua News Agency. March 7.

———. 2018c. "'Chengshi qiang ren dazhan': Qiang ren rongyi liu ren nan" "城市抢人大战"：抢人容易留人难 ["Cities' War for Workers": It's easy to grab people and it's hard to keep people]. Xinhua News Agency. May 4.

Xu, Xin, Ahmed El-Ashram, and Judith Gold. 2015. "Too Much of a Good Thing? Prudent Management of Inflows under Economic Citizenship Programs." International Monetary Fund. May 1. Working Paper No. 2015/093. https://www.imf.org/en/Publications/WP/Issues/2016/12/31/Too-Much-of-a-Good-Thing-Prudent-Management-of-Inflows-under-Economic-Citizenship-Programs-42884#.

Xue, Longyi, Mark Y. Wang, and Tao Xue. 2013. "'Voluntary' Poverty Alleviation Resettlement in China." *Development and Change* 44 (5): 1159–1180.

Yang, Dali L. 1996. *Calamity and Reform in China: State, Rural Society, and Institutional Change Since the Great Leap Forward*. Stanford, CA: Stanford University Press.

———. 1997. *Beyond Beijing: Liberalization and the Regions in China*. New York: Routledge.

———. 2006. "Economic Transformation and Its Political Discontents in China: Authoritarianism, Unequal Growth, and the Dilemmas of Political Development." *Annual Review of Political Science* 9 (1): 143–164.

Yang, Fan. 2016. "Buman gaokao ming'e xuejian shu wan jiangsu, hub'i jiazhang zhengfu kangyi" 不满高考名额削减数万 江苏、湖北家长政府抗议 [Dissatisfied with the reduction of tens of thousands of places for college entrance examination, Jiangsu and Hubei parents protest government]. Radio Free Asia, May 15.

Yang, Jin, Zuhui Huang, Xiaobo Zhang, and Thomas Reardon. 2013. "The Rapid Rise of Cross-Regional Agricultural Mechanization Services in China." *American Journal of Agricultural Economics* 95 (5): 1245–1251.

Yang, Philip Q. 1994. "Explaining Immigrant Naturalization." *International Migration Review* 28 (3): 449–477.

Yang, Yuanyuan, Alex de Sherbinin, and Yansui Liu. 2020. "China's Poverty Alleviation Resettlement: Progress, Problems and Solutions." *Habitat International* 98: 102135.

Yang, Yujeong. 2021. "The Politics of Inclusion and Exclusion: Chinese Dual-Pension Regimes in the Era of Labor Migration and Labor Informalization." *Politics and Society* 49 (2): 147–180.

Yılmaz, Zafer, and Bryan S. Turner. 2019. "Turkey's Deepening Authoritarianism and the Fall of Electoral Democracy." *British Journal of Middle Eastern Studies* 46 (5): 691–698.

Young, Jason. 2013. *China's Hukou System: Markets, Migrants, and Institutional Change*. London: Palgrave Macmillan.

Yu, Xianghua, and Xuejian Chen. 2012. "Zhongguo laodongli shichang de huji fenge xiaoying yi qi bianqian—gongzi chayi yu jihui chayi shuangchong shijiao xia de shizheng yanjiu" 中国劳动力市场的户籍分割效应一起变迁—工资差异预计会差异双重视角下的实证研究 [Empirical research on the effect of the household registration system evolution on labor market segmentation in China: From dual perspectives of employment opportunities and wage gap]. *Jingji yanjiu* [Economic Research]. 12: 97–110.

Zenz, Adrian. 2019. "'Thoroughly Reforming Them towards a Healthy Heart Attitude': China's Political Re-education Campaign in Xinjiang." *Central Asian Survey* 38 (1): 102–128.

Zhan, Shaohua. 2017. "Hukou Reform and Land Politics in China: Rise of a Tripartite Alliance." *China Journal* 78: 25–49.

Zhang, Jinlong. 2015. "Bei Wei Juntian Zhi Yanjiu Shi" 北魏均田制研究史 [A history of the studies of the equal-land system in the Northern Wei Dynasty]. *Wen Shi Zhe* [Journal of Chinese Humanities] 5 (350): 108–127.

Zhang, Jipeng, Ru Wang, and Chong Lu. 2019. "A Quantitative Analysis of Hukou Reform in Chinese Cities: 2000–2016." *Growth and Change* 50 (1): 201–221.

Zhang, Li. 2008. "Conceptualizing China's Urbanization Under Reform." *Habitat International* 32 (4): 452–470.

———. 2012. "Economic Migration and Urban Citizenship in China: The Role of Points Systems." *Population and Development Review* 38 (3): 503–533.

Zhang, Li, and Meng Li. 2016. "Local Fiscal Capability and Liberalization of Urban Hukou." *Journal of Contemporary China* 25 (102): 893–907.

———. 2018. "Acquired but Unvested Welfare Rights: Migration and Entitlement Barriers in Reform-Era China." *China Quarterly* 235: 669–692.

Zhang, Li, and Li Tao. 2012. "Barriers to the Acquisition of Urban Hukou in Chinese Cities." *Environment and Planning* 44 (12): 2883–2900.

Zhang, Li, and Gui-xin Wang. 2010. "Urban Citizenship of Rural Migrants in Reform-Era China." *Citizenship Studies* 14 (2): 145–166.

Zhang, Mingqiong, Chris Nyland, and Cherrie Jiuhua Zhu. 2010. "Hukou-Based HRM in Contemporary China: The Case of Jiangsu and Shanghai." *Asia Pacific Business Review* 16 (3): 377–393.

Works Cited

Zhang, Shangqiang, and Dan Fan. 2004. "Huji Yang, tianling he tianjinzhi" 户籍样、田玲和"均田制 [On household prototype, land law and jun land system]. *Yunnan minzu daxue xuebao (zhexue shehuikexue ban)* 云南民族大学学报 (哲学社会科学版) [Journal of Yunnan University (Philosophy and Sociology Edition)]. 1: 94–102.

Zhang, Xiaobo, Jin Yang, and Reardon Thomas. 2017. "Mechanization Outsourcing Clusters and Division of Labor in Chinese Agriculture." *China Economic Review* 43: 184–195.

Zhang, Yinghong. 2003. "Ziyou qianxi: Li women hai you duo yuan" 自由迁徙：离我们还有多远 [Freedom of movement: How far away are we still?]. *Sociology Research*, China Academy of Social Science. 12: 16–18.

Zhang, Zongping, and Zhen Guo. 2013. "Woguo gongzi shuiping chaju fenxi: Qishi xing gongzi xianxiang" 我国工资水平差距分析：歧视性工资现象 [Analysis of China's wage gap: The phenomenon of discriminatory wages]. *Journal of South China Agricultural University* (Social Science Edition). 4: 94–102.

Zhao, Gang. 2006. *Zhongguo tudi zhidu shi* 中国土地制度史 [History of China's land system]. Beijing: Xinxing Publishing.

Zhejiang Provincial Government. 2015. "Zhejiang xing renmin zhengfu guanyu jinyibu tuijin huji zhidu gaige de shishi yijian" 浙江省人民政府关于进一步推进户籍制度改革的实施意见 [Zhejiang provincial government notice on further promoting the reform of the household registration system]. Hanzhou.

Zhengzhou City Government. 2018. "Zhengzhou shi rencai gongyu jianshe he shiyong guanli zhanxing banfa de tongzhi" 郑州市人才公寓建设和使用管理暂行办法的通知 [Notice of Zhengzhou City's interim measures for the management of the construction and use of talent apartments]. Zhengzhou.

Zhu, Jieming. 2005. "A Transitional Institution for the Emerging Land Market in Urban China." *Urban Studies* 42 (8): 1369–1390.

Zimmermann, Klaus F., Amelie F. Constant, Amelie F. Constant, and Liliya Gataullina. 2009. "Naturalization Proclivities, Ethnicity and Integration." *International Journal of Manpower* 30 (1/2): 70–82.

Zuo, Cai (Vera). 2015. "Promoting City Leaders: The Structure of Political Incentives in China." *China Quarterly* 224: 1–30.

Zweig, David. 1992. "Urbanizing Rural China: Bureaucratic Authority and Local Autonomy." In *Bureaucracy, Politics, and Decision Making in Post-Mao China*, edited by Kenneth G. Lieberthal and David M. Lampton, 334–359. Oakland: University of California Press.

Index

administrative upgrading, 103
agricultural *hukou,* 40, 45, 49, 50–51, 71–72, 187. *See also hukou* system (internal citizenship)
agricultural population, rural population *versus,* 190
agriculture, mechanization in, 130–31, 135, 140–41, 143, 145, 215
Anhui, 37
assimilation, 158–59, 172–73
authoritarian citizenship: 4–10; factors of, 4; future research regarding, 185; as particularistic, 177; rights and responsibilities, 22–24; security logic of, 56–57; theorizing, 8–20
authoritarian redistribution, 13–14
authoritarianism, 22–26

Beijing: age transfer requirements in, 230n13; assimilation in, 173; demand for *hukou* in, 160–61, 165–66, 169, 174; education in, 164; high-skilled quotas in, 95; *hukou* demand in, 149–50; *hukou* transfer quotas in, 229n43; migrants/migrant workers in, 116–17; selective municipalities in, 110; top receiving firms in, 96; willingness to pay (WTP) in, 160, 166–68
belonging, 24–25, 52, 186
birthright citizenship, 9, 87–89

black *hukous,* 69, 88. See also *hukou* system (internal citizenship)
blind migration, 30–31, 57–58
blue-print *hukou,* 100. See also *hukou* system (internal citizenship)
bottom-up development: motivations for, 3–4; net naturalizations and, 145; overview of, 13, 82–83, 114, 128–32, 146–47; policy development and, 140–41; rural resident naturalization and, 121

cadre transfers, 105, 106
Canada, 95, 99–100
central economic planning, 30, 32, 62–64
central reforms, 66–71
Chinese Communist Party (CCP), 23, 29, 66, 69
choice experiment, 211
Chongqing, 72, 110
citizenship: belonging and, 52, 186; central effects on access to, 16–17; in democracies, 7; downward shift of, 64–65; elements of, 6; entitlements of, 6; imperial origins and, 26–29; inclusive, 22; individual effects on access to, 16–17; institutions, 22–26, 56, 178; as internally inclusive and externally exclusive, 24; local effects on access to, 16–17; manipulation of, 184; membership, 24–26, 60–65; purpose of, 6; responsibilities of, 23–24, 30, 33;

273

274 *Index*

citizenship (*continued*)
    studies of, 5–6; rights, 8, 23, 32, 33, 39, 40,
    177, 185; universal membership in, 6–7;
    varieties of, 6–8, 186
city tier, 144
city-entry-barrier index, 197–98
cluster analysis, 208
coercion, 150–56, 174
collective *hukou*, 187. See also *hukou* system
    (internal citizenship)
command economy, 29–30, 32, 39, 221n13
Comprehensively Deepening Reform
    Commission (CDR), 67–68, 69–70
contingent valuation, 210
corruption, in *hukou* system (internal
    citizenship), 76
COVID-19 pandemic, 184–85
Cultural Revolution, 63
Custody and Repatriation Centers, 38–39,
    89, 152, 169

danwei (work units), 31, 46
decentralization: of citizenship membership,
    65; of development policies, 64;
    economic development policy and,
    122; economic incentives and, 65;
    fiscal, 64; of *hukou* naturalizations, 22,
    46; of *hukou* policies, 64–65; internal
    citizenship regimes in, 178; municipal
    government control and, 223–24n37,
    228n33; reforms of, 10, 40, 42
demand, for *hukou*: destination
    attractiveness, 160–62; discrimination,
    170–71, 218n15; distance, 191; household
    decisions, 172; and identity, 169–70;
    rights, 161–69
democracy, citizenship and, 6–7, 22
development: foreign capital for, 124–25;
    horizon and sustainability of, 147;
    incentives of, 16; policy origins in,
    121–23; policy outcomes and, 134–46;
    policy variation regarding, 121–23. *See
    also specific types*

early reform period, 34–39, 38
economic development: access and, 83;
    citizenship membership expansion
    and, 60–65; city tier and, 144;

    decentralization in, 122; incentives for,
    133; labor and, 61, 176; as liberalizing
    force, 114; local, 78; local calculus
    regarding, 120–21; market forces and,
    63; policies for, 14, 121–23; redistribution
    and, 83; reforms for, 33–46; social
    welfare programs and, 61; Xi Jinping's
    viewpoint regarding, 176. *See also
    specific types*
economic incentives, 60–79, 83
economic planning, logic of limited
    inclusivity and, 62–64
education, 51–52, 61, 82, 122–23, 163, 222n20
elections: in China, 8, 23, 39–40, 220n4,
    223n33; democratic citizenship and, 5–6,
    7, 22; non-democracy and, 56, 217n5;
    registration, 7
employer-selected migration, 95,
    139–40, 203
entitlements, 6, 57. *See also specific types*
ethnicity, migration control, 58–60; as
    security concern, 118, 138
exclusion: in citizenship, 14; of *hukou*
    rights, 85; in *hukou* system (internal
    citizenship), 58; local-level, 14; pressures
    of, 79–80; security imperatives for,
    56–59; security incentive and, 56–60;
    security-driven, 65–79, 75; stability and,
    56–60; systemic, 56

family planning certificate, 93, 173,
    200–201, 237n7
family-based citizenship, 92–94, 102, 106,
    141, 200–202; low-skilled programs and,
    205–6; naturalization and, 36–37, 38,
    62–63, 64, 81, 200–202
Finance and Economic Affairs leading small
    group, 70
firms: foreign, 81–82, 94–95, 124–25; local
    government relations with, 97, 123, 140;
    policy interests, 78–79, 122–23; quotas,
    policy development and, 101–2, 140
fiscal chauvinism, 118–20, 123, 138–39
floating population, 35, 50, 55, 79, 191. *See
    also* migrants/migration
food insecurity/food rations, 31, 32–33, 34,
    119, 184–85
forced naturalization, 103–4

foreign economy, capital, 124–25, 126, 128, 139–40, 145; foreign direct investment (FDI), 128, 139, 140, 145; foreign owned production, 135, 143; for local development, 81–82. *See also* outward-oriented development

Foshan, 154–55

Fujian, 74, 110

general-pool models, 95–97, 139–40, 203–4

Germany, 86, 92–93

globalization, 81, 229n46. *See also* foreign economy

governance, structure of, 122

Great Leap Forward, 31, 32–33, 63

Guangdong: active policies in, 231n19; education in, 82; *hukou* policy reforms in, 148; local policy experimentation in, 45; migrant integration in, 74; points policies in, 95; population of, 238n12; research design in, 17–18

Guangzhou, 97, 100, 103–4

Guo Shengkun, 71

Haikou, 97

Hainan, 126

Han majority group, 59–60, 118

Handan, 77

Hangzhou, 97

Harbin, 73

health care: as a social right, 39, 61, 161, 169; health insurance programs, 46–47, 51

high-skilled labor: benefits of, 81–82; certifications, 203; competition for, 125–26; human capital of, 124; naturalization openness and, 141–42; as naturalization pathway, 80–81; in outward-oriented development, 145; overview of, 94–98; points policies for, 103–4; policy development and, 139–40; in policy indexes, 202–4

ho khau system (Vietnam), 25, 87, 180–81

Hong Kong, 95

Hu Jintao administration, 46, 67

Hubei, 120, 209

hukou population, 189–90. *See also* floating population, migrants/migration

hukou reforms: acceleration of, 68; condemnation regarding, 66–67; early, 153–55; financial cost excuse regarding, 71; forced transfers, 152–56; local economic development and, 78–79; municipal-level interests of, 74–79; policy publishing of, 75; provincial coordination of, 71–74; public opinion regarding, 75–76; responsibilities in, 69

hukou system: assignments under, 30; as blood-based rule, 85; changing, 9, 41, 223n26; as citizenship membership institution, 9–10; classifications of, 187; as coercive institution, 152; corruption in, 76; demand for, 156–74; development timeline of, 27; dual management system of, 72; functions of, 115–20; for government resource protection, 11–12; history of, 21–22, 26–29; identification in, 32; illegal sale of, 38; imperial origins of, 26–29; as labor allocation tool, 55; as land taking compensation, 129–30; marketization of, 11; migrant workers in, 10–11; overview of, 1–2, 15–16, 25–26, 52–53; as permit-based system, 87; rights and, 33; statistics regarding, 2, 3; status in, 169–70; types of, 187–88; varying access to, 10–11, 12–13. *See also* demand, for *hukou*

hukou transfers: children, 88, 172, 201; education-based transfers, 38, 97–98, 105–6, 203–4; family-based, 92–94, 107, 202; forced, 103–4; general-pool models, 95–97, 139–40, 203–4; graduate returnees, 102; high-skilled, 80–1 (*see also* high-skilled labor); land and, 82–83, 154; long-term resident, 81, 98–99, 109, 188, 189, 204–7; military, 101–2, 105, 106; newborn registration, 88–89, 200–201; *nongzhuanfei*, 38, 40, 63, 99, 205, 206; point-based, 95–97, 103–4; quotas, 64, 95, 103–4, 120, 140, 148, 229n43; work-based programs, 38, 64, 205–6

human capital, 124, 128. *See also* labor

276   *Index*

inclusion: for development, 60–65; economic incentive of, 60–65; economically driven, 65–79; expansion of, 60; limited, in central economic planning, 62–64; in local citizenship, 55; by local governments, 80–81; membership, 81–84; pressures of, 79–80; security imperatives for, 59–60; systemic, 56; in top-down development, 83

individual *hukou*, 149, 187. See also *hukou* system (internal citizenship)

industrialization, 57

integration, of rights, 49

internal citizenship, 3–4, 8–9. *See also* local citizenship

internal migration, 1, 57–58, 190. *See also* migration

internal naturalization regimes: family-based citizenship in, 92–94; high-skilled naturalization in, 94–98; investment-based, 99–101; measuring, 90–91; military-government assignments, 101–2; overview of, 91–92; residence-based transfers in, 98–99; rural return, 101–2. *See also* local citizenship

international naturalization, 158–59

investment-based naturalization, 81, 99–101, 106, 107, 207

iron rice bowl welfare, 222n17

Jiangsu, 120

Jiangxi, 74, 110

Jiayuguan, 154–55

jus sanguinis principles, 87–88

Karamay, 154–55

Kunming, 97

Kyrgyzstan, 182–83

labor: allocation, 29–32, 55; labor discipline, 30; labor force/market, 61, 62, 78, 124–25, 176; labor protests, 10–11, 60 (*see also* high-skilled labor land); confiscation, 129–30, 131, 154, 155–56, 205; construction, 234n22; conversion of, 233n9; distribution system of, 28; expropriation, 103, 106; fiscalization, 131;

land-for-*hukou* exchanges, 82–83; law and, 129; price, statistics regarding, 215; and urbanization, 128–29; use rights, 47, 78, 82–83, 163–64, 235n13

landless peasants, 131, 192

Li Keqiang, 50, 54, 70

Linfen, 134

local citizenship: acquisition of, 87–89; belonging in, 24–25; birthright, 87–89; defined, 225n50; development of, 25; federal systems and, 220–21n6; inclusion in, 55; institutions, 24–25; membership, 29–32, 34–39, 79–84; migrant exclusion from, 80; naturalization, 89; overview of, 15–16; pathways for, in early reform period, 38; regimes of, 40; varying access to, 10–11, 12–13

local development, 81–84

local naturalization: by city size, 49; controls of, 80–81; defined, 9; processes of, 9–10; reforms to, 49

local political rights, 39–40

local public security bureaus, 76–78, 89, 90, 116

local social welfare bureaus, 78

local state corporatism, 227n23

low-skilled labor, 126, 128–29, 206. *See also* labor

manufacturing sector, *hukou* reforms and, 79

Mao Zedong era: *hukou* system under, 21–22, 72; internal migration under, 35–36; population changes in, 35–36; ration-based economy of, 119; redistribution policies of, 62; rise of local citizenship in, 29–33; transfer types during, 105; urban-centered industrialization policies of, 57; work unit in, 222n17

market forces, into the economy, 63

market socialist system, 61

membership: categories of, 36; and citizenship, 2, 5, 11–12; citizenship responsibilities with, 28–29; defined, 5; enforcement of, 30–31, 38–39 (*see also* Custody and Repatriation Centers); *hukou* and, 9; institutions, 6–7; local, 25–26, 33; loss of, 26, 32, 69, 88;

manipulation of, 40–46, 79–84, 177; in non-democratic citizenship, 8, 22, 24; particularistic, 4, 6, 24, 56, 59, 177; redistribution and, 13–16, 34–35, 48–50; universal, 6–7

migrant workers: access to *hukou* by, 223n29; in Beijing, China, 116–17; during COVID-19 pandemic, 184–85; discrimination of, 171; economic development from, 79; high-skilled, 81–82, 94–98, 202–4; in *hukou* system (internal citizenship), 10–11; leading small group, 70; measurement of, 191; motivations of, 79–80; net naturalization and, 142, 144; new residency program of, 73; population measuring and, 233–34n18; protests of, 60; residence-based naturalization and, 99; statistics regarding, 50, 54; for steel industry, 63; temporary residence policy for, 34–35; transfer of *hukou* of, 77–78

migrants/migration: children born to, 88; control release regarding, 34; defined, 222n25; demand for *hukou* by, 156–74; detaining of, 39; discrimination of, 170–71; economic development and, 120–21; fiscal chauvinism and, 123; Great Leap Forward and, 32; *hukou* demand by, 156–57; internal, 1, 57–58, 190; internal reforms of, 34–35; land use rights of, 78, 235n13; long-term, for integration, 67; as low-end population, 116; measuring population of, 190–92; membership restrictions on, 38–39; mobile population of, 191; municipal government viewpoint regarding, 75; naturalization process and requirements of, 70–71; neighborhood danger zones of, 116; policy experimentation regarding, 37; public security and, 114; in rural areas, 103; security concerns regarding, 116–17; sending areas, 37; social detachment of, 116; statistics regarding, 55, 215; as three-withouts persons, 39; as undesirable, 115–16; willingness to pay (WTP) by, 157–58, 166–68. *See also* migrant workers

Ministry of Finance, 72

Ministry of Human Resources and Social Security (MHRSS), 70

Ministry of Land and Resources, 72

Ministry of Public Security (MPS): central level, 66, 68–69, 72; local level, 76–78, 89, 90, 116

moderate municipalities, 108, 109, 110, 111

multilevel citizenship, 52, 186, 218n11

municipal governments: interests, of *hukou* reforms, 75–79; level of analysis of, 196–97; management by, 228n39; moderate, 108, 109, 110, 111; open, 107–9, 110, 111; selective, 107–8, 109, 110, 111

National Development and Reform Commission (NDRC), 67–68, 69

national identification card system, 37

naturalization: coercion in, 153–55; correlations of, 159; database regarding, 90; defined, 9; in early reform period, 36–37; education-based, 97–98; estimates, 104, 105, 111, 142–46, 208–10, 216; family reunification, 36–37; family-based citizenship in, 92–94; forced, 103–4, 154–55; high-skilled, 81–82, 94–98, 202–4; hyperlocal, 235n11; identity and, 170; internal regimes of, measuring, 90–91; investment-based, 99–101, 207; local citizenship, 89; local, process of, 40; military-government assignments, 101–2; pathways for, 80–81; points policies for, 95–97; policies for, 10; policy experimentation for, 37; process and requirements of, for migrants, 70–71; residence-based, 98–99, 204–7; restructuring of, 42; rural return, 101–2; statistics regarding, 127

New Zealand, 95

New-Type Urbanization Plan: city-size categorization in, 224n41; considerations regarding, 55; evidence of reform outcomes in, 50–52; membership and rights in, 48–50; membership restrictions in, 73; overview of, 47–48; people-centered urbanization in, 130; questions regarding, 55

Ningbo, 97

278 *Index*

nonagricultural *hukou,* 40, 43, 44, 45, 47, 49, 71–72, 188. *See also hukou* system (internal citizenship)
nonagricultural population, urban population *versus,* 189–90
notification-based registration systems, 86–87, 218n17

Office of Custody and Repatriation, 38–39, 89, 152, 169, 223n29
open municipalities, 107–9, 110, 111
Organization Department, 228n36
outward-oriented development: high-skilled workers and, 121; motivations for, 3; naturalization rates and, 144–45; overview of, 13, 81–82, 114, 124–28, 146; policy development and, 139–40. *See also* foreign economy

pension, demand for *hukou* and, 161, 163, 164, 168–69
People's Bank of China, 69
permit-based systems, 86–87
planned economy, 31. *See also* economic planning
points-based policies, 95–97, 103–4
policy: experimentation, 37, 43–45, 46; implementation, 150–51; indexes, 200–210; list and results table for, 213–16; patterns of, 107–12. *See also specific types*
policy development: in bottom-up development, 140–41; net naturalization and, 142–46; origins of, 121–23; outcomes of, 134–36; in outward-oriented development, 139–40; pathways to, 123–24; security incentives for, 138–39; in top-down development, 141–42
political rights, 23, 39–40. *See also* elections
population management, public security and, 114
poverty alleviation: relocation, 83, 133–34, 154; poverty counties, net naturalization and, 144, 145–46
principal component analysis (PCA), 204, 207
propiska system (Soviet Union), 25, 31, 49, 87, 181–83

protests: coercion and, 151; effects of, 76; of institutional barriers, 63; of land confiscation, 131; of migrant workers, 60; rights versus rules consciousness, 219n23; social, 75, 76; in Target Responsibility System, 229n40
provincial-level policies, for *hukou* management, 42–43, 71–74
public opinion, of *hukou* reforms, 75–76; lobbying, 7

real estate, *hukou* policy benefits to, 78. *See also* land
redistribution: centralized, 39; as co-opting groups, 59; countryside neglecting in, 57; economic policy and, 62, 83; elections and, 56; of food, 31, 32–33, 119; increasing urban citizenship rights through, 32–33; in industrial sector, 31; limiting, 57; to privileged groups, 56, 57; process of, 13–14; rights, 49; security incentives and, 57; segregation and, 57; socioeconomic, 22–23, 61; surveillance and, 59; unequal, 4–10; into urban centers, 57
Reform and Opening Up policy, 33–34, 124
Republican Era, 27, 28
residence permit system, 50, 73, 188, 224n45
resident *hukou,* 188. *See also hukou* system (internal citizenship)
rural citizenship, 46–47, 82–83, 102–3, 131–32
rural areas: collectivization, 31–32; development firms, *hukou* policy benefits to, 78; land use rights, 47, 82–83; productivity, 130, 140–41
rural *hukou*: definition, 187, 188; right of return, 101–2. See also *hukou* system (internal citizenship)
rural population, agricultural population *versus,* 190
rural-to-urban transfer programs: cap of, 63–64; control of, 40; dissolution of, 64–65; increase of, in Sichuan Province, 71–72; overview of, 38, 101–2, 154–55, 204–6; statistics regarding, 205, 206. See also *hukou* transfers

security: access and, 83; balancing, 65–79; concerns regarding, 66; ethnicity concerns regarding, 118; as *hukou* system function, 115–18; imperatives, 59–60; incentives, 56–60, 75, 83, 138–39

segregation, 7, 57, 183

selective municipalities, 107–8, 109, 110, 111

selectorate theory, 13–14

self-supplied grain *hukou,* 34. See also *hukou* system (internal citizenship)

Shaanxi, 134

Shanghai, 100, 110, 169

Shantou, 154–55

Shanxi, 134

Shenyang, 97

Shenzhen, 74, 95, 97, 100, 103–4, 125, 154–55, 204, 209, 231–32n26

Sichuan, 43–45, 71–72

social welfare: bureaus, 78; and development, 61; as redistribution, 22–23, 61; reforms, 46; as rights, 7, 8, 23, 39–40; urban programs, 51, 62

socialist model of development, 32

South Africa, 183

Soviet Union, 25, 29–30, 31, 49, 87, 181–83, 221n13

Spain, 23

Special Economic Zones, 121

spouses, registration of, 202

stability, as *hukou* system function, 115–18

subnational citizenship, 25. *See also* local citizenship

surveillance, information gathering and, 28, 48, 59, 77, 89, 116

survey methods, 210–11

Target Responsibility System, 228n36, 229n40

technology transfer, 124–25

temporary residence policy, 34–35, 188

three-withouts persons, 39

Tianjin, 110

top-down development, 4, 13, 83, 114, 121, 132–34, 141–42

transaction model of citizenship, 23–24

United States: Department of Motor Vehicles in, 86–87; discrimination in segregation policies in, 7; investment path to citizenship in, 99–100; notification system in, 86–87; nursing tiers in, 230n14; permanent resident status in, 93; voter registration laws in, 7; welfare system in, 218n10

universities, enrollment policies of, 119–20

urban *hukou,* 169, 188. See also *hukou* system (internal citizenship)

urban population, nonagricultural population *versus,* 189–90, 209

urban resettlement, 133–34

urban-rural economy, 40

urbanization: 54, 60, 82, 128–29; reforms, 47–48, 67, 69, 156; upgrading, 174

Uzbekistan, 183

Vietnam, 25, 87, 180–81

voluntarism, 149–56, 173–75

welfare: as rights, 49, 51; spending, 37; system, 71, 218n10, 222n17

Wen Jiabao, 67

Western Development Plan, 133

willingness to pay (WTP), 157–58, 160, 166–68, 210

work, as citizenship responsibility, 23, 30, 33

Wuhai, 154–55

Wuhan, 97, 126, 209

Xi Jinping: 67, 68, 70, 176; administration of, 67–68

Xi'an, 2, 11, 126, 127, 219n22

xiangsui system, 26, 28

Xinjiang, 58–59, 110

Yunfu, 95–96

Zhang Gaoli, 69–70, 71

Zhanjiang, 97

Zhengzhou, 126

Zhongshan, 95

Zhuhai, 154–55

Also published in the Shorenstein Asia-Pacific Research Center Series

United Front: Projecting Solidarity through Deliberation
in Vietnam's Single-Party Legislature
Paul Schuler (2021)

Fateful Decisions: Choices That Will Shape China's Future
Edited by Thomas Fingar and Jean C. Oi (2020)

Dynasties and Democracy: The Inherited Incumbency Advantage in Japan
Daniel M. Smith (2018)

Manipulating Globalization: The Influence of
Bureaucrats on Business in China
Ling Chen (2018)

Poisonous Pandas: Chinese Cigarette Manufacturing
in Critical Historical Perspectives
Edited by Matthew Kohrman, Gan Quan, Liu Wennan, and
Robert N. Proctor (2017)

Uneasy Partnerships: China's Engagement with Japan,
the Koreas, and Russia in the Era of Reform
Edited by Thomas Fingar (2017)

Divergent Memories: Opinion Leaders and the Sino-Japanese War
Gi-Wook Shin and Daniel Sneider (2016)

Contested Embrace: Transborder Membership
Politics in Twentieth-Century Korea
Jaeeun Kim (2016)

The New Great Game: China and South and
Central Asia in the Era of Reform
Edited by Thomas Fingar (2016)

The Colonial Origins of Ethnic Violence in India
Ajay Verghese (2016)

Rebranding Islam: Piety, Prosperity, and a Self-Help Guru
James Bourk Hoesterey (2015)

Global Talent: Skilled Labor as Social Capital in Korea
Gi-Wook Shin and Joon Nak Choi (2015)

Failed Democratization in Prewar Japan:
Breakdown of a Hybrid Regime
Harukata Takenaka (2014)

New Challenges for Maturing Democracies in Korea and Taiwan
Edited by Larry Diamond and Gi-Wook Shin (2014)

Spending Without Taxation: FILP and the Politics of Public Finance in Japan
Gene Park (2011)

The Institutional Imperative: The Politics of
Equitable Development in Southeast Asia
Erik Martinez Kuhonta (2011)

One Alliance, Two Lenses: U.S.-Korea Relations in a New Era
Gi-Wook Shin (2010)

Collective Resistance in China: Why Popular Protests Succeed or Fail
Yongshun Cai (2010)

The Chinese Cultural Revolution as History
Edited by Joseph W. Esherick, Paul G. Pickowicz, and
Andrew G. Walder (2006)

Printed in the USA
CPSIA information can be obtained
at www.ICGtesting.com
JSHW020827070824
67719JS00001B/1